PATHWAYS TO SUCCESS THROUGH

IDENTITY-BASED MOTIVATION

PATHWAYS TO SUCCESS THROUGH IDENTITY-BASED MOTIVATION

Daphna Oyserman

OXFORD
UNIVERSITY PRESS

Oxford University Press is a department of the University of
Oxford. It furthers the University's objective of excellence in research,
scholarship, and education by publishing worldwide.

Oxford   New York
Auckland   Cape Town   Dar es Salaam   Hong Kong   Karachi
Kuala Lumpur   Madrid   Melbourne   Mexico City   Nairobi
New Delhi   Shanghai   Taipei   Toronto

With offices in
Argentina   Austria   Brazil   Chile   Czech Republic   France   Greece
Guatemala   Hungary   Italy   Japan   Poland   Portugal   Singapore
South Korea   Switzerland   Thailand   Turkey   Ukraine   Vietnam

Oxford is a registered trademark of Oxford University Press
in the UK and certain other countries.

Published in the United States of America by
Oxford University Press
198 Madison Avenue, New York, NY 10016

Cataloging-in-Publication data is on file at the Library of Congress
ISBN 978-0-19-534146-1

9 8 7 6 5 4 3 2 1
Printed in the United States of America
on acid-free paper

CONTENTS

Imagine a twelve-year-old boy; on the one hand, he wants to do well in school and hopes to become an all 'A' student. On the other hand, schoolwork is not all that interesting; it is not clear how well he will do; and when he looks around to figure out what boys care about and value, what their goals are, and how they act, he sees girls outperforming boys academically. How do these competing sets of knowledge ("I want to do well," "Girls outperform boys") influence the interpretation he is likely to make of his experiences at school? School and gender are salient for most children from an early age, so he is likely to notice that gender and school performance seem to go together. If schoolwork is associated with girls, then gender is an easy at-hand interpretation for any difficulty he might experience with schoolwork. The interpretation goes something like this: "Of course this schoolwork is hard for me, I am a boy and boys do not do schoolwork as well as girls." This interpretation undermines effort; it implies that trying is a waste of time and that he might as well shift his attention elsewhere. Does this example suggest that boys are doomed to underachieve compared with girls, or are there small changes in context that can make a boy's feelings about his gender compatible with school attainment, just as being a girl currently does?

The question is not just about gender, the same scenario can be played out by substituting racial-ethnic, national, or religious heritage or social class for gender. In each case, the question is how to make sense of group-level differences. A large number of books promise to explain the secrets behind group-level differences in attainment by turning to group-level effects to explain group differences. In contrast, I focus on the dynamics of what I term *identity-based motivation*, highlighting how immediate situations and their interpretation matter, yielding what may appear to be fixed between-group differences.

My own path to considering when and how identities can fit together to bolster or undermine goal-focused behavior began in 1983. I had just arrived in Ann Arbor, Michigan, to pursue doctoral studies at the University of Michigan; I was outside in the play area of the university family housing unit. A neighbor was filling me in on the local scene. After telling me where the grocery store and bus line were, she asked if I knew about Devil's Night, which occurred the night before Halloween. No. I did not. It turns out that this was a night of youth mischief, the "trick" in "trick or treat" that took place in the neighboring city, Detroit. Tricks used to be annoying things like egging windows, toilet-papering trees, or placing rotten vegetables on front porches. By the 1980s, they included fire setting; according to the Detroit Free Press, more than eight hundred fires were set on Devil's Night in 1984.

Although the tricks were never very nice and certainly annoying to all, fire setting is really a whole new category. I wondered what the youth who were setting fires were imagining about their futures. Surely they were not thinking something along the lines of "I will set a fire and this may ruin my life if I get caught in a felony and am jailed" or "I will set a fire and someone might die in this fire; it will be on my conscience and forever change the person I become." On the flip side, I wondered about youth in fire-setting neighborhoods. What about the ones who did not set fires? Perhaps they had a particular way of imagining possibilities for their future selves that highlighted the risks of participating in Devil's Night. Were there particular kinds of future selves or particular ways that these future selves were structured that helped sensitize these youths to risks? If so, was that generalizable to other situations in which identities might be motivating? What would that mean for researchers interested in the development and function of self-concept?

My research since then has involved an expanding series of steps meant to address these questions. First, I compared Detroit's high school students with their peers in a continuum of facilities—schools for truants, group homes, the county detention center, and the state prison (Oyserman, 1993; Oyserman & Markus, 1990a,b; Oyserman & Saltz, 1993). My focus was on youths who were "at risk" either because of their own behavior (e.g., they were involved with crime and delinquency) or because of their context (e.g., they attended middle schools that fed into high schools in which graduation rates were low). I asked open-ended questions about the youths' future selves, what they expected to be like, what they feared they might be like, and what they hoped they could be like. I asked both about the immediate future (what they could be next year) and the more distant future (what they could be as adults). The open-ended format meant that respondents could describe what they were trying to become or trying not to become without bias from content provided by the question itself. I assumed that if I understood how responses of youth who did well in these contexts differed from those who did poorly, I could use the insight to develop preventive interventions relevant to all teens.

This first set of studies revealed three themes: two involved commonalities across youth and the third revealed subtle but potentially important differences between youth who were in school and those who were in jail. Commonalities were striking, whether in school or in jail all youths *had* possible selves for the near (next year) and for the far (as adults) future. Moreover, content of far future possible selves was quite similar across youth. All imagined adult future selves that embodied the American Dream: they hoped to have a house, car, and nice things. In terms of content of their next year's possible self, most responses focused on identities in school and in relationships with family, friends, and schoolmates. None said they hoped to be delinquent. Some were concerned that they might end up being jailed or killed or as gang members, thugs, or drug dealers. This high level of similarity in imagined future selves for youths in currently varying circumstances suggested that any differences in behavior could not be explained by their imagined possible selves or by the content of possible identities alone. Differences were subtler. Youths differed in whether positive and negative aspects of a future identity seemed to come to mind at the same time and in whether they had strategies to attain any or all of their future identities. These differences distinguished youths in different circumstances. Less delinquent youth had "balanced" future identities that included both a negative and a positive possibility in the same domain. Less delinquent youth also had strategies—things they were doing now to attain their future selves.

Subsequent studies built on these results. A first critical question was whether these differences in the structure of possible selves were associated with changes over time in academic engagement, including grades and school attendance (Oyserman, Bybee, Terry, & Hart-Johnson, 2004). The answer was that they were. Controlling for prior grades, students did better over time if they had not only positive and negative images of a future identity but also strategies to work toward their positive and to avoid their negative future identities. The next critical question was what these differences in the structure of possible selves meant more broadly, what was the underlying process that resulted in these subtle differences as well as commonalities. I term this broader perspective *identity-based* motivation, it has become a topic of sustained interest and is the theory described in this book (e.g., Oyserman, 2001; 2007, 2008; 2009; 2013; Oyserman & Destin, 2010; Oyserman, Elmore, & Smith, 2012; Oyserman & James, 2011; Oyserman, Smith, & Elmore, 2014).

As detailed in Chapter 1, identity-based motivation theory makes three core predictions. First, subtle features of the immediate situation influence which identities come to mind and what these identities imply for behavior. For example, a situation may make gender or race-ethnicity salient. However, the influence of being a boy or a girl, Black or Latino is not fixed; it depends on the situation. The situation might imply that boys and girls are different or the same, responsible or irresponsible, and so on. Second, once an identity (and its implications for behavior) comes to mind, people prefer to act in ways that are consonant with it. But whether they take such action depends on how relevant the identity and behaviors feel to the situation as it unfolds and how any difficulty in holding on to the identity and engaging in the behavior is interpreted.

For a number of years my students and I focused on the ways in which social identities, especially racial-ethnic identities, synced or failed to sync with children's school-focused possible selves and desire to do well in school (e.g., Altschul, Oyserman, & Bybee, 2006; 2008; Oyserman, 2008; Oyserman, Brickman, Bybee, & Celious, 2006; Oyserman, Gant, & Ager, 1995; Oyserman, Harrison, & Bybee, 2001; Oyserman, Kemmelmeier, Fryberg, Brosh, & Hart-Johnson, 2003; Oyserman & Fryberg, 2006). If achievement was experienced as embedded in racial-ethnic identity, academic outcomes improved. At the same time we began to ask how cultural factors might play a role in which identities came to mind and what their content might be (Oyserman, 2007; Oyserman et al., 1995; Oyserman, Sakamoto, & Lauffer, 1998; Oyserman & Sakamoto, 1997). These studies suggested a complex interplay between individualism, collectivism, racial-ethnic identities, and possible selves.

Much of this research focused on a particular social-racial-ethnic identity. Across studies, the content of racial-ethnic identity mattered. Children who believed that doing well in school was included in their racial-ethnic identity worked harder and did better in school, whether we looked at the period from eighth to ninth grades (Altschul, Oyserman, & Bybee, 2006) or the period from ninth to twelfth grades (Oyserman, 2008). Could I develop an intervention that set conditions for all youths to see this connection between school and identity? The School-to-Jobs (STJ) intervention that I detail in this book is the result of this development process (Oyserman, Bybee, & Terry, 2006; Oyserman, Terry & Bybee, 2002). This is a brief, culturally sensitive, portable, and testable intervention. I tested it twice, using a randomized clinical trial funded by the W. T. Grant Foundation and the National Institutes of Health. After these tests and before writing this book, I went back and tested the effects of each of the active components in separate experiments to make sure that effects were real and stable. I hope that this book will serve as a useful and stimulating tool. Although its content is my own, the basis on which it stands is collaborative. I thank my students and colleagues as well as the parents, children, and adults who participated in the studies and my own children and family. All made this book possible. My own children reminded me of the importance of the work, the tenuousness of parenting in the face of social contexts, and the importance of persisting. As one said to me when I explained that I was heading back to Detroit on a Saturday morning for an STJ session, "No offense Mom, but are you sure anyone will go to school on Saturday for you?"

INTRODUCTION AND READER'S GUIDE

This book focuses on gaps between aspiration and attainment and how situations can increase or decrease them. These gaps represent the shortfall between the self that one aspires to become and the outcomes one actually attains and the reverse, the too small gap between the self one fears becoming and the self one actually becomes. Making progress toward aspired selves (or away from feared selves) requires that people take action. People do plan to act at some point, when the time is right. Unfortunately, people also procrastinate and under or misinvest. They start too late and once they start, they commit too little effort before turning their attention elsewhere, or they fail to use effective strategies. As a result, their high hopes and earnest resolutions often fall short. Rather than considering these to be personal failings or character flaws, I focus on situational constraints and affordances, opportunities that trigger or impede taking action.

To understand when and how the future self can matter, this book starts with identity-based motivation (IBM) theory, a situated social cognition theory which predicts that people prefer to act in identity-congruent ways but that the identity-to-behavior link is opaque for a number of reasons. In Chapter 1, I operationalize what I mean by these terms, outline the predictions of IBM, and summarize evidence supporting an IBM approach. As described in that first chapter, even very young children can imagine future selves. They can tell you about the adults they want to be when they grow up. Moreover, these future selves are often quite positive and education-linked. Children's future selves also sometimes but not always also matter for their behavior. Whether a child wants to be a cheese maker or a veterinarian, he or she will work harder on school tasks when this adult self is on their mind and feels relevant to their current choices. Given these results, the main source of aspiration-attainment gaps for children does not appear to be the lack of a future self or an insufficiently positive future self. Instead, the source of the gap is that these future selves are not always experienced as relevant—mattering in the moment.

The reader may wonder why I focus so much on schooling. In Chapter 2 I articulate why. Pathways to success go through school. People interested in happiness, well-being, health, life satisfaction, saving for retirement, voting, and almost any other index of an involved citizenry should care about education. Education matters not only for the children themselves but also for society. This implies two core challenges: First, intervening to reduce school dropout rates and, second, figuring out which interventions are likely to be usable, feasible, scalable, and thus sustainable. As outlined in Chapter 2, dropout rates do not seem to be influenced by the failure to value college or to expect success, as would be predicted by expectancy-value theories. Instead, most children, even those from very low-income backgrounds, value education and aspire to attend college. They are right to have these aspirations, since academic attainment predicts one's life chances. However, dropout rates are high, particularly among low-income and minority children. Intervention to reduce dropout must consider what the process to drop out is, so that intervention can target core vulnerabilities. There is clear evidence that intervention can reduce school failure. Unfortunately most interventions aimed at school failure are long and complicated, undermining usability and feasibility. More importantly, even when they have outcome evidence, they do not test the underlying process model, so what the active components actually are is opaque. This matters for researchers using interventions to test theories, since it is unclear if the outcome was produced in the way the theory envisioned. While practitioners and educators wanting to use an intervention may think that they do not care about theory, they actually do. Without testing the underlying theoretical process model, it is impossible to scale programs that work, because what needs to be replicated and scaled is the active ingredients (the things that yield change), not their operationalization in a particular setting (specific activities that embody the active ingredients in one setting but may not in another). Chapter 2 outlines what educators should be looking for in selecting an intervention.

An important implication of identity-based motivation theory is that small interventions can have large effects as long as they harness motivation by focusing on the three components of identity-based motivation. In Chapter 3 I detail my translation of identity-based motivation theory into the STJ intervention, which I developed and tested using a randomized clinical trial funded through the National Institutes of Health. I articulate the translation of theory to intervention: the questions that needed to be asked and answered in developing STJ, thumbnail sketches of the activities, and the evidence from the randomized clinical trial that the intervention improves academic outcomes by changing identity processes. Translation always requires testing, and, with funding from the Department of Education (Institute for Educational Studies), my colleagues and I are currently testing how teachers can use STJ in their homerooms.

Chapter 4 provides the full manual and all the tools that I used. This means that the specific activities, exactly as described in this book, were tested using the process; fidelity and outcomes measures are also exactly as described in this book (manual section). This section is for readers who want to implement STJ, test themselves on how well they are doing, and quantify effects on children. After reading the first three chapters of this book, readers will be able to make changes to the intervention without losing track of the active ingredients that must be kept for the intervention to be effective.

Why read this book? I hope you will read this book if you are interested in motivation, if you wonder why aspirations and attainments are so often mismatched, and if you want to know when motivation actually matters for behavior. You will find this book useful whether you are interested in utilizing what you learn to make changes in your own life or others' lives or if you are just curious about how motivation works. Reading this book will provide you with insight into the underlying process of motivation and rule out seemingly plausible but empirically unsupported alternatives.

Who should read this book? The book was meant for use in classrooms and the real world outside the classroom; students, researchers and policy makers, schools and other service providers, practitioners in a variety of settings, and parents will all find it useful. It is written to be accessible both to people in the world outside universities (policy makers, parents, educators) and those within university settings—students and researchers in developmental, social, clinical, and community psychology as well as in social work, counseling, and education courses. The book can be used in program development and evaluation classes as well as in self, identity, and motivation courses. Schools and other social service settings wanting to use the intervention can use the book to run the STJ intervention. Because the theory and decision points are described, tailoring can be done by focusing on the core components without fear of changing active ingredients and thus undermining the effectiveness of the intervention. The manual was tested with twelve- and thirteen-year-olds; its tone and the format of activities fit an audience of this age. The manual is set up to be used while running an intervention so that headings, type set and so on make accessibility 'on the fly' possible. The principles and many of the activities can also be used in other settings, as described in Chapter 3. Parents interested in motivational processes in their children and understanding what kind of intervention is likely to work and why will also find this book of use.

How should this book be read? This book can be read differently for different purposes. Having taught program evaluation in the past, I am aware that few programs are actually developed from an empirically tested theory. Instead, programs often report a variety of theories as reference points, even though none of the theories were specifically tested in the way they are used and much of the program is not really based on any particular theory. This makes it very difficult to explain to students what theory-driven intervention development and evaluation might look like. This book provides a blueprint of a brief intervention that is rooted in both a general framework and a particular empirically validated theory; it is set up so that it can be ported—moved from one setting to the next, because the active ingredients are made explicit. Students and researchers interested in developing theory-based, testable interventions will find the book useful in three ways: as a case study of a particular development and translation process (Chapters 1, 3, and 4), as a springboard for thinking about how social problems connect and how intervention at different levels can have carryover consequences (Chapter 2), and as a springboard for thinking about how to use intervention to create pathways for success (Chapters 1 through 4).

The book also works well in classes on self, identity, and motivation because it articulates the theory, provides empirical tests of the components, and demonstrates that the theory is robust enough to withstand the test of translation to intervention and randomized clinical testing of the intervention, with longitudinal follow-up. Moreover, it provides the actual translation to activities, a critical step that is missing if students just read articles summarizing that an intervention worked without a detailed explanation of what was actually done. Using the book in this way, readers should start with Chapters 1 and 3 and work in groups to think about activities that they would want to connect to create an intervention. The manual (Chapter 4) could be used as a backdrop for these. Chapter 2 is grounded in the assumption that "knowing is for doing"—that is, how people think about themselves in the moment reflects their sense of the action possibilities in that context. This chapter concretizes the evidence that valuing something, aspiring to it, expecting it to occur, and having strategies to get there all may be necessary but not sufficient unless contextual features are taken into account.

While the manual tested focuses on educational outcomes, identity-based motivation theory can be used for interventions meant to improve academic performance, health, well-being, and happiness across age groups. Therefore another way to use this book in policy, classroom, and research settings is as a blueprint for how to translate identity-based motivation theory into a testable intervention and then to evaluate it. Practitioners can use this book as the means to ground the STJ intervention into the specifics of their own setting and to know exactly how to make translations and adjustments to fit their setting without inadvertently changing a core active component. For researchers and practitioners interested in using this intervention in their own research and practice, this book provides a comprehensive overview of the theory and empirical support for it, articulation of the steps I took to translate the theory into the intervention, the manual itself, and the tools for process (delivery fidelity, enactment fidelity) and outcome (child results) assessment I used.

Parents can use this book to understand the motivational process and think through ways to help their children see the future as starting now and not later. For parents, reading about the nature of the evidence and why education matters may help in thinking about their children's developmental progression. While the manual is not intended as a parenting guide and was used in small groups, not one on one, it does provide parents with some clear dos and don'ts. For example, do help you children experience the future as starting now, not later, but don't worry yourself or them if they do not know what they really want to be when they grow up. The path to the future runs through school in any case.

IDENTITY-BASED MOTIVATION

PEOPLE EXPERIENCE THEMSELVES ACROSS TIME—recalling who they were and imagining who they will become. This consciousness of the self over time (Tulving, 1985; Wheeler, Stuss, & Tulving, 1997) and the ability to mentally "time travel" is a general human capacity (Epstude & Peetz, 2012) that develops by about age five (Atance, 2008; Atance & Jackson, 2009; Atance & Meltzoff, 2005; Russell, Alexis, & Clayton, 2010). For this reason, the future self can play a role in current choices from an early age. Indeed, when asked, people report imagining their future selves; they can describe both positive and negative possible identities their future selves might have (Dalley & Buunk, 2011; Norman & Aron, 2003). People say they care about whether they are making progress toward attaining their positive and avoiding their negative future identities (Vignoles, Manzi, Regalia, Jemmolo, & Scabini, 2008). They even report that their future selves are truer versions of themselves than their present selves, which are limited by the demands of everyday life (Wakslak, Nussbaum, Liberman, & Trope, 2008).

Given all that, it might seem unnecessary to test whether people's current actions are influenced by their future identities. Surely it has to be the case that future identities matter. Yet uncovering the circumstances in which the future self and other aspects of identity matter for behavior has turned out to be difficult. It is not always apparent that identities matter in spite of people's feelings that they must. Figuring out the underlying process is critical to reducing the gap between aspirations and attainments and is the focus of this book. Does the future self really make such a difference in behavior? In the next sections, I provide a perspective and research evidence to answer the question.

SELF, SELF-ESTEEM, IDENTITY, AND THE FUTURE SELF

While often used interchangeably, the terms *self, self-esteem,* and *identity* are based on different concepts (Oyserman, Elmore, & Smith, 2012). Self-esteem is the positive or negative regard one has for oneself. Identities are descriptors (e.g., homeowner, middle-aged), personal traits (e.g., shy, outgoing), and social roles (e.g., mother, daughter) and the content that goes with these traits, descriptors, and roles (e.g., proud, worried). *Self* is an overarching term—including self-esteem; past, current, and future identities; and the ability to experience oneself, sometimes termed self-awareness or metacognitive experience. The terms *past, current,* and *future self* are often used as a shorthand to mean all of these things with a temporal twist. Early and influential writing about the self and all of its aspects came from William James (1890), who articulated the idea that the self is temporal and has motivational power. His idea was that people include in their identities the traits, possessions, and relationships they have as well as the traits, possessions, and relationships they aspire to attain, and that they judge themselves based on their progress toward their aspired identities. A person's sense of worth (self-esteem) rises as he or she becomes more like the aspired identity.

James even had a formula: Self-esteem is the proportion of aspired identities one has attained and made into current identities. To feel good about oneself, one has to attain one's aspirations. Self-esteem increases as the number of attained identities relative to aspired possible identities increases and it falls as the number of attained identities relative to aspired possible identities decreases. Self-esteem would be 100 percent if all aspired identities were attained. To calculate a person's self-esteem, one need only take the number of aspired identities a person has already attained as the numerator (top of the fraction) and the number of aspired identities a person has overall as the denominator (bottom of the fraction). James assumed that decline in self-esteem is painful, and he articulated two ways to improve self-esteem—increase effort so that more aspired identities are attained and reduce or prune aspirations so that those that cannot be attained are dropped.

These seemed like excellent predictions. In fact, they were so intuitive that they were assumed to be true. The implication was that having possible future identities would lead to working to attain them and any aspired identities that could not be attained would be dropped. According to Google's search engine, Google Scholar, the modern formulation of this thesis—that future selves guide attention, motivation, and action as described by Hazel Markus and Paula Nurius, has been cited in thousands of academic papers (Markus & Nurius, 1986). It took a while, but eventually personality and social psychologists began to collect data on the content of people's positive and negative possible future identities and the relationship between future self and current self-regard (Coleman, Herzberg, & Morris, 1977; Cross & Markus, 1991; Little, 1983; 1989; Markus & Nurius, 1986; Palys & Little, 1983). Some psychologists even sought to establish links between the future self and behavior (Dalley & Buunk, 2011; Hoyle & Sherrill, 2006; Murru & Martin Ginis, 2010; Ouellette, Hessling, Gibbons, Reis-Bergan, & Gerrard, 2005; Oyserman & Markus, 1990a, 1990b; Ruvolo & Markus, 1992). A few asked if there is evidence that people give up on those aspired future identities that are impossible to attain (King & Hicks, 2007; King & Raspin, 2004; Pizzolato, 2007). As detailed next, the results suggest that reality is a bit more complicated than the simple prediction that having aspired future identities promotes striving toward goals.

Before describing these studies, I should note that, prior to this new look at the future self, there was research on the future self from a human development perspective that emphasized the transition to adulthood as the time for identity development (Erikson, 1963, 1980). From this perspective, each life phase involves a critical task, which, if successfully completed, bolsters self-esteem and well-being. The task for the transition to adulthood is exploration and commitment to a future self (Coleman, 1978; Erikson, 1963; 1980; Marcia, 1980; McGuire & Padawer-Singer, 1976). Human development researchers sought to establish ways to measure the extent to which adolescents and young adults were actively trying on and exploring future possible identities. The identities of interest were occupational and relational (Erikson, 1963), but the same approach was taken more generally to other identities, including exploring and committing to racial-ethnic identities (Phinney, 1990, 1992). The new look at the future self by social and personality psychologists freed the future self from a particular life phase or content and reframed the focus of enquiry. Instead of asking about the extent to which adolescents and young adults were exploring and committing to a future identity, researchers focused on the content of the future self and its association with self-esteem (or well-being more generally) and behavior, as detailed in the next two sections.

Content of the Future Self

Figuring out how to examine the content of future identities is not without methodological complications.[1] However, some commonalities emerge across the now voluminous literature on possible identities and the future self (for reviews, Oyserman & James, 2008, 2011). Given a chance, people describe their future selves in terms of positive and negative identities related to core achievement and generative developmental life tasks as well as material and lifestyle markers and milestones. Life tasks include attaining positive and avoiding negative schooling (e.g., college-bound "me," high school dropout "me"), employment (e.g., veterinarian "me," unemployed "me") and generative milestones in sustaining family relationships (e.g., parent "me", divorced "me") and community participation (e.g., volunteer, voter, or citizen "me"). Positive and negative possible identities related to lifestyle and material milestones markers include healthy "me," homeowner "me," drug addict or out-of-shape "me." Fewer possible identities focus on personality traits separate from those traits nested in attaining schooling, employment, and other milestones.

During the school years, near future (next year) possible identities typically focus on academic attainment, with a lesser focus on social relationships and lifestyle or material issues (for reviews, Oyserman & Fryberg, 2006; Oyserman & James, 2008). Although most of this research has been conducted in schools in the United States, some studies have been conducted in different settings and provide evidence for cross-setting and cross-cultural stability in pattern of response. From this research, it seems that the focus on school is universal. Whether respondents are in school or at home, are American or Chinese, are doing well in school or

---

1. In studying the future self, researchers ask participants to report on what they imagine themselves to be like. The hope is that by accumulating responses across various studies, it will be possible to get a sense of both the range of responses and what these responses imply for well-being and future outcomes. The reality is that this is hard to accomplish, because the way the question is framed influences the answer provided (Schwarz & Oyserman, 2001). Open-ended responses differ from closed-ended checklists. Responses to questions about a particular life domain (e.g., future career selves, future academic selves) will differ from responses to open-ended questions (e.g., future selves). Responses to questions without a specific time frame (e.g., the future) will differ from those with a particular time frame (e.g., next year). Responses to questions with a particular valence (e.g., "Tell me about your desired or hoped for future self", "Tell me about your undesired or feared future self") will differ from those without one (e.g., "Tell me about your future self"). On the one hand, there is no one correct way to ask about the future self because researchers should choose questions that fit their theoretical focus. On the other hand, this makes it difficult to read and synthesize what the literature can actually tell us about the future self (Hoyle & Sherrill, 2006; for a summary of existing measures with adolescents, see Oyserman & Fryberg, 2006; for a summary of existing measures more generally, see Oyserman & James, 2011). In spite of this difficulty, it is important to try to make sense of what is known about the content of the future self.

not, come from low- or higher-income families, and are White or minority, their future selves are dominated by schoolwork but also involve social relationships and material possessions in that order (Bi & Oyserman, 2014; Oyserman, Bybee, Terry, & Hart-Johnson, 2004; Oyserman & Destin, 2010; Oyserman & Fryberg, 2006; Oyserman & Oyserman, Johnson, & James, 2011; Zhu, Tse, Cheung, & Oyserman, 2014).

When asked about undesired or feared possible selves, these same topics emerge, as do various ways of becoming "off track," including pregnancy and too early parenthood, drug use, crime, and delinquency. These responses are even obtained for youth in detention and correctional facilities (for specific examples, Clinkinbeard & Murray, 2012; Clinkinbeard & Zohra, 2012; Iselin et al., 2012; Oyserman & Markus, 1990a, 1990b; Oyserman & Saltz, 1993). Differences by gender, race-ethnicity, and social class, to the extent that they have been studied, do not appear to be as marked as differences based on developmental shifts in the life tasks people are approaching (e.g., Anthis, Dunkel, & Anderson, 2004; Knox et al., 2000; Oyserman & Fryberg, 2006; Segal et al, 2001).

While this research is interesting, the general finding that the content of future selves maps onto people's developmental life tasks implies that most of them aspire to pretty much the same things. Take schoolchildren; if almost all schoolchildren can imagine a future self in a later time in which they are doing well in school, what about these future selves can distinguish children who do their homework well from those who do it poorly or not at all? Did the few children who failed to report such school success for their future selves give up on these possible identities or did they never have them? As detailed next and in the section on identity-based motivation, there is some content-based research that reports associations between how the future self is considered and behavior.

Positive and Negative Future Selves and Behavior
In this section I consider two core questions. First, is it more motivating to imagine positive future identities to be attained or negative future identities to be avoided? Second, are there costs to self-esteem and well-being of focusing on positive or negative future identities? Recall that William James predicted that self-esteem would be lower if current (attained) identities were relatively few in number compared with future (aspired) identities. He did not really consider negative future identities in considering self-esteem. However people do report having them: they can envision futures in which they have failed school, lost their jobs, had an accident, gained weight, lost health, and so on (for a review, Oyserman, Destin, & Novin, in press).

Most researchers have followed James's lead and focused mostly on positive possible identities. Markus and Nurius (1986) took a modified version of James's approach and measured the association of self-esteem and number of positive possible identities. They showed a positive association between the number of positive possible identities and self-esteem. Follow-up research commonly counted up the number of positive future identities a person reported and looked for associations with positive outcomes (e.g., with grades, Anderman, Anderman, & Griesinger, 1999; plans, Oettingen, Pak, & Schnetter, 2001; physical symptoms, King, 2001; optimism for the future, Gonzales, Burgess, & Mobilio, 2001; Meevissen, Peters & Alberts, 2011; Peters, Flink, Boersma, & Linton, 2010; Sheldon & Lyubomirsky, 2006). Sometimes the predicted association was found, other times it was not (see, for example, Dalley & Buunk, 2011; Oettingen, Pak, & Schnetter, 2001).

Some researchers compared positive and negative possible identities. For example, Ogilvie (1987) found that negative future self-images were more associated with self-esteem than positive ones. That is, the correlation between feeling close to becoming like one's negative future identities and lower self-esteem was greater than the correlation between feeling close to becoming like one's positive future identities and higher self-esteem. Some studies found that positive and negative possible identities are equally behaviorally motivating (Murru & Martin Ginis, 2010; Ouellette, Hessling, Gibbons, Reis-Bergan, & Gerrard, 2005). Other studies found that thinking about negative feared future identities is more motivating than thinking about positive desired ones (Dalley & Buunk, 2011). Indeed, sometimes thinking about a positive future identity has no consequence for behavior or is even associated with a reduction in effort (Gonzales, et al., 2001; Oettingen, et al., 2001). This heterogeneity of effects implies that despite its intuitive appeal, it is not enough to have a future orientation or set of future possible identities. Positive future selves do not of themselves predict positive consequences, nor do negative future selves of themselves predict positive or negative consequences (see also Oyserman, Destin, & Novin, in press; Smith, James, Varnum, & Oyserman, 2014).

Beyond Content and Valence: A Future Self Is Necessary but Not Enough

Rather than making a broad claim that the future self is (always) a guide to behavior, it seems that we should be asking a more targeted set of questions. First, why the future self does not always matter and, second, how and when it does. Just because the future self can matter does not mean that it always will.

Consider homework, healthy diet, and exercise. Homework might feel like a worthwhile investment while envisioning a desired possible "college graduate" identity or an undesired possible "high school dropout" identity, but otherwise it might feel like a chore to be shirked. The same is true for health. A healthy diet and exercise might feel like a good investment while envisioning a desired possible "healthy" identity or an undesired possible "flabby" identity, but they might simply feel onerous and restrictive otherwise.

People often seem to neglect their future selves in favor of their present selves (Anderson, Dietz, Gordon, & Klawitter, 2004; Benzion, Rapoport, & Yagil, 1989; Shapiro, 2005; Thaler, 1981). They procrastinate. They start too late and quit too soon. Worse yet, they fail altogether to act in ways that would enhance their chances of attaining their positive and avoiding their negative possible future identities. Students skip their homework and avoid studying. They go out with friends, play computer games, or spend hours on social media instead of reviewing their notes, thus ending up with worse grades than they otherwise could have attained. Weight watchers push the button and wait for the elevator instead of taking the stairs; they don't pass up the second dessert or third roll and don't eat their kale, ending up less fit and healthy than they had aspired to become. Indeed, as many a study has documented, simply imagining one's future self is not enough to lead to positive behavioral engagement (Oettingen, Pak, & Schnetter, 2001; Strauss, Griffin, & Parker, 2012; Vansteenkiste, Simons, Soenens, & Lens, 2003).

MAKING JUDGMENTS INVOLVES MAKING MEANING

To further understand why possible future identities do not always direct current behavior and why, at other times, they do, it is useful to take a step back and ask what is known about how people make judgments (Higgins, 1998; Schwarz, 2002; 2012; Smith & Collins, 2010). To form a judgment, people need to figure out what their experiences mean (Heider, 1958; Weber, 1967). To do so, they need to consider their situation. Not surprisingly, then, people are highly sensitive to their immediate environment, automatically picking up cues about what content and what way of thinking is relevant in the moment (Bargh, 2014; Bargh & Ferguson, 2000). In this way, contexts influence what is on people's minds. People pay attention to what is on their minds in forming judgments of how frequent, likely, or typical events are (Tversky & Kahneman, 1973). People do not pay attention to why information is on their minds, assuming that things on their minds are relevant to the judgments they are making (Higgins, 1998). They include accessible information in their judgments unless context provides reasons to exclude this information (Bless & Schwarz, 2010).

Everyday Theories

People make sense of what comes to mind using a variety of everyday theories, often focused on explaining to themselves their experience of ease or difficulty in thinking (Schwarz et al., 1991; Schwarz, 1998). Judgments—such as "Do I like this?" "How hard should I try?" "Should I keep going?" "Should I pay attention?"—are often based on how thinking feels and not just on the content that comes to mind. This very important distinction between content and experience might seem hard to grasp without a specific example. Luckily, the classic study on this distinction focused on identity. Schwarz and colleagues (Schwarz, Bless, Strack, Klumpp, Rittenauer-Schatka, & Simons, 1991) showed that participants who were asked to make a judgment about their assertiveness or unassertiveness were more influenced by how hard or easy it was to come up with examples than by the examples themselves. This might sound reasonable; if it is hard to come up with examples of times one acted assertively, maybe there are not that many and one is not really all that assertive. Schwarz and colleagues were able to disentangle whether the interpretation was a reasonable conclusion drawn from one's own life or a conclusion that the researcher artificially created by setting up a feeling of difficulty. They did so in two steps, as detailed next.

First, Schwarz and colleagues (1991) asked participants to give examples of times they were assertive or unassertive; then they asked separate groups of participants to either give fewer than this average number of examples (six) or more than this average number of examples (twelve). Six and twelve were chosen because they represented the average minus or plus a standard deviation (*standard deviation* is a statistical term referring to the square root of the squared difference from the mean). Since it was less than most people gave when not constrained, giving six examples felt easy for the average participant. Since it was more than most people gave when not constrained, giving twelve examples felt hard for the average participant. Participants paid attention to that feeling. In the twelve-example condition, in spite of having come up with many examples of times they had been assertive, they rated themselves as less assertive than participants in the six-examples condition who had come up with fewer examples. They also rated themselves as less assertive than participants who were asked to come up with many examples of times that they had not been assertive. Twelve examples of being assertive felt difficult to do, so the average participant became convinced that he or she was not assertive. But the same thing happened for participants asked to come up with examples of being unassertive. Twelve examples of being unassertive felt difficult to do, so the average participant became convinced that he or she was in fact assertive.

Experienced Difficulty and Its Interpretation

The effect of difficulty on motivation and engagement is a core theme in psychological work. Experienced difficulty can be a cue to increase focused attention. William James (1890) discussed difficulty in terms of the will to overcome distraction, his insight being that will power is not needed unless a task would otherwise not be the immediate focus of attention. Empirically, this seems to be true up to a point. As difficulty increases, so do motivation and effort and the perceived attractiveness of the difficult-to-attain goal (for a review, see Brehm & Self, 1989). This effect is not linear. Anticipating or experiencing a task as too easy makes it seem not worth the effort. Anticipating or experiencing a task as impossible has the same effect; effort stops abruptly if a task is perceived as being impossible (Brehm & Self, 1989; Silvestrini & Gendolla, 2013). Between these two extremes, increased difficulty increases engagement. Effects in these studies were found by manipulating task difficulty rather than by manipulating people's *interpretation* of what their experience of difficulty meant.

While these and other studies did not directly manipulate the theory people used, the judgment participants were asked to make drew their attention to one particular way of interpreting difficulty. In the case of tasks, an accessible possible interpretation seems to be "if it is very difficult, it must be impossible"; in the case of self-judgments, an accessible possible interpretation seems to be "if it is difficult, it must not be true" (Greifeneder, Bless, & Pham, 2011; Schwarz, 1998, 2004, 2010). Follow-up studies show that people are sensitive to situational cues as to which theory to use to interpret why certain information is on their minds and what an experience of ease or difficulty implies (Labroo, Lambotte, & Zhang, 2009; Xu & Schwarz, 2009). Among other interpretations, experienced difficulty may mean that one does not know or lacks expertise, that something is not true, is dangerous, or is novel or sophisticated (Schwarz, 2012). These studies show that people are not good at distinguishing between thoughts and feelings that stem from the object of judgment and thoughts and feelings that just happen to occur at the same moment (for reviews, see Schwarz, 1998, 2004, 2010; Schwarz & Clore, 2007). This means that the very same processes that make people sensitive to their circumstances can lead them astray; but as I outline in this book, it also means that interventions can be helpful.

What Does an Identity That Comes to Mind Imply?

Future Self and Current Behavior. As the prior section highlights, having a future identity is not the same as having it on one's mind and experiencing it as relevant to current judgment, choice, and behavior. On the one hand, one's future self may or may not be on one's mind. If a particular future identity does not come to mind, it is unlikely to influence behavior. On the other hand, even if a future identity does come to mind, whether and how it influences behavior will depend on the everyday theory used to interpret it. Is the future experienced as distant and hence not relevant to current choice? Is thinking about or working toward that future self experienced as difficult or as easy, and if so, what is ease or difficulty interpreted to mean? For a child, the adult self involves the distant future; it is possible, not for sure, and may be experienced as far away and disconnected from the present. Thus even if accessible, one's imagined adult self may or may not feel relevant to the school task at hand.

As documented in temporal construal theory, people's lay intuition is that that which is far away may be of value but does not require current action (Trope & Liberman, 2003). This intuition—that things that are close by require action while things that are far away do not—has also been studied under the rubric of "authorship". Authorship involves causality. That is, people's mental systems are sensitive to temporal and spatial proximities; that is, things that are nearby are assumed to be related (e.g., Ebert & Wegner, 2010). Synthesizing this work implies that even though judgments and hence actions are commonly based on what comes to mind at the moment of judgment (Higgins, 1998), a future self may come to mind but not be experienced as relevant to current judgment and action. After all, the future is far, distant, separate from the here and now. Anything that is not immediate is experienced as mattering less for current choice (see temporal construal theory, Chapman & Elstein, 1995). Distant goals are perceived as less dependent on a particular set of current actions (Liberman & Förster, 2008).

Even though people have a lay theory that they should act in identity-congruent ways, these findings imply that only those identities that seem relevant to the task at hand should shape action (Oyserman, Bybee, & Terry, 2006). A number of experiments test this prediction by manipulating whether children experience a connection between their future adult selves and their present selves. Two of these involved the School-to-Jobs intervention to improve academic attainment (Oyserman, Bybee, & Terry, 2006; Oyserman, Terry, & Bybee, 2002). In one seven-week intervention, children were randomly divided into two groups. One received the intervention and the other had school as usual. In the intervention, children were led to believe that their next year's selves were connected to their adult selves; as a result, they attained better grades in school than those in the no-intervention control group (Oyserman, Bybee, & Terry, 2006). Activities provided the connection message—for example, by having children link their next year's and adult possible selves on a time line in one session and then, in another session, having them link their next year's and adult possible selves through strategies for action on a poster board.

In addition to these intervention results, we also tested these ideas in separate experiments. We started with the supposition that one way in which children can experience connection is by seeing education as a path from their present to their future selves. Indeed, how twelve-year-old children described their future selves as adults in ten years was associated with how much time they later spent on homework as well as their end-of-year grades, even when controlling for prior academic attainment (Destin & Oyserman, 2010, study 1). Children who described their ten-years in the future adult selves as dependent on their educational attainments (e.g., "I will be an engineer if I go to college") spent more time on homework and had better end-of-year grades than those who described this future self without reference to educational attainment (e.g., "I will be a musician with my own band if I practice enough"). In a follow-up experiment, to test whether this effect is causal, we assigned children to two groups. Those who were induced to see their adult future selves as education-dependent were six times more likely to hand in the next day's homework than those induced to see their adult selves as education-independent (Destin & Oyserman, 2010, study 2).

Other studies tested the possibility that the active component is not specifically about school as a path to one's future self but the feeling of certainty provided by any path metaphor associated with the future self. Thus first-year college students were asked to imagine their best possible academic selves in four years' time and to write the key words illustrating these future selves (Landau, Oyserman, Keefer, & Smith, 2014). Where they wrote the key words differed by condition. One third of the students were randomly assigned to write these key words on a path, the others wrote the words in a container, or simply on lines located in the same part of the page. They were then given the opportunity to engage in academic tasks (a different one in each study). Across studies, students in the path condition were more interested in study aids, they planned to study more, they worked harder on mental math tasks, and they felt more certain that they knew the steps to take to attain their possible selves than the students in the other conditions.

Social Identities and Current Behavior. The idea that future identities influence behavior only if they come to mind, are experienced as relevant to the task at hand, and influence the interpretation of experienced difficulty can be applied to current identities as well (Oyserman, 2007, 2009). In one set of studies we asked African American, Hispanic, and American Indian schoolchildren in the United States and Arab Israelis in Israel to complete a novel math task, one that they had not done before, so they did not already know whether they could do it (Oyserman, Gant & Ager, 1995, Study 2; Oyserman, et al., 2003, studies 2 and 3). We predicted that children would work harder on this and other school tasks if their racial-ethnic identities were on their minds and if racial-ethnic identities were experienced as relevant to school attainment. To test this prediction, we asked half the children about their racial-ethnic identity (what is it, what does it mean in your everyday life) *before* giving them the math task and the other half of children *after* giving them the math task.

We coded children's responses to the racial-ethnic identity questions and looked at whether content of racial-ethnic identity mattered and if so, if it mattered only when accessible prior to action (before doing the math task). That is what we found. Students mostly described their racial-ethnic identity in terms of connection to their in-group—feeling proud, connected, a part of the group. This content, though positive, was not particularly relevant to school. Indeed, accessible racial-ethnic identity did not improve performance for these children. However, some children described school attainment as something that their group and larger society valued. This content clearly was relevant to school. For these children, performance improved when racial-ethnic identity was accessible—that is, when they were asked about it before they did the math task. This positive effect was found for each of the racial-ethnic groups we studied.

To demonstrate the generalizability of these effects beyond racial-ethnic group membership, in a follow-up experiment we focused on gender (Elmore & Oyserman, 2011). Like race-ethnicity, being a boy or a girl may or may not be relevant to school attainment. We asked boys and girls to describe their possible selves, solve the same novel math problem, and estimate how far they would go in school. Before answering these questions, all children were first asked to interpret one of four graphs. Half of the children saw a graph in which gender was not mentioned. The graph either showed the percentage of people in their state who graduated high school or the average income of people in their state. These were the control-group children, since gender did not figure into the graphs they were shown. In the control group, girls did better at the math task than boys; they described more school-focused possible selves and they believed that they would go farther in school than boys did. This pattern of girls outperforming boys is consistent with the national data, especially for low-income and minority children (EPE Research Center, 2007; Roderick, 2003).

However, the pattern shifted for the other half of the children. These children saw gender-dependent graphs. Some saw a graph of high school graduation (women graduate at a higher rate than men); others saw a graph of average income (men earn more than women). Children in these conditions were given a cue that their gender group matters and either facilitates or undermines success. As predicted, boys' performance could be improved or undermined depending on which cue they received. Compared with boys in the control condition and boys in the women-graduate condition, boys in the men-earn-more-than-women condition described more school-focused possible selves. Not only did they think they could be getting better grades, they also performed better on the math task and even reported that they would go farther in school and do better occupationally as adults. Taken together, these studies provide support for the prediction that whether an identity matters is a function of whether it is *accessible* and *experienced as relevant* to the choices afforded by the current situation.

IDENTITY AS A MEANING-MAKING LENS: IDENTITY-BASED MOTIVATION

In this section I synthesize the literature reported in the prior sections to consider what research on meaning making implies for when and how identities matter for the meaning people make of their situation and their choices over time. As noted above, both current and future selves can be psychologically relevant to choice. An identity is psychologically relevant if it is accessible in working memory, and experienced as connected to available behavioral options. Current and future selves can have the same, competing, or different desires. If the current self is psychologically relevant, people may ask, "Is this fun?" or "Am I enjoying myself?" or "Do others [boys, Latinos, etc.] act this way?" In contrast, if the future self is psychologically relevant, people may ask "Is this important for the person I may become?" "Am I making progress toward my goals?" or "Do successful people do this?" The two perspectives may produce the same or differing results—for example, acting like a boy may or may not help in attaining one's future identity as an "A" student.

Identity-based motivation (IBM) theory implies that people are likely to overlook possibilities for action. That is, there are more potential possibilities for action than people typically notice or pay attention to. Overlooking possibilities can be useful if people limit their choices to those that improve their future chances; however, this is not always the case. Even identity-congruent choices may not be recognized as choices. People overlook choices for a number of reasons. They act on the identities that come to mind and seem psychologically relevant in the moment. They act to the extent that experienced difficulty in taking or sustaining action is interpreted as meaning that an accessible identity is important (not impossible) to attain. At the same time and for the same reasons, people sometimes engage in actions that undermine their desired future selves.

Consider the following common situations: feeling depleted at the end of a long day, being pressed for time as a deadline approaches, and looking for fun. Does the depleted student recharge with a delicious mound of fresh fruit, a walk, a pile of fries, by going out with friends? Does the out-of-time student cut and paste from his own or someone else's work, pay someone to write that term paper, or delay working on other assignments to complete the assignment? Does the fun-seeking student watch a movie or shoplift? All of these and many more are potential choices, but people are unlikely to consciously and systematically weigh the pros and cons of all options for dealing with hunger, stress, and boredom before deciding. Instead, their choices both large and small are likely to be channeled by what feels *identity-based* and *identity-congruent* in the moment.

Taking an IBM approach does not imply that the future self never matters for current action. Rather, it implies that the future self does not always have behavioral implications and that without an understanding of the situational cues that link future self to current action, interventions, no matter how well-meaning, are unlikely to succeed. By focusing on when the future self has behavioral implications, IBM implies that small changes in context can have big effects if these changes (1) make the future seem relevant to the present, (2) make strategies feel identity-congruent, and (3) facilitate interpretation of experienced difficulty as a signal of task importance, a cue that this is "for me" and not "a waste of my time." These three ingredients are crucial. Consider the following situations: an elementary school student faced with her spelling words, a middle school student who cannot solve his algebra homework, and two friends with a tough eighth-grade writing assignment. How much effort, how many different strategies, how much recall of the writing rules the teacher taught is enough? As I will demonstrate, these choices are fluid, not fixed traits. Small interventions can help students experience their future possible selves as psychologically relevant to the present, see strategies to attain that self as identity-congruent, and experience difficulties as energizing rather than undermining of goal-focused investment.

Action Is (Sometimes) Future-Focused

Identity-based motivation (IBM) theory starts with this seeming paradox: People can imagine their future selves and do care about this aspect of themselves; at the same time, they may often fail to take future-focused action (Oyserman, 2007, 2009). IBM theory predicts why that might be. In doing so, it focuses on the possibility that the average person has the capacity to act in a future-oriented way but that this capacity is not necessarily evoked in context. It shows how small changes in context can increase or decrease the likelihood that people will act in service of their future selves. It is not that an IBM approach disregards individual differences in capacity; rather, it assumes that given a reasonable level of capacity, the future self will matter only if it feels psychologically relevant in context.[2]

2. Individual differences in capacity—sometimes termed impulsivity, willingness to delay rewards (Ersner-Hershfield, Garton, Ballard, Samanez-Larkin, & Knutson, 2009; Frederick, Loewenstein, & O'Donoghue, 2002), or future orientation (e.g., Keough, Zimbardo & Boyd, 1999; Nurmi, 1991; Raynor, 1969; Steinberg, Graham, O'Brien, Woolard, Cauffman, & Banich, 2009; Zimbardo & Boyd, 1999)—have been related to culture (Gupta, Hanges, & Dorfman, 2002; Seginer & Halabi-Kheir, 1998), social class (Lamm, Schmidt, Trommsdorff, 1976), parenting (Webley, & Nyhus, 2006), and school context (Chen & Vazsonyi, 2013).

Contexts influence which identities come to mind, whether they feel relevant to the current situation, and how they are interpreted to make sense of experienced difficulty.

Accessibility. The first element of IBM theory is that people act on that aspect of the self that is accessible at the moment of judgment. The importance of accessibility is familiar to anyone who has been told to put a photograph of a desired achievement at eye level in a place where it will be seen (by the desk, on the refrigerator) so that the desired goal does not slip from one's mind. Accessibility is a necessary element for action since it sets the direction and endpoint to strive toward (or in the case of a negative self, to keep away from). But, as anyone who has tried this approach may be painfully aware, imagining a possible identity, even one that is highly desired, is not in itself sufficient to produce action. People can still eat cake or the rest of the leftover pizza even while looking at the bikini image on the refrigerator door.

Psychological Relevance. This frustrating disjuncture between an accessible future self and current behavior occurs in part because in order to influence behavior, an identity must not only come to mind but also seem relevant to the task at hand. Having a future self is not in and of itself enough to spur a person to action, but this fact is not intuitively obvious. Indeed, for a long time social scientists assumed that it was (e.g., Duval & Wicklund, 1972; Miller, Galanter, & Pribram, 1960). IBM theory outlines three reasons why future selves (and identity in general) do not necessarily spur action. First, even important future selves can be experienced as psychologically distant and irrelevant to the current situation. Second, the strategies to attain one's future self may not feel like things a person such as oneself would do. And, third, a "see it be it" frame provides no sense of how to interpret difficulties along the way (see Oyserman, 2007; 2009; Oyserman & Destin, 2010; Oyserman, Elmore, & Smith, 2012 for detailed presentation of the model).

A few examples can help make to these ideas clear. First, consider the "What do you want to be when you grow up?" question asked by concerned adults wanting to help a child stay on course. After getting an answer, these adults typically exhort the child to work hard in school or risk failing to attain the desired future. As in the case of the would-be thin person pinning a photograph depicting a skinny future self to the refrigerator, these methods imply that to "see it" is to "be it." But seeing it is not being it. There is still the question of relevance: Is skipping homework today really going to matter for a self that is more than a decade away in the future? Is a piece of cake now really going to matter in an hour, let alone after that? As these examples imply, the act of imagining a future self is not sufficient; even if it on one's mind it does not necessarily require that any action be taken now. People can consider retiring in 30 or 40 years or that their newborn will be a college student in 18 years, if these future identities as retiree or as parent of a college student feel distal, they will not start saving (Lewis & Oyserman, 2014).

Here is another example. Consider an eight-year-old boy with a college-bound future self and a spelling test on Friday. If his college-bound self does not come to mind, memorizing the words will not be experienced as an investment in that future self. If his college-bound self feels far away, he may not see how it matters whether Friday's spelling words are memorized or not. If memorizing the words feels hard, he might even think of that as evidence that he does not have the right stuff to make it to college. If making flash cards, writing the words over and over, covering the words with his hand and saying out loud what is hidden, or other effective strategies feel like "not me" things to do—things girls or nerds do—he might fail to use effective memorization strategies. Of course failing to use effective strategies makes the task harder and success less likely than it needs to be. In short, one's future self is not a magnetic force field inexorably drawing behavior toward it. Rather, relevant possible identities may be obscured at the moment of choice. Even if they're on one's mind, they may seem too far away to matter or may seem to be pointing to a path people like oneself do not take.

(Mis)Interpretation of Experienced Ease and Difficulty. Experiencing difficulties is likely to be a ubiquitous concomitant of goal striving. But what does this experience imply? It could bring to mind content and associations related to importance or impossibility. Accessible content and associations shape how difficulty is interpreted—as either a signal that goal achievement is impossible or as a signal that goal achievement is important. Difficulties can plausibly signal either interpretation, and being sensitive to both possibilities is rooted in an evolutionary press for survival (Charnov, 1974; Nesse, 2009). Consider an organism foraging for food. On the one hand, sustaining and even increasing effort in the face of difficulty reduces the chance that the organism will give up too soon and prematurely move on to another area (Nesse, 2009). At the same time, a mechanism for turning attention away from an unattainable goal is also necessary so that the organism does not starve owing to its inability to redirect attention toward more fruitful targets (Charnov, 1974). Hence people should be sensitive to both the possibility that their efforts would be better spent elsewhere as well as to the possibility that they should ramp up engagement for tasks worth extra effort.

Putting It Together. Each of the three ingredients of identity-based motivation influences effort and engagement, as detailed in the general model is presented in Figure 1.1. Each of the experiments reported in this section tests an aspect of the model—for example, testing whether manipulating psychological relevance influences readiness to act or if manipulating interpretation of experienced difficulty influences psychological relevance. Of necessity, each experiment can test only a piece of the full process tested in the School-to-Jobs intervention described in Chapter 3. Experiments are important because they test whether

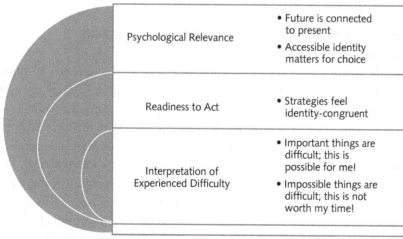

FIGURE 1.1
The three ingredients of identity-based motivation.

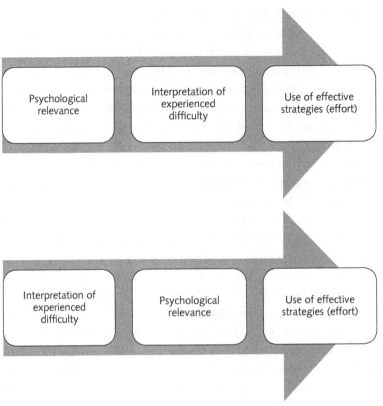

FIGURE 1.2

An example of the identity-based motivation process. The models are drawn as linear sections; manipulating one ingredient can have downstream consequences for other ingredients. *Note:* In the first sequence, something about the situation makes a certain way of seeing oneself seem possible; this influences how difficulties are interpreted and therefore whether strategies are effectively used. In the second sequence, something about the situation influences which interpretation of experienced difficulty comes to mind; this influences which identities seem relevant in the moment and therefore whether strategies feel identity-congruent.

each posited active ingredient has the intended effect immediately; this provides a reason to keep a component in the general model for intervention. Because each experiment tests a smaller, linear piece of the model, in Figure 1.2 I draw a set of linear relationships with the left-most section manipulated and its effects on the middle and subsequent sections tested, as detailed in the remaining sections of this chapter.

The Effects of Making the Future Feel Psychologically Relevant on Current Choice

Making the future feel psychologically relevant to the present is important because otherwise even if the future self comes to mind, it is likely to be experienced as important but distant and thus requiring no current action (Wakslak, Nussbaum, Liberman, & Trope, 2008). Indeed, the more vividly the present is experienced, the more effort is required to control the impulse to take small rewards in the present over larger rewards in the future (Metcalfe, & Mischel, 1999). Small changes in framing can flip children's preference for small but immediate versus larger but later rewards (Bandura & Mischel, 1965). On average people are more willing to make future-focused choices if a connection between their current and future selves has been made (Ersner-Hershfield et al., 2011; Pronin, Olivola, & Kennedy, 2008). For example, they are less tempted to engage

PATHWAYS TO SUCCESS THROUGH IDENTITY-BASED MOTIVATION

in delinquent activities (van Gelder, Hershfield, & Nordgren, 2013). Studies like these demonstrate that an accessible future self can influence current choices but only if the future self is made to feel psychologically relevant to these current choices.

Consider homework. Homework is not designed to be more fun than current alternatives, and students are unlikely to do their homework because they have nothing more fun do with their time. Why do homework then? IBM theory predicts that homework is done because it is imbued with meaning via its link to the future. If this link to the future were missing, homework would not get done and there would be no reason not to have cake for breakfast, ice cream for lunch, and donuts for dinner. As an initial test of this prediction, we used the same novel math task we had used in prior studies and found that nine- to twelve-year-old children who reported that they could vividly imagine their adult selves also spent more effort on the task and produced more solutions (Nurra & Oyserman, 2014).

To further test the prediction that the psychological relevance of the future self matters for choice, we asked other nine- to twelve-year-olds about their adult future selves and how old they would be at that time; then we had them do something else (Nurra & Oyserman, 2014). We divided the children into groups and asked the question about their future selves in a different way to each group to see whether the way in which the question was asked influenced their sense that their future selves were psychologically relevant to the present situation. Across the different ways of asking the question, almost all children focused on the job they would have as adults, and they thought that they would be in their early twenties when they became this future selves.

However, the way the "What will you be as an adult?" question was asked did influence the effect of the future self on current behavior. In one study we showed children a picture of two circles labeled "me now" and "me as an adult" and asked them to describe their adult selves. The children were divided into two groups. In one group the two circles overlapped and in the other group they did not. Seeing overlapping circles led children to report that their adult selves were easier to imagine and led to improved schoolwork. In another study we divided children into three groups. The first group was asked about their adult selves, the second group was asked about their far-adult selves, and the third group was asked about their near-adult selves. Children in this third group worked harder at school tasks. We found the effect not only immediately but also on grades when we followed up later. Indeed, in two separate samples, children led to consider their adult selves as connected to their current selves got better grades at the end of the marking period three months later. Across studies we checked to see if the effect was due to children actually saying that they would become their adult selves at a younger age. This was not the case. Nine- to thirteen-year-olds think they that will be their adult selves when they are about twenty-two years old, and that did not change. What changed is that they felt a need to get going on their schoolwork. My students and I are currently examining whether this same effect can be found for children in kindergarten and early elementary school. Children as young as age five understand the idea of a future self, but does seeing that self as connected to the current self encourage them to delay gratification or consume their rewards immediately?

Of course getting going on a future that seems distant is important not only for children. We tested this with college students as well (Landau, Oyserman,

Keefer, & Smith, 2014). In these studies, instead of overlapping circles and adult future selves, we asked first-year college students to imagine themselves at the end of their undergraduate careers, having attained their best possible academic selves. Then we had students write down keywords that described these selves. Some students were given a lined sheet of paper or asked to enter their responses onto lines on a computer screen. For other students, the sheet of paper or computer screen included a picture. The picture was either an image of a path or an image of containers. Students in these conditions either wrote their possible selves on the path or put them into a container. Across studies, we found that the path image improved outcomes. Students were more likely to take offered information on university study and academic resources (study 1), worked harder on mental math tasks (study 2), planned to spend more time studying (study 3), and performed better on actual course exams (study 3). The way the path was considered mattered. When we gave students an image of a figure walking on a path we found our results, when the image did not imply agency (e.g., being a passenger on a train) nothing happened (study 4). Students using a journey metaphor to frame their academic possible selves reported feeling that their academic possible selves felt connected to their current selves (study 5) and that they knew what to do to attain those possible selves (study 6). Using a journey metaphor did not change students' possible selves; it changed students' belief that they should and could get going now and indeed resulted in actual engagement and an improvement in performance.

The Effects of Making Strategies Feel Identity-Congruent on Current Choice

The prior section demonstrated the influence of the first component of IBM, showing that one's future self influences choices if that future self is both accessible (on one's mind) and experienced as psychologically relevant to the present self. A few different ways of making the future self feel psychologically relevant to the present self were described. In this section, I turn to the second ingredient of IBM, the strategies-identity association. This ingredient focuses on the idea that choices are more likely to bolster rather than undermine the attainment future selves if at the moment of choice relevant strategies are experienced as identity-congruent rather than incongruent.

To test this prediction as it relates to school and career identities, my students and I asked low-income and minority eighth-grade students in Detroit classrooms what they expected to be doing in ten years and, if they expected to have a job, what kind of job that might be (Destin & Oyserman, 2010). Like the younger students previously described, all of the students expected to be working in ten years (at about twenty-three years of age). About half the students described their possible future career attainments as contingent on their school success and the other half did not. We called these different ways of thinking education-dependent and education-independent. We followed the students over the course of the school year and found that those with education-dependent future career selves spent more time on homework and earned better grades than did those with education-independent future career selves. This positive influence of an education-dependent future self on using homework as a strategy remained significant even after controlling for prior school grades.

To test if we could get more children to use homework as a strategy to attain their future selves, we went to another Michigan school with similar demographics. We divided the children into two groups. One group was shown a graph of the average earnings of Michiganders by level of education. The data were real, taken from the U.S. Census. Although we did not say that education is the path to a successful future self, they could see in the graph that as education increased—from less than high school, to high school graduate, to college, to graduating college, and to professional degrees—income rose as well. The other group was shown a graph of the average earnings of the average Michigander and of top athletes, actors, and musicians. We used these careers both because they were the common choices among the students in the prior studies with education-independent future-self descriptions and because other research suggests that these are salient career identities among low-income and minority children (Guiffrida, 2009). Again, the data were real. Although we did not say that education is not the path to attaining a successful future self, the students could see in the graph that compared with the average person, top musicians, athletes, and actors had very high and quite similar earnings. Thus the education-dependent condition drew explicit attention to the connection between education and adult wage-earning identities while the education-independent condition made no mention of education. Then students received a survey of "everyday behaviors" to fill out on their own. The study was ostensibly over.

The survey asked children how much time they planned to spend that night on homework and studying as well as on other leisure-time activities (watching TV, listening to music, playing video games, playing sports, using the computer). After they handed in the survey, the experimenter left the room. Their teacher offered children a chance to do extra-credit homework that night. We asked the teacher to let us know which children handed in that homework. Then we compared the two groups. Did considering their future as education-dependent change students' use of homework as a strategy? It did. The children in the education-dependent group not only said they planned to spend more time on homework and studying that night than did the children in the education-independent group, they were also almost eight times as likely to do their extra-credit homework. The positive influence of making the future feel education-dependent remained even after we added controls for teacher, prior grade point averages, and gender. Making the future feel education-dependent did not influence the amount of time children planned to spend on other activities. Compared with children in the education-dependent group, children in the education-independent group did not report that they would spend more time on sports or music or other leisure activities.

In these studies we manipulated whether the future self was experienced as education-dependent or education-independent. We found the same pattern of effects in field studies examining the effect of making strategies for healthy living (such as getting regular exercise or drinking water) feel identity-congruent or incongruent (Oyserman, Fryberg, & Yoder, 2007). Low-income and minority children and adults were divided into two groups. One group reported on the effectiveness of various strategies for healthy living. Members of the other group were first asked about their socioeconomic status and race, thus bringing these identities to mind. People in the first group consistently rated strategies for healthy living as more effective than did people in the second group, implying that these strategies did not feel identity-congruent. In a final set of studies, we manipulated whether these strategies felt identity-congruent or not. Strategies that felt identity-congruent were also experienced as more effective.

The Effects of Manipulating Interpretation of Experienced Difficulty on Current Choice

IBM theory predicts that interpretation of experienced difficulty, rather than difficulty itself, matters. That means that motivation, effort, task persistence, and success will either increase or decrease as a response to experienced difficulty depending on what experienced difficulty is interpreted to mean. To test this prediction, we asked students to describe their future selves or to complete a difficult task (an intelligence test or a standardized writing test) (Oyserman, Novin, Smith, Elmore, & Nurra, 2014; Smith & Oyserman, 2014). Sometimes students were middle schoolers from the Detroit area and were primarily African American or Latino and from low-income families, other times students were undergraduates from the University of Michigan and were primarily white or Asian American from well-off families. In each study, before completing the task, students were divided into three groups. The first group just completed the task with no initial framing. They formed our control group. The other groups were first asked how much they agreed or disagreed with four questions. The questions either led them to consider that important school tasks are difficult, thus making difficulty an indicator of importance, or led them to consider that impossible school tasks are difficult, thus making difficulty an indicator of impossibility. Students in the difficulty-implies-importance group were more likely to describe school-focused future selves and strategies to attain them. They also outperformed students in the other two groups on both the intelligence test and the writing test. The control group and difficulty-implies-impossibility group did not differ from each other, implying that control-group students also acted as if they interpreted task difficulty as implying impossibility. The two interpretations of experienced difficulty were not correlated—holding one did not predict holding the other. Each interpretation of experienced difficulty had significant and separate associations with relevant constructs (e.g., academic self-efficacy, belief that school is the path to attaining adult possible selves), grade point average, and likelihood of graduating high school. Moreover, each interpretation of experienced difficulty had effects separate from children's belief in the malleability of intelligence (for malleability of intelligence readings see: Blackwell, Trzesniewski, & Dweck, 2007; Dweck, 1999; 2006).

Across studies we found that it was easy to shift students from one interpretation of difficulty to the other. This means that for any child, experienced difficulty at school tasks may be interpreted as implying that school success is identity-congruent, important to attain, and hence worth the effort. At the same time, it also means that for any child, experienced difficulty at school tasks may also be interpreted as identity-incongruent, impossible to attain, and hence not worth the effort. Either interpretation can be brought to mind by features of the situation. As we showed in the gender study, important social identities like gender can instigate this same process of interpreting difficulty (Oyserman, 2007, 2009; Oyserman & Destin, 2010).

SUMMARY

By taking into account research on how salient information influences judgment and behavior, we may close what appears to be a puzzling gap between the high value placed on education and the actual school attainment. School-focused possible identities may not come to mind or may feel too far in the future to be relevant in the moment. Even if the possible identity feels relevant, working on one's school-focused possible identities is likely to be difficult. What does this difficulty mean—are school-focused and feared off-track possible identities "truely" possible or do they contradict other important social identities? Is attaining one's school-focused possible identity plausible or not worth the effort?. To judge what difficulty means teens must answer the following implied questions: "Why is engaging in this so hard for me; is this really the true me?" and "Do *we* (i.e., members of my group) have possible selves like this?" Likewise, they must judge whether particular behavioral patterns and strategies (e.g., asking for help) are likely to work and if they contradict in-group identity (e.g., "will asking the teacher for help actually help me succeed in school?"). Similarly, with regard to feared off-track possible selves, an effective way to work on avoiding becoming like these possible selves is to focus on school—spending time doing homework, going to class, paying attention while there, and staying after school for extra help. But if these strategies do not feel like in-group things to do or if difficulty is interpreted as meaning that they are not self-relevant, youths will have difficulty engaging in these strategies even if they believe them to be effective.

Successful movement toward positive school-focused possible selves and away from feared school-focused possible selves requires ongoing behavior; it is not enough to complete one homework assignment or stay after class just once. If the possible self rarely comes to mind or mostly feels too far away to matter, this sustained pattern of engagement is unlikely to occur. A similar lack of sustained engagement is triggered if one is uncertain of the identity-congruence of strategies for working on the possible self. Finally, working on any important possible self is difficult, and if this difficulty is interpreted as meaning that it is impossible to attain, then difficulties will undermine effort. In contrast, if difficulty is interpreted as meaning that the possible self is important to attain, then difficulties will bolster effort.

2

A FOCUS ON EDUCATION

AMERICAN STUDENTS ASPIRE TO GET GOOD GRADES and succeed in college (Rosenbaum, Deil-Amen, & Person 2006; Trusty, 2000). This is true across the socioeconomic spectrum (for a review, see Oyserman, 2013). American parents share these goals. They have high educational aspirations and expectations for their children even if their own educational and economic attainments are low (Entwisle et al., 2005; Kim, Sherraden, & Clancy, 2012; Madeira, 2009).[1] Parental

1. In this paper I do not distinguish between aspirations and expectations. This is in contrast to other researchers who find it useful to make that distinction, with an aspiration involving hopes and dreams (e.g., "if you could be anything at all, what would you most hope and want to be?") and an expectation involving subjective estimation of what is actually possible (e.g., "if you had to bet money on it, what will you be?"). Logically, the two are different. Hopes will be higher than expectations, since expectations imply that one could really do it and hopes imply only that one would want it to transpire. Researchers also assume that expectations are more likely to be linked to behavior than hopes, in part because expectations involve predictions of one's own competence. An expectation is something one believes one has the skills and competence to attain; in that sense it is akin to how the term *efficacy,* or *self-efficacy,* is used. In education, expectancy-value theories (e.g., Wigfield & Eccles, 2000) predict that people will take action to attain valued school outcomes if they expect that they have the skills to attain these outcomes. Because aspirations are not defined as being linked to skills, within a value-expectancy framework, they are less central.

Although all of these arguments are compelling, as I outline next, the parents and children who respond to surveys and are of interest to us here do not seem to be following this logic. The way that data on aspirations and expectations are collected in survey research is typically to ask children and their parents, first, how far they would ideally like to go in school and, second, how far they realistically expect to go in school. The logical pattern of aspiration being higher than expectations is typically found with aspirations 10 to 15 percent higher than expectations (Elliott, 2009; Madeira, 2009). This pattern generally holds for low-income students as well (Kirk, Lewis, Scott, Wren, Nilsen, & Colvin (2012). However, other features of the pattern of relationship between the aspiration and expectation questions suggest that children and parents do not distinguish between the aspiration and expectation questions as researchers intend for them to.

First, responses to expectation and aspiration questions are *highly correlated* even for low-income children and their parents, for whom college graduation is simply less likely to occur no matter how high their aspiration (Madeira, 2009). Consider that only one in ten 24-year-olds whose family earnings are in the bottom 25 percent have college degrees, compared with almost eight in ten twenty-four-year-olds whose family earnings are in the top 25 percent (Mortenson, 2005). Second, *expectations sometimes exceed aspirations*, which is a logical inconsistency (Boxer, Goldstein, DeLorenzo, Savoy, & Mercado, 2011). This means that what respondents are telling us about their educational aspirations and expectations may not yield the nuanced differences researchers had hoped to learn about. To respondents, educational aspirations and expectations may be one and the same. There are a number of reasons why this may be the case. I consider five of them: temporal distance, self-serving biases, social desirability, positivity bias, and questionnaire structure.

First, consider temporal distance. College is a distant goal and parents and students may focus on how much they value the outcome rather than estimating the obstacles along the way (e.g., Lieberman & Trope, 2008). This would result in expectations being nearly as

aspirations and expectations seem to matter at least in part by influencing children's imagined future identities—whether children imagine that they might or could attain all "A" grades, be college graduates, and so on (for a review, see Wildhagen, 2009). The effect of parental educational visions for their children is still apparent when their children become young adults, predicting return to school among dropouts (Sacker & Schoon, 2007).

high as aspirations, especially for respondents without direct experience of the process of getting into and graduating college. They simply would not be able to distinguish educational expectations from desires if they did not see what might block desires from translating into successful outcomes.

Second, consider positivity bias. In considering whether they will attain a positive outcome, people search for the reasons this might occur and fail to search for the reasons it might not. As a result, people tend to believe that their chances of attaining positive outcomes are higher than would be warranted (Mezulis, Abramson, Hyde, & Hankin, 2004). Thus respondents may assume that they will attain what they want even if they are aware that many other people have failed to attain their educational goals. They simply will not assume that they will encounter the difficulties others have experienced.

Third, consider self-serving biases. In considering whether they will attain a positive outcome, people may find it difficult to come up with reasons to show that this will happen. This difficulty may be experienced as threatening because it might imply that the positive outcome is unlikely. Questions about how far one wants, expects, or desires to go in school may be threatening to low-income and minority students who are aware of stereotypes about their group. After threat, there is an increased tendency to restore a positive emotional state by seeing oneself in a positive light (e.g., Roese & Olson, 2007). Just thinking that educational aspirations may not be attained (a thought process necessary to answer the expectation question) may motivate disregard of this possibility.

While I have just suggested psychological processes as to why answers to expectation and aspiration questions may not be distinguished in the way the researcher intended them to be, there are also reasons that focus more on the nature of the interaction between the respondent and the questioner. Consider social desirability. Responses to both expectation and aspirations questions may be influenced by the knowledge that college is valued in society. A social desirability explanation highlights the difficulty of asking people to self-report something undesirable about themselves. People may know that failing to say that they expect and want to go to college will be viewed negatively, so they do not do it. Finally, consider questionnaire structure. A typical questionnaire asks the same question about educational attainment twice, first asking about desired attainment and then about expected attainment. Using a closed-ended response format increases the efficiency of data collection but systematically shifts responses (Schwarz & Oyserman, 2001). In this case, having considered how far in school one wants to go (the first question), respondents may have their desired goal on their minds and not probable impediments along the way. As a result, their answers to the second question (how far do you expect to go?) will be highly similar to their answers to the first question (how far do you want to go?). Had the expectation question come first, responses to both questions might be lower.

All of these disparate factors converge in predicting what is actually found: First, children's educational expectations will be as high as their education aspirations. Second, children's educational aspirations will be high. Third, many participants, particularly those who are low-income and minority group members, will give essentially the same response to the "expectation" and "aspiration" questions. This does not mean that their responses are false or that they are not motivated but rather that the participants are not necessarily making the nuanced distinctions between wants and expectations that researchers wish to make. Therefore, in the sections below, though I use whichever term was used in the research, I do not assume that whether the term expectation or aspiration was used matters much because respondents do not separate expectations and aspirations as much as researchers do.

High aspirations are the rule, and not just among economically privileged or educationally advantaged Americans. In the United States, most children plan to go to college no matter if they are living in families receiving free and reduced-cost school lunches (Kirk, Lewis, Nilsen, & Colvin, 2013). This remains true in families at or below the poverty line (Elliott, 2009) and in juvenile detention facilities (Toldson et al., 2010). Almost half of neglected and abused children placed in foster care aspire to go to college (Kirk, Lewis, Nilsen, & Colvin, 2013). Even in developing countries such as Ghana, where only primary school is free and most adults have less than a primary school education, three in four children aspire to attend college (Chowa, Masa, Wretman, & Ansong, 2012).

In contrast to these positive aspirations, the reality is that too few children make it through the education pipeline to attain necessary degrees and certification. Teachers, school administrators, and policy makers are increasingly concerned about education's leaky pipeline.[2] The assumption is that people act in ways that fit their values and expectations (e.g., Feather, 1982; Wigfield, 1994). Yet students fall to the wayside in spite of their high aspirations. As outlined in this chapter, this leaky pipeline has serious consequences for both society and the individuals who did not manage to get through the pipeline. Failure to get through cannot be attributed to lack of desire to attain an education or low expectations of success, because children start out expecting to be college-bound. Rather, dropout seems to entail a gradual disengagement and refocusing of attention to other goals. Therefore intervention should aim at keeping children's college-bound identities on their minds, making these identities feel psychologically relevant in the moment, and facilitating their interpretation of experienced difficulty in school as implying importance, so that students do not disengage and do not direct their attention elsewhere.

TOO LITTLE EDUCATION IS COSTLY FOR INDIVIDUALS, FAMILIES, AND SOCIETIES

Societies with higher educational attainment have higher economic growth (Gylfason, 2001) and more civic engagement. Increasing compulsory education increases voter participation (unless barriers to registration are made too high, Milligan, Moretti, & Oreopoulos, 2004). In contrast, high school dropout is costly; in the United States, dropouts cost an estimated $200,000 more over an individual's lifetime in lost tax revenues and increased expenditures for health and welfare as compared with graduates (Building A Grad Nation, 2012; Chapman, Laird, Ifill, & KewalRamani, 2011; Jordan, Kostandini, & Mykerezi, 2012; Levin, Belfield, Muenning, & Rouse, 2007).

At the same time, individuals with higher educational attainment have better lives (Gylfason, 2001). In the United States, twenty-something graduates of four-year colleges earn 96 percent more than same-aged high school dropouts, 53 percent more than same-aged high school graduates, and 28 percent more than same-aged associate degree holders (National Center for Education Statistics, 2010). Higher education also improves lives in the next generation. Women who have not gone to college are more likely to be single than to be

---

2. The leaky pipeline metaphor is used to describe education as a means to channel children's energy toward adult success, with leakage implying that some children are left behind, outside the pipeline.

married when they give birth; the reverse is true for women with college degrees; 51 percent of births to women who did not attend college are to single mothers, while only 8 percent of births to women who graduated college are to single mothers (all comparisons are for white mothers in their twenties and thirties DeParle & Tavernise, 2012). These positive consequences of education are magnified as wage inequality increases, as it has in the United States since the 1970s (Acemoglu & Pischke, 2001).

On the flip side, not finishing high school is really not a viable choice. All but a tiny (and shrinking) proportion of jobs require at least a high school diploma, and jobs without this degree requirement pay less. Compared with high school graduates, American high school dropouts are estimated to earn $130,000 less over their lifetimes and to be at greater risk of incarceration (Building A Grad Nation, 2012; Levin, Belfield, Muenning, & Rouse, 2007). Each extra year of compulsory schooling increases lifetime wealth by about 15 percent (Oreopoulos, 2007).

Moreover, even controlling for wealth effects, education is associated with much better outcomes, including increased life happiness, more job satisfaction, higher prestige and more interesting work, more trust in others, and a lower likelihood of unemployment, divorce, arrest, and teenage parenthood (Oreopoulos & Salvanes, 2011). Each additional year of compulsory schooling reduces the risk of ill health, unemployment, and unhappiness in adulthood (Oreopoulos, 2007). In adolescence, school failure is associated with poorer well-being, including lower self-worth (Mercer, 2010; Nation et al., 2003), higher risk of obesity (Joe, Joe, & Rowley, 2009), too early initiation of sexual activity and engagement in risky sexual practices (Clark et al., 2005; Kirby, 2002) as well as increased risk of smoking, drinking (Bryant & Zimmerman, 2002), and drug use (Bachman, O'Malley, & Johnston, 1980; Barnes & Welte, 1986; Dewey, 1999; Ellickson, Tucker, Klein, & McGuigan, 2001; Maton & Zimmerman, 1992; Paulson, Coombs & Richardson, 1990; Zimmerman & Maton, 1992; Zimmerman & Schmeelk-Cone, 2003).

Clearly, the carryover consequences of the leaky education pipeline for well-being are grave. Researchers have rightfully spent a lot of time trying to understand the causal process. For both theoretical and applied reasons, it is important to know more than just that problem behavior and educational failure are associated. The order in which they usually occur matters, thus, if for the average child problem behavior is the starting point and educational failure is more like the consequence, then intervention should focus on preventing problem behavior. The reverse is also true. If for the average child educational failure is the starting point and problem behavior is more like the consequence, then intervention should focus on preventing educational failure. The causal process cannot be fully ascertained because no one would want to run an experiment in which children were assigned to school success or school failure to see whether problem behaviors emerged or to have or not have problem behaviors to see whether school failure emerged. However, it is possible to look at processes over time across children.

Using this temporal distribution method, poor school performance has been demonstrated to precede or at least exacerbate problems (Kirby, 2002). For example, academic difficulties and school misbehavior predict subsequent cigarette smoking above and beyond the impact of prior cigarette smoking on later smoking (Bryant, Schulenberg, Bachman, O'Malley, & Johnston, 2003). The same is true for substance use (Bryant & Zimmerman, 2002; Zimmerman & Schmeelk-Cone,

2003) and self-esteem (Mercer, 2010). This is not to argue necessarily that all of these problems have the same or even largely overlapping etiology but rather that higher educational attainment is a resource that is associated with other positive consequences across the life span (e.g., Adler & Rehkopf, 2008; Lantz et al., 1998). Therefore intervention to reduce risk of dropout and school failure is likely to have spillover effects for well-being and healthy behavior.

LEAKY PIPELINE, NOT PERSONAL CHOICE

Intervention is necessary because, in spite of high aspirations, high school dropout remains a serious problem in the United States. Between 22 and 31.2 percent of incoming ninth graders won't leave high school with a diploma (the higher estimate uses what is called the cumulative promotion index; see Woolley et al., 2013). Risk of dropout is higher among economically disadvantaged, rural, urban, and minority youth (African American, Latino, and American Indian). Dropout rates range from 32 to 38 percent among minorities and up to 50 percent among economically disadvantaged students (Children Trends Database, 2013; Johnson, Strange, & Madden, 2010). The same issues arise for college graduation. Less than a third of Americans are college graduates, and as many as half of those who start college do not finish (Bureau of Labor Statistics, 2010; Building A Grad Nation, 2012; National Center for Education Statistics, 2010).

A reader may wonder whether high school and postsecondary education is not simply a personal choice. The evidence clearly suggests otherwise. Early dropouts have such bleak life prospects and too little education is so costly that is unlikely that dropout is simply a choice of present over future self (Oreopoulos, 2007). Rather, the evidence suggests that leaving school too early is both multiply determined and usually involves a cumulative process of increasing disengagement with school (Fine, 1991; Orfield, Losen, Wald, & Swanson, 2004). That is, while some students may not aspire to school success, many who do have this aspiration gradually focus their attention on other things anyway. If aspiration were all that mattered, this should not happen. It is this latter process that is the focus of identity-based motivation (IBM) theory. As detailed in Chapter 1, to be useful, a future self must be accessible and psychologically relevant, linked to strategies, and yield a productive interpretation of difficulty. These three elements are not necessarily in place without intervention.

Consider, for example, a longitudinal analysis of ninth graders in St. Paul, Minnesota (Uno et al., 2010). When asked in ninth grade, three quarters reported that they expected to go to a four-year college. Only one quarter did not expect to go to college. To see if having a college-bound identity in ninth grade mattered, the researchers recontacted the full cohort fifteen years later, when they were in their late twenties. They wanted to know how many finished college and whether having a ninth-grade college-bound identity predicted finishing or not. On the one hand, not having a college-bound identity was an excellent predictor. Virtually none of these ninth graders had finished college by their late twenties. On the other hand, having a college-bound identity did not guarantee college completion. About 40 percent of students with a college-bound identity had completed college by their late twenties, but about 60 percent had not.

Although the researchers did not collect data about the intervening process, their results imply that interventions cannot assume that creating a college-bound identity is sufficient. The identity may not come to mind, strategies may not feel identity-congruent, and difficulties along the way may be misinterpreted as implying that being college-bound is unlikely rather than productively interpreted as implying that school tasks are important and worth extra effort. The question for teachers, practitioners, and policymakers is how to support students to translate valuing schooling, expecting to go to college, and aspiring to become college graduates into a higher rate of college attendance and graduation (Mello, 2009; Mello, Anton-Stang, Monaghan, Roberts, & Worrell, 2012; for a review, see Oyserman, 2013). As noted in the opening paragraphs of this chapter, children and their parents value education and aspire to academic success, implying that dropping out cannot be due only to low expectations or lack of valuation of education. Even if expectations and values are in place, the future self can still feel psychologically irrelevant to the current situation. In order to sustain the needed effort over time, a student's "college-bound" future identity needs to be accessible and experienced as psychologically relevant; it must also provide a motivating interpretation of experienced difficulty in school (Oyserman, 2007, 2009).

Taking a situated approach, dropping out can be thought of as contextually scaffolded. Dropout-prone contexts make it difficult to see the psychological relevance of the future self to current action. They also facilitate misinterpreting difficulties in school as meaning that school-focused identities and strategies to attain them are not relevant or not possible for people like oneself. If these key components of IBM are not present, students' attention will drift elsewhere, resulting in too little engagement with school. Indeed, time-use analyses demonstrate that American students often have drifting attention. The average student spends the lion's share of his or her time socializing (Arum, Roksa, & Cho, 2011) and only about fourteen hours a week studying—far shy of the recommended amount of some thirty hours for most students (Babcock & Marks, 2010). Allocating sufficient time to academics is critical for success in school (Astin, 1993; Pascarella & Terenzini, 2005; Kuh, Kinzie, Buckley, Bridges, & Hayek, 2006) and earnings afterward (Babcock & Marks, 2010). While a variety of barriers related to social class, race-ethnicity, and gender have been identified as additional reasons for underperformance separate from study time (e.g., Steele, 1997), these factors do not address underperformance among nonstereotyped groups and do not explicitly focus on time allocation.

INTERVENING TO REDUCE THE ASPIRATION-ATTAINMENT GAP

Considered together, then, educators, policy makers, parents, and concerned citizens face two core challenges with regard to education. First there is the challenge of patching the leaky pipeline and thus reducing the educational aspiration-attainment gap; second is the challenge of choosing a usable, feasible, scalable, and sustainable intervention to do so. Reducing high school dropout rates and increasing completion of college or other forms of post–high school education is a common good, improving both individual and societal well-being and yielding a fuller participation of citizens in modern society. As outlined in this section, choosing a usable, feasible, scalable, and sustainable intervention is a challenge.

A number of programs and interventions provide outcome evidence and at least a broad theoretical rationale, but fewer involve randomized trials with long-term follow-up, manualization, and testing of the fidelity of implementation.

These limitations are important for both implementation and policy purposes. To move beyond simply asserting that a program works it is necessary to be able to unpack both *what* exactly works and *how* it does so. Otherwise the program cannot be used elsewhere, since it is not clear what the active components were. To be usable, feasible, scalable, and thus sustainable over time an intervention must also provide a test of the process model so that practitioners will know what the core components are and whether any changes they need to make to go to scale are likely to undermine these components. This challenge is addressed by the School-to-Jobs intervention.

What Sort of Empirical Evidence Should a Practitioner Look For?

An empirical test, particularly through random assignment to treatment or control, assures the practitioner that there was not something different about the children or their setting prior to the intervention that could provide an alternative explanation of any result. Showing positive outcome effects in a randomized trial means that something good happened. The question is what happened? Simply knowing that a program has demonstrated significant effects on outcomes of interest does not provide an answer to this question. As a first step, evidence should be provided that the outcomes were based on delivery of the program with fidelity. As a second step, evidence should be provided that the theoretically active components were actually changed by the intervention. The most clear-cut way to document fidelity is to observe and code intervention delivery for evidence that the manual was followed. The clearest and most straightforward way to document that the intervention produced effects through the theoretically relevant process is to assess each of the active components of the model and test that the program yielded its effects through the predicted mediational pathway. The clearest and most straightforward way to document that each of these active components matters is to manipulate each of them and show that each has the expected effect on the outcome of interest.

Once a program has yielded this basic evidence of effectiveness, practitioners still must ascertain whether it is usable and feasible for them in their setting and with their skills and resources and whether it is scalable beyond the initial test site. For a program to be usable, the practitioner needs to know *what to do* to deliver it. For a program to be feasible, the practitioner has to *be able to deliver* the intervention within the limits of time, skills, funding, and other resources. Usable and feasible programs are likely to be sustained over time in a particular location. For a program to be scalable, it needs to be adoptable across practitioners and structures that differ in their resources and capacity. Often programs underspecify the theoretical process model and core active components on which success is premised. If this happens, an intervention may fail to scale simply because features of the particular context in which the program was initially tested and adopted are not made explicit.

Current practice can be severely limited by not testing the theoretical process model. Without a clear test, it is not possible for teachers to know whether they have omitted key components of the model of change when they intentionally or unintentionally modify an intervention to address developmental, cultural, or other factors. Nonmanualized, long, and/or complex interventions are especially vulnerable to unintentional movement away from such key components.

Indeed, teachers are less likely to implement programs that seem unlikely to work because they are too demanding to be implemented with fidelity or because the underlying program rationale is underspecified or not accepted by the teachers (Beets et al., 2008).

In undertheorized intervention models hidden features of context may often prove to be stumbling blocks for scalability. For example, say an intervention improves academic attainment by bolstering productive parent involvement. Whether this can be scaled depends on whether the characteristics of the initial setting are taken into account in the process model. Say the initial test took place in a high-parent-involvement context so that the goal was not to engage parents but to channel their energy. The scalable version of the program would need to broaden the process model so that another resource could be substituted in low-parent-involvement contexts unless promoting parent involvement were included explicitly in the program. The same would be true for any active component; a reader would need to figure out what was the context in which the intervention was tested and whether or not that context was reflected in the process model. Only then could a reader hope to ascertain what changes might be necessary for the program to fit into another context and whether those changes would undermine what made the intervention successful in the first place.

How to Intervene?

In their desire to do good, teachers and others often forget that no one likes to be told what to do. People often react to obvious attempts to influence them by doing the opposite because they sensitive to the possibility that others are trying to limit their choices. This well-documented response, termed reactance, can have quite negative consequences if not considered in developing interventions. Early adolescence in particular is a time in which youth are particularly sensitive to the possibility that their autonomy is being undermined rather than supported (Chirkov & Ryan, 2001; Grandpre et al., 2003; Miller et al. 2006; Steinberg & Silverberg, 1986). It is also a time of increased risk, as youths attempt to make sense of what their experiences of ease and difficulty at various endeavors—including schoolwork, sports, and socializing—might mean for their possible future selves (Oyserman & James, 2009). But attempts at direct persuasion run the risk of being challenged by teens seeking opportunities to demonstrate their independence from authority figures (e.g., Koepke & Denissen, 2012; Mazor & Enright, 1988; Steinberg & Silverberg, 1986) and their autonomy from social influence more generally (Hill & Holmbeck, 1986). How should concerned adults proceed? Should they try to intervene to convince teens that their experienced difficulty at schoolwork signals that schoolwork is important and worth the effort, or should they remain silent and hope that students do not interpret their experienced difficulty at schoolwork as signaling that schoolwork is impossible and not worth their effort?

Psychological reactance theory predicts that a persuasive appeal, once perceived as a threat to one's self-determined thought or behavior, will elicit a motivation to restore this threatened freedom (Brehm, 1966). Restoring this freedom may involve embracing the derogated attitude or performing the unsanctioned behavior (Brehm, 1966; Brehm & Brehm, 1981). This has been termed a "boomerang effect" (Wicklund, 1974). Boomerang effects are common in the adolescent intervention literature; examples include interventions to increase exercise and healthy eating and to reduce the likelihood of risky behaviors, including risky sexual behavior, alcohol and drug use, smoking, delinquency, or disordered eating patterns (Burgoon, Alvaro, Grandpre, & Voulodakis, 2002). Thus exposure to the tobacco industry's antismoking messages was documented to increase adolescents' interest in smoking (Farrelly et al., 2002), and exposure to prevention messages from a patient who had recovered from an eating disorder increased teens' perceptions that girls with eating disorders were pretty and in control of their lives (Schwartz, Thomas, Bohan, & Vartanian, 2007). Boomerang effects were also found in public responsibility campaigns; for example, the distribution of handbills against littering resulted in increased littering (Reich & Robertson, 1979).

Because teens commonly express reactance in response to adults' attempts to influence their personal goals, rejecting adults' suggestions or even endorsing their opposite to reassert autonomy (Brehm, 1966; Erikson, 1963; 1980; Lapsley & Yeager, in press), researchers seek strategies to make messages persuasive without threatening autonomy (Aronson et al., 2002; Yeager & Walton, 2011; Walton & Cohen, 2011). Although message-undermining reactance has been more fully considered in the domain of health (e.g., Dillard & Shen, 2005; Whitehead, 2005), there is no reason not to expect reactance to occur for messages meant to promote a particular way of thinking about effort at school. Hence, in developing an intervention, it is critical that the intervention message be something that comes from participants rather than being perceived as something that teachers or other adults are trying to make participants accept.

When to Intervene?

A final question a practitioner or policy maker may ask is when to intervene to reduce the risk of school failure and dropout. Although any time is possible, the middle school years are particularly critical for a number of reasons. First, almost 40 percent of dropping out occurs by ninth grade and only 15 percent of students who fail ninth grade go on to graduate high school (Chapman, Laird, Ifill, & Kewal Ramani, 2011; Herlihy, 2007). This implies that intervention should occur prior to ninth grade.

Second, by middle school it is possible to predict that a student will not graduate high school using the following simple criteria: a failing grade in an English or math class, an unsatisfactory behavior mark in at least one class, or attendance falling to 80 percent or less (Balfanz, Herzog, MacIver, 2007; Neild, Balfanz, & Herzog, 2007). Reduced effort, increased behavior problems, and reduced attendance in middle school all contribute to a diminished likelihood of a successful transition to high school (Cairns, Cairns, & Neckerman, 1989; Finn, 1989). These statistics imply that interventions that improve middle school outcomes in these areas will reduce the risk of dropping out.

Third, the middle school transition occurs during the pubertal shift and involves a change from a small to a larger, more impersonal setting in which one can let go of past selves and focus on the future. For all these reasons, not only one's next-year self but also one's high school and adult self should be easily cued and made to feel relevant to current choices. Given the evidence that the cumulative disengagement from school that eventuates in dropping out rarely results from students' diminished desire to do well academically, interventions can leverage this desire to attain positive outcomes. A middle school intervention that makes the future feel close, that makes strategies feel identity-congruent, and that provides a productive interpretation of difficulty at school should improve academic outcomes and reduce disengagement (Oyserman, 2013).

What Sort of Evidence Exists?

An enormous number of programs exist, as do meta-analyses (e.g., Durlak et al., 2011) and syntheses of them (e.g., Snipes, Fancsali, & Stoker, 2012). The bottom line seems to be that a number of programs meant to improve academic outcomes provide evidence that they do, although not all used randomized designs to test outcomes. Some programs provide impressively lengthy follow-ups. Unfortunately these programs are typically long and complex (e.g., intervention lasts a full school year (Felner et al., 1982; Ialongo et al., 1999) or intervention lasts all of elementary school through sixth or eighth grade (Flay, Allred, & Orway, 2001; Hawkins et al., 1999). Even these programs do not test the theorized process model underlying effects; they lack detailed intervention manuals, usability-enhancing checklists, and fidelity protocols. Thus, for example, although Flay et al. (2001) report that their intervention includes curricular material, only Ialongo et al. (1999) and Oyserman et al. (2006) describe detailed intervention manuals with outlines and checklists including the specific themes that need to be covered to ensure fidelity of intervention.

Complex, multi-component, or lengthy programs pose usability and feasibility obstacles that limit their scalability and staying power (Durlak & DuPre, 2008). Beyond the problem of length and complexity, a careful read of the published results shows that there are serious limits to their methodological rigor. While some involve random assignment (Ialongo et al., 1999; Rotheram, 1982; Oyserman et al., 2006) others do not (Felner, Ginter, & Primavera, 1982; Flay, Allred, Orway, 2001; Hawkins et al., 1999). Although underlying theoretical rationales for the interventions differ, in looking at the published literature, I did not find any that tested the underlying process model directly except for the school-to-jobs program (Oyserman et al., 2006).

Lack of evidence from randomization, lack of a clear theoretical rationale, and lack of testing of the theorized process model all limit scalability. Without these it is not possible to determine which elements of the program constitute active components or how particular activities can be modified to fit differences in age, culture, and other contextual features. A final limitation of current practice is a lack of detailed intervention manuals, usability-enhancing checklists, and fidelity protocols. Thus, although Flay et al. (2001) report that their intervention includes curricular material, only Ialongo et al. (1999) and Oyserman et al. (2006) describe detailed intervention manuals with outlines and checklists, including the specific themes that need to be covered to ensure fidelity of intervention. Without an intervention manual, it is not clear what counts as implementation of a program. Without a fidelity checklist, it is not clear whether the program was implemented as intended. Without this information, how can a practitioner or policy maker hope to replicate successes in one setting to successes in another setting?

Indeed, while recommendations for program guidelines include making sure that the program has an outcome evaluation and is theory-based, including appropriate timing and sensitivity to sociocultural factors, so few test fidelity of implementation or the theoretical process model that these criteria are not even listed as recommendations (e.g., Nation et al., 2003). While guidelines do note the need for well-trained staff and sufficient dosage, it is difficult to know what to train for without an intervention manual and difficult to know if training succeeded without a test of fidelity. Moreover, without a manual it is difficult to provide a theoretical rationale for sufficient dosage (beyond rule-of-thumb rationales that big problems require large-scale and long intervention). By looking at features of programs with positive outcomes and assuming that these features are necessary, program guidelines sometimes include recommendations that may have the unintended effect of limiting scalability, usability, and feasibility. For example Nation and colleagues' (2003) review of reviews looking at preventive interventions to improve school outcomes or reduce substance use or behavior problems recommends comprehensive interventions with varied teaching methods. While big may be great in some circumstances, it may not be possible in others. A new form of intervention suggests that small interventions can have big effects as well (Oyserman & Destin, 2010; Yeager & Walton, 2011).

HOW THE SCHOOL-TO-JOBS PROGRAM AND IDENTITY-BASED MOTIVATION THEORY FIT INTO THIS PICTURE

My examination of the school-based intervention literature suggests that the school-to-jobs (STJ) intervention described in Chapter 3 addresses a number of limitations of current research and practice. First, other than STJ, published interventions do not typically provide a test of the theoretical mediational process, meaning that even academic outcome-tested interventions are only loosely based in theory. Second, other than STJ, even published interventions that meet some criteria for usability and feasibility (e.g., randomized trial, empirical test of fidelity of implementation) do not meet other criteria (e.g., brief, manual-based). Third, well-meaning practice can undermine rather than support engagement by providing feedback to students in ways that imply that schoolwork is a chore, that success rather than difficulty is diagnostic, or that the future is distant and not currently relevant.

This is not to say that the core notions motivating other interventions contradict identity-based motivation theory. Far from it. With regard to theory, school-based preventive interventions to improve academic outcomes and reduce school failure and problem behavior are typically loosely based in social control theories (e.g., Hirschi & Gottfredson, 1990; Hirschi, 1986, 2004). Social control theories predict that students will be less involved in crime and more connected (bonded) to normative institutions (school, parents) if they perceive teachers and parents as noticing, caring about, and responding systematically to good and bad behavior. Related promising intervention and program ideas focus on how children make sense of themselves and their possibilities. These ideas are being translated into a variety of programs focused on children's possible selves and mindsets (for a review, see Snipes, Fancsali, & Stoker, 2012).

It is not that the ideas are problematic or unlikely to explain part of the leaky educational pipeline; rather, it is figuring out how to translate a broad idea into a specific intervention that is problematic. As noted previously, if a program is not evaluated with random assignment, it is hard to tell if what worked was the program and not something else. If a program does not have a manual and a fidelity checklist, then practitioners and policy makers cannot tell if they are doing what worked when the program was initially evaluated. If the program does not test its process model, then even if the program works, practitioners and policy makers cannot tell what about it worked. Without this knowledge, they cannot know what changes to individual activities or to program components more generally are feasible while sustaining the program's active ingredients. A process evaluation is particularly important because programs often include elements that seem to have good face value but are not part of the theoretical model. For example, they aim to improve not only the quality of teacher management and responsiveness (as would be suggested by social control theory) but also the quality of education, making it unclear what the active elements are (e.g., Ialongo et al., 1999; Hawkins et al., 1999). Having lots of elements means that it is hard to tell which element mattered. It also makes replication more difficult because there are simply more ways for problems to arise.

In addition, programs sometimes also address student motivation and identity, including providing a behavioral profile of what a good student is, a road map of how to get there, and reinforcement for successes. Indeed, an examination of the theoretical roots of interventions that assessed academic outcomes and provided follow-up data suggests that all involve active components of identity-based motivation (e.g., Battistich et al., 1989; Cauce, Comer, & Schwartz, 1987; Cook et al., 1999; Cook, Murphy, & Hunt, 2000; Elliott, 1995, 1997; Enright, 1980; Flay, Acock, Vuchinich, & Beets, 2006; Flay & Allred, 2003; McTigue & Rimm-Kaufman, 2011; Rimm-Kaufman, Fan, Chiu & You, 2007). As I detailed in Chapter 1, however, getting the theory clear and operationalizing specifically matters. Otherwise what might seem like very similar activities can result in opposite effects. For example, in Chapter 1 I described studies with elementary school students. Students asked to think about their near future as adults differed from students asked to think about their future as adults or about their far future as adults. Imagining a near future as an adult increased attention to schoolwork but imagining a future or a far future as an adult did not.

SUMMARY

Children and parents value education; they expect and aspire to be college-bound. These values, expectations, and aspirations are important but not enough, resulting in a leaky educational pipeline for society and an aspiration-attainment gap for children. Failure to finish high school and college is prohibitively expensive for individual children, their future families, and society as a whole. Costs come in the form of lost wages and productivity, reduced well-being and health, and less civic engagement.

At the high school level, midway markers of increased risk of failure have been identified. These markers are a failing grade in an English or math class, an unsatisfactory behavior mark in at least one class, or attendance falling to 80 percent or less. To reduce the risk of failure, intervention that addresses these issues is needed and many interventions exist. However, it is almost impossible for practitioners and policy makers to make informed decisions about which interventions to use, since even when outcome evaluations exist, the intervention process itself remains opaque Moreover, often interventions are not manualized or, if manualized, they have not been tested for fidelity. As a result neither what was specifically intended to happen nor what actually did happen can be ascertained.

Even when manual and fidelity materials are available, programs fail to provide an empirical test of their process model, so that it is unclear whether the program, even if delivered as intended, has its effects through the predicted mechanism. Knowing this may seem pragmatically unnecessary, but it turns out to be pragmatically essential. Without a test of the process model, practitioners and policy makers will not know which pieces of the intervention as delivered actually had the expected effects. This means that they cannot know which pieces can be changed and, if changed, in what way, so as not to lose the active ingredients that made the intervention successful in the first place.

TRANSLATING IDENTITY-BASED MOTIVATION TO INTERVENTION

PATHWAYS TO SUCCESS FROM SCHOOL TO JOBS AND LIFE

3

IN THIS CHAPTER I DESCRIBE the School-to-Jobs intervention, a brief intervention that translates the components of identity-based motivation (IBM) into a testable, usable, feasible, and scalable intervention for use in schools and other settings to improve academic outcomes. To develop the intervention, I took the core IBM principles and translated them into a framework and set of activities that have coherence and meaning. These core principles, as detailed in Chapter 1, are that identities, strategies, and interpretations of difficulty matter when they come to mind and seem relevant to the situation at hand. Because thinking is for doing, context matters, and identities, strategies, and interpretations of difficulty can be dynamically constructed given situational constraints and affordances. Therefore the framework and set of activities I developed were sensitive to the context in which education and educational success or failure occurs, the processes by which children succeed or fail to attain their school-success goals, and the action children need to take if they are to succeed. The intervention was fully tested twice (Oyserman, Bybee, & Terry, 2006; Oyserman, Terry, & Bybee, 2002), using random assignment to control (school as usual) and intervention conditions so that it would be possible to know whether the effects were due to the intervention and not to other differences in the children themselves. Importantly, the tested intervention was manualized and fidelity to both manual and underlying theorized process was also tested. In these ways, the intervention stands as a model for development. STJ is currently being used in England and in Singapore. Each country gives the intervention its own name to fit the context.

This chapter is divided into three parts. In the first part, I outline the choices I made in developing the intervention. In the second part, I outline the sequenced activities that constitute the intervention (they are detailed in the manual that forms Chapter 4). In the third part, I describe the evidence that the intervention succeeded in changing academic outcomes and that changes occurred through the process predicted by IBM. Throughout, I link back to Chapter 1 to clarify which aspects of IBM are being cued in the activities and the underlying process model being tested. I also link back to Chapter 2 to clarify why particular outcomes are targeted. I make these links explicit so that readers can use their understanding of IBM and of the proximal predictors of school failure to effectively use the implementation manual in Chapter 4 and can make informed decisions if they need to change a particular activity to fit their setting. An understanding of IBM allows readers to avoid falling prey to assumptions about what needs to happen or how motivation works. Instead, decisions about activities to use are guided by evidence. That way any needed changes in activities do not undermine the efficacy of the intervention. Having a feel for what can be changed and how requires a clear understanding of the model. The implementation manual that follows in Chapter 4 lays out exactly how to run each intervention activity. Chapters 1 and 2 form the training needed prior to reading the implementation manual in Chapter 4.

DEVELOPING THE SCHOOL-TO-JOBS INTERVENTION

Setting the Stage

My goals were twofold: First, to develop an intervention that would work in the contexts I wanted to benefit—that is, schools serving low-income and minority students who might otherwise be at risk of failing to make it through education's leaky pipeline. Second, to develop the intervention such that it was universally relevant. For an intervention to work, it needs to take place in a location and at a time when potential participants would be receptive to the message. It must be in a format that engages participants, is feasible for others to use, is simple enough to replicate and scale up, is cost-efficient, and brief. To be socioculturally sensitive, an intervention has to take into account the social context of school and the important actors in children's lives (other students, teachers, caregivers and parents, community members).

Interventionists sometimes suffer from a correspondence bias—believing that big or important problems require big and lengthy interventions. But big interventions are not necessarily needed. My goal, after all, was to improve academic outcomes by leveraging the three components of IBM as active ingredients.[1] In developing the School-to-Jobs program I was not proposing to teach skills or change values. Teaching skills is what teachers already do and, as noted in Chapters 1 and 2, I had no evidence that school-relevant values needed changing. Instead, there is evidence that teachers' and students' efforts would yield better outcomes if they matched. Our goal was to set in motion a process by which students would notice that classroom, coursework, and other educational opportunities were there, relevant to their futures, and meant to be engaged in, even when and especially when it felt difficult or they experienced failure, so that attendance, grades, and overall performance would improve.

What Is in a Name?

In visiting schools running my intervention, I have sometimes been introduced to staff or students as the possible-self or School-to-Jobs lady. Maybe that was

---

1. In Chapters 2 and 3 I use active ingredients to describe those parts of interventions that actually influence outcomes of interest and to distinguish active from inert ingredients. That is, interventions often include activities, elements, and even whole components that do not actually influence the outcomes of interest in the intended direction—they are inert (make no different) or worse yet, iatrogenic (make things worse). In contrast, active ingredients, like the fluoride in toothpaste actually yield the intended effect. Other ingredients may be needed, just as toothpastes include flavoring, but may not be the best way to attain a goal. Examples of that would be sugar or alcohol in a children's cough syrup.

because my name is hard to pronounce, but I think it was because this was the name that identified who I am. Names identify. A descriptive name that feels right is definitely better than a name that fails to describe or feels wrong. As I thought about what to name the intervention I was developing and testing, I wanted the name to provide a sense of meaning and clarity to participants and stakeholders. I did not really understand the importance of a name until, in the initial piloting one of the consistent pieces of feedback from participants was that they wanted to be able to choose a uniquely identifying name for their group. So that is now one of the first things participants do. Just like participants, organizations have also given different names to my intervention to fit the context in which they are working. That is just as it should be, since names, like identities, are context-dependent in their meaning.

Given that, the name I chose for the intervention is School-to-Jobs (STJ). I wanted a name that focuses on what the intervention is meant to do and makes concrete the idea that school is the path to a particular future—to having the kind of job one would want to have. The name is meant to reflect the core idea that the future starts now and that engaging in school now is the way to get there. I just as well could have chosen other versions of this theme, such as "School-to-Life" or "School-to-Success." I did not choose "School-to-College" because college, as described in Chapter 2, is highly aspired, but not so commonly attained, and is in any case only a means to the life that comes after. Indeed, in the current version of the program, we are using the name "Pathways to Success," as the title of this book suggests.

I did not choose names like "Future Self," "Aim High," "Future Star," or "College-Bound," which would have made sense if the goal had been to raise hope or increase aspirations or valuation of college. Values, hopes, and aspirations are important, of course, but in my experience in Detroit (and as is true generally as noted in Chapter 2), I found no problem of low aspirations, low valuation of education, lack of college-bound expectations or imagined future selves. Pretty much all the middle school students in my studies aspired and expected to go to college and get a job, even though the high school graduation rate in Detroit and other American urban centers is not good. There was no need for an intervention to change values or raise hopes. Values were in place and hopes were high.

There was a need for an intervention to leverage these values and hopes into action, to make the future feel near and connected to the present rather than far and disconnected. This is the core focus of the STJ intervention. Specifically, the goal is to create a sense that this future starts now, not later; that students can use effective strategies to attain their school-success possible identities; and that it is normal to experience difficulties and even failures along the way to school success and any other important goal.

Where Should the Intervention Occur?

Before choosing a name though, I thought about how best to create the changes I was targeting. Little research focuses on the effects of context on intervention success. That said, practitioners are aware that some settings (e.g., prisons, probation) may have unique affordances and constraints (Hammett, Gaiter, & Crawford, 1998) and may interact with client characteristics (Andrews, Zinger, Hoge, Bonta, Gendreau, & Cullen, 1990). Having done research in a variety of settings and having had clinical and academic training in preventive and crisis intervention, I considered it obvious that I had to think carefully about the fit between intervention goals and the place where the intervention would be made. Of course sensitivity to contextual affordances and constraints is also central to IBM's focus on the dynamic construction of identities, strategies, and interpretations of difficulty in context. IBM highlights the situated nature of meaning and the dynamic construction of identities, strategies, and interpretations of difficulty. This means that change that takes place in one setting—for example, in a church group—may or may not come to mind in a context that feels different, such as school.

Students who are unsure about whether they can engage in effective strategies to attain their school-related possible identities may feel convinced while alone or with a counselor or in another setting, but unless this comes to mind in school, it may not matter. People do not necessarily transfer skills and mindsets from one setting to another. An intervention is more likely to work if the context in which change is to occur matches the context in which the intervention occurs.

If the goal of the intervention is to improve academic outcomes and this requires action in a particular setting, then the intervention should occur in that setting. To do well in school, students have to publicly engage in a set of behavioral strategies in school. They must participate actively in class, ask questions, stay after class, pay attention, and hand in homework. All of these activities are more likely to occur if students believe that other students will not see these strategies as *identity-incongruent*. Doing well in school also requires that time be spent on homework and studying. This meant that some intervention time would have to be spent with caregivers in the school setting as well. Thus, in my case, the answer to the *where* question was surprisingly clear. The setting of the intervention had to target the setting in which change was needed. That is, if children needed to engage more with school, the intervention would have to take place in school and with students who saw one another every day. It would also need, at some point, to include parents and other adults, since the students' new school focus would have to be sustained in nonschool hours and they would have to be able to engage not only their parents but also others in creating a path from middle school to successful adulthood. School is a natural context for the STJ intervention because the change the intervention is seeking to make must occur in school.

Other settings are likely to be important for other outcomes. A program using IBM principles to help youths who are aging out of foster care might consider which setting best exemplifies the goals for these youths. In that case, perhaps a community college setting that provides relevant post–high school training would be best, given the plan for such youths to become independent wage earners much earlier than other eighteen-year-olds. The same might also be true for dropout recovery programs working with youth who are no longer likely to graduate high school through the regular means. In the same way, a program using IBM principles to help students sustain a focus on science, technology, engineering, and math (STEM) coursework and majors must be located in the setting that actually matters for STEM. This could be a lab, hospital or other setting. An intervention is unlikely to work if it cues extraneous identities or is not located in the setting where relevant identities, strategies, and interpretations of difficulty are needed.

When Should the Intervention Occur?

Turning from place to time, I reasoned that an intervention is more likely to work if it occurs at a time when change feels necessary and possible. Interventions are mistimed if they occur either too soon, before participants feel change is needed, or too late, once participants feel that change is impossible. If the goal of the intervention is to improve academic outcomes, I reasoned, it had to occur at a time when academic change is possible and students are interested in change. Therefore I focused on *the beginning* of a school year that was itself at a *transition point*.

The beginning of a transition is the natural time for any intervention to occur (Mrazek & Haggerty, 1994). This is true whether the transition is a school transition (Seidman & French, 1997, 2004) or another transition, such as the transition to parenthood (Glade, Bean, & Vira, 2005). Having chosen school as the context, my choice about time included two elements: when during the school year and when during the course of schooling. The beginning of the school year is the best time to start changing, since the first weeks of school constitute a fresh start for everyone; September captures the moment of highest energy and most focus on potential success, much like the point at which New Year's resolutions still ring true. In the beginning of the school year, teachers do not already know the students, so students have a chance to form a positive impression. Moreover, change that occurs prior to the first marking period means that students still have a real possibility of changing their academic outcomes. That is because the best predictor of grades is prior grades. If I waited until later in the school year, the students would have had little real viable chance to improve. Their teachers would already have formed an impression of them and their prior academic investment (as reflected in their first-quarter grades) would have a huge weight in what seemed possible. If no change was feasible, the intervention would have felt irrelevant, students would not have engaged, and it would have been less likely to work.

In addition to starting at the beginning of the school year, I focused on the year prior to a major transition, the shift to high school. This is a time when change is on the horizon, so the idea of thinking about the future is relevant. I chose the last year of middle school as the time to intervene; this is a high-risk time—as documented in Chapter 2—and fits the transition criteria. In Detroit, middle school is sixth to eighth grade, so the intervention focused on the fall of eighth grade. School systems with a seventh-to-ninth-grade junior high have a similar inflection point, as do schools with primary to secondary school shifts. The goal is to catch students the year prior to the shift or in school systems that first have a sorting exam in the year prior to the examination. Just as the beginning of the year is a time when change is possible, the year preceding an important transition offers an important opportunity to change course.

Transition points such as the transition to high school are salient to youth as a time to imagine the future; it is therefore a time for which the intervention makes sense. Since initial development and testing, my students and I have also tried the activities with sixth graders, and they are understandable to them. With some revisions, the activities could work just as well for students trying to pick themselves up and get back on track. Examples include students in summer school to regain course credits and be allowed to start high school and students in general equivalency programs seeking an alternative to high school. Colleagues have engaged with both of these groups.

Targeting an Audience: With Whom Should the Intervention Intervene?

Having considered where and when to intervene, a third core question was with whom to intervene. To answer this question, I returned to the core IBM components and to my training in preventive intervention and asked myself which students would be helped by an IBM-based intervention—students already exhibiting problems, students at risk though not yet exhibiting problems, or students generally. I chose to focus on a universal intervention—something that was accessible to and useful for all students—for two reasons. First, cuing IBM components should be useful for all students since it is a general process model of human motivation. Second, I did not see a way to deliver the intervention as intended if only some students received it. If the intervention was not universal but for a selected set of students—the good students, the bad students, the students with low standardized test scores or low grade point averages —the selection criteria would suggest that only some students needed or would benefit from intervention. If the better students were chosen, this would imply that only the clever students needed to engage in current action to attain their future selves and to interpret their failures as highlighting the importance of the goal. If only the underperforming students were chosen, this would imply that only these students were failing to do these things. Any selection seemed to miss the point. IBM theory predicts that missing opportunities, starting too late, and quitting too soon are human shortcomings and that all of us can improve.

Moreover, choosing students who were already showing signs of problems or of promise would have mislabeled the intervention as something only certain students needed or could benefit from. Much intervention research documents the potential of iatrogenic effects when problem individuals are brought together because of their problem (Dishion, McCord, & Poulin, 1999; Poulin, Dishion, & Burraston, 2001). The problem can become an identity and thus increase rather than decrease risk. IBM theory highlights the need for strategies to feel identity-congruent, which could best happen in a nonselective context.

By making the intervention universal, children in STJ were not identifiable as the good students, the band members, or the low performers; they were just students. The main focal context was school. Being engaged with school is not just a private value or a personal plan; it requires doing things very publicly. Others see if you are raising your hand to ask a question or if you are doodling, they see if you are handing in homework, staying after class for help, or getting in trouble with the teacher. If I wanted children to do these "engaged" behaviors and not a variety of disruptive behaviors, the intervention had to involve public activities. Engaging with school had to feel identity-congruent for all students; this would be easier if they experienced all other students as also wanting to be engaged with school. Taken together, these factors implied that the core of the intervention had to involve a universal set of group-based activities in school.

You Cannot Make Me: Considering Reactance

Another important consideration was reactance, the tendency to react negatively to situations in which one's freedom of choice is constrained by saying, doing, and believing the opposite of what some authority is trying to make one say, do, or believe. Reactance is likely an endemic problem in intervention, since in many cases the sought-after change is something that someone other than the targeted participant wants to see occur. A clear way to circumvent this problem is to create a situation in which participants experience messages as coming from inside, from their own experiences and those of their peers, rather than from an outside source. If activities are structured so that they are appealing (everyone participates), seem open and without a heavy-handed persuasion attempt yet are structured such that the intended message is likely to emerge from participants themselves, reactance can be avoided. Since people are sensitive to normative influences from similar others, having the activities take place in a group setting could increase chances of positive change as long as these principles were upheld. This can be seen in the fidelity checklist provided in Chapter 4. In each session, observers note not only whether the intended sequence of activities was followed but also whether the intended message was heard and if it came from participants rather than from trainers.

Dosage Duration and Intensity: How Many Sessions and at What Frequency?

Having considered where, when, and with whom the intervention would occur, I turned to a final question about the framework of intervention—dosage. This term refers to the number and intensity of treatment episodes—in my case, class sessions devoted to activities. Just as with questions related to timing, questions related to dosage are critically important in calibrating if an intervention is likely to succeed. It might seem obvious that an intervention should last as long as needed to obtain an effect and no longer, and that it should be intensive enough to be noticed but not so intensive as to make the experience seem separate from everyday context and experience. Community action and prevention science converge on the notion that intervention should be simple and short and provide a clear link between theory and intervention if they are to be sustainable over time (e.g., Borrelli et al., 2005; Wandersman, 2003; Weissberg & Greenberg, 1998).

Yet in making dosage choices there are many ways to go wrong. Something that occurs too infrequently is unlikely to matter even if it eventually occurs many times, since people may not even notice that something different is going on (Yerkes & Dodson, 1908). Something that is very intensive may be noticed but fail to yield lasting effects if it feels like an experience separate from the everyday context or reality—a problem that is frequent for weekend retreats, summer camps, and other intensive experiences. Even if intensity and frequency over time are planned, an intervention might still not yield an effect if the planned process is too long, too complicated, or otherwise unwieldy.

Very brief one- to three-session interventions, sometimes called motivational interviews, have been found to work, implying that more is not necessarily better (Miller, 2000). Positive effects for small interventions are found even for behaviors that seem difficult to change (Miller, 2000) and for macrolevel outcomes like economic trends (Klein, 1992; see also Brown & Detterman, 1987). Small interventions can have large effects if they cue an already available but underused alternative set of cognitive structures, everyday theories, or heuristics.

My goal was to develop a small intervention that would have big effects, and my prediction was that STJ would have a large effect on academic outcomes if it evoked an IBM pattern of responding. All that was needed was to build a set of activities so that the IBM components came to mind in a connected way enough times in a school context that other school contexts would evoke this pattern as well. The desired pattern was to experience the future as psychologically relevant to the present and to interpret experienced difficulties and failures along the way as evidence that school success is important but not impossible to attain. That is, the intervention needed to facilitate the accessibility of the IBM set of active components: The future starts now; it is education-dependent; I can use strategies to work toward school success; and when it feels difficult, that just means I should work harder, because school-success is important.

Weighing intensity and duration issues together with the timing issue I discussed earlier, I settled on activities that would take place twice a week starting at the beginning of the school year and ending prior to the beginning of the first marking period. Realistically I could not start at the very beginning of the school year, since students in the schools I was targeting do not necessarily start coming to class on the first day of school and schools may still be finalizing their hiring decisions. If the intervention was short, I would need everyone to be present at the start. In addition, class periods are relatively short, so each activity had to have a core point and the points had to build from week to week. To provide a sense of closure, a final in-school session had to give students a chance to put everything together so that parents could be brought in at the end in after-school sessions. Taking all of this into account, I decided on an eleven-session in-school intervention, with two after-school sessions that would include students and their parents or adult caregivers.

School as a Context of Intervention

Interventions in School Are Often Long. In contrast to my reasoning, as noted in Chapter 2, educational interventions are often very long, spanning years or whole segments of schooling (e.g., all the primary school years or all the middle school or high school years). Perhaps that is because the implicit assumption of interventionists is that skills and habits are difficult to teach and easy to forget. If the intervention involves teaching a skill or creating a habit, enough time to practice the skill and enough intensity to automatize the habit is needed, not more. Habit formation may require less time than imagined (Gollwitzer, 1999; Wood & Neal, 2007). Once something is a habit, people may be less sensitive to particular costs and rewards of the behavior in a given setting (Fuhrer, 2000; Lally & Gardner, 2013). This would imply that intervention timing should build on research on habit formation and habit change.

Yet interventions span much longer periods than are needed for habit formation; this is problematic for a number of reasons. When an intervention spans such a long time frame, even if an outcome evaluation suggests that the intervention works, it is difficult to know what this means. How can one distinguish timing of intervention effects from dosage of intervention effects and from other extraneous effects (e.g., whether the child moves to another school system)? How can the intervention be scaled to another setting if it is not clear what exactly was done and what would have been enough repetition, practice, or time? Moreover, lengthy interventions are increasingly difficult to apply in schools and school districts experiencing less certainty about budgets, staffing, content, and testing requirements. Two possible reasons that educational interventions are so long are that developmental theories might predict the need for long interventions just as a general assumption, without delving into the process of learning or habit formation, and that education itself spans many years (Yeager & Walton, 2011).

Intervention in Unstable Systems. To the extent that systems are stable, long interventions might be plausible. However, systems are not necessarily stable, whether the system of interest is the family (where the child lives and with whom), the school (which school the child attends, which teachers are at that school), or the community (especially school-focused policies and funding). Flux in student body, teaching staff, and policy supports means that interventions are effectively shorter than planned since the parts are all moving.

Teacher flux is an issue generally, especially in low-income and minority schools (Ingersoll, 2001; Loeb, Darling-Hammond, & Luczak, 2005). In the schools where I worked, teachers, principals, and policies shifted. As many as a third of the students who had started the school year in a particular school were no longer at that school at the end of the school year. The size of the student body at these schools remained more or less constant because as children were leaving the school, others were entering.

This flux seemed to have multiple causes, often seemingly rooted in poverty and the press of economic instability. Children might move because the head of household needed to change addresses, sometimes quickly and without official notice, so that bill collectors would not be able to track them down. Children might switch households, so that they were temporarily or more permanently residing with a different head of household. These moves might be due to family tensions, behavioral issues, or school issues. Moves affected the continuity of attendance at the same school even though the school district had a school-of-choice policy, so children could have stayed in the same school. Even so, parents and caregivers valued education and wanted their children to do well, but they were themselves pressed for time and wanted the school to do its job of educating children.

In developing the STJ intervention, I was very mindful of these setting issues. I wanted to develop an intervention that was brief enough that it was likely that students and teachers who started together would complete the set of activities and then have the IBM mindset no matter where they later ended up. I wanted to include parents, but not in a way that set up a barrier for their participation. I needed to involve other adults so that students would get a sense that everyone took the path from school to jobs and that school was worth the effort.

Including Parents. I still needed to consider both how and when to involve parents and other adults. I wanted to start with school and engagement in school in the school setting. However, I also wanted to establish the school-home linkage, so that children and parents could communicate about the ideas of STJ (i.e., the future starts now, school now leads to desired adult futures, difficulties and failures along the way are normal for important goals, school strategies are identity congruent). To make this happen, I decided that parents would be invited in after the in-school sessions were completed and that activities would be structured to focus on communicating and linking school to future careers. Similarly, we would include other community members only at the end, after parents had been brought in. In this way, STJ entailed engaging family, school, and community contexts. The goal of STJ is not to get a job or learn to write a resume or plan for a particular career; therefore we did not want particularly special community members but just adults who were not the students' parents and had jobs. The particular activities we chose and our rationale for choosing them are discussed below.

Translating IBM into a Set of Sequenced Activities

An IBM perspective clarifies that meaning is situated and that thinking is for doing. In order for the intervention to work, it had to occur at the time and place that it was needed, with the people that mattered, be long enough and intensive enough, and not any longer or more intensive than needed. It had to feel easier to engage than to disengage, so that students would experience the intervention as something they wanted to do rather than had to do. It had to be interesting, so that students were thinking and structured and that the elements of IBM were cued repeatedly.

As noted in Chapters 1 and 2, students already generally believe that education is valuable; they already want to do well in school. The problem is that in context, these things do not come to mind, the future seems far away and disconnected from education, and difficulty is misinterpreted as meaning that the task is irrelevant. Given that students already had the values and identities, there is no value in discussing these ideas in the abstract. Therefore STJ is not a group discussion or a set of lectures. Rather, it is a set of activities. Students do something. They produce something. They can then see that everyone else has also done so.

The group process is important for two reasons. First, identities, strategies, and interpretation of difficulty matter in context and not out of context. If the intervention was to work, it had to help students in the context in which they were. Second, identities, strategies, and interpretation of difficulty are social constructs. As summarized in Chapters 1 and 2, students needed to see that others like them held these identities, strategies, and interpretation of difficulty. By seeing that everyone is engaging in the tasks, students are reassured that considering the future, having difficulties, and developing strategies all are identity-congruent—things that students like themselves do and experience.

Each activity is different. There is movement and not too much talking. The talking that occurs is targeted to focus on the simple core point of each activity so that the message builds gradually across sessions and is retained in memory in the form of the activity. In each of the early activities, products are individual. The group process starts with these products.

Moreover, activities are sequenced so that they start out being almost deceptively simple and fun. They are quite structured, so that what participation entails is clear. The reader can see this in the manual in Chapter 4. Initial activities have a very structured setup of how things unfold and provide explicit participation structure. This makes sure that everyone participates and makes sure that what counts as successful participation is simple. Trainers provide specific and clear feedback rewarding participation, so that students can get engaged. This is done because it is critical that each student participate and become part of the group. Experienced difficulty early on might otherwise be misinterpreted as implying that STJ is impossible, not something one cares about. Engaging everyone side-steps a group dynamic in which some students feel that this is not for them and refuse to engage. If students are to experience a sense that everyone imagines a future, that this future connects with current actions, that school is the path to future successes, and that difficulties are normative for important tasks, everyone has to participate.

At the same time the group dynamic had to be fostered and structured. As can be seen in Chapter 4, the early activities, especially session 1, set the stage and help students practice engagement. STJ is not therapy. It is not meant as a place to discuss deeply personal matters that raise issues of confidentiality. The context must be structured so that each student has a place no matter his or her temperament or bent—whether a student is outgoing or shy, feels knowledgeable at the moment or not. Student engagement is closely structured in initial sessions so that it is simple and virtually guaranteed. The reason for this is that each student participates, participation is about equal, and each student is successful. This motivates their willingness to keep engaging even as activities become more demanding. Moreover, by seeing that all the other students are participating, each student learns the implied norm that this is something everyone is doing and that they all have some skills and abilities to get through school and to training beyond. Structure also makes the context feel safe.

Developing an Intervention to Capitalize on Identity-Based Motivation

Dynamic Construction. IBM theory focuses on people's everyday theories about themselves and the situated consequences of these theories for motivation. As described in Chapter 1, these everyday theories include three elements: identities, strategies to attain these identities, and the interpretation of experienced difficulty in working on tasks that seem related to these identities. Identities are images of the person one is, might become, or fears becoming. They can be focused on individual traits, such as being conscientious, or on social identities, such as being a student, a girl, a daughter. These social identities can include a variety of content and strategies—being a girl can imply that one cares about school, and this can involve paying attention in class.

Being a girl can also imply that one cares about one's appearance, and this can involve paying attention to fashion. Of course there is no one way or one right way to be a girl, so which content comes to mind and which strategies seem to fit is not fixed. Strategies are the links to behavior cued by these identities. Strategies sometimes but not always also serve to focus one's attention on others in the context in which behavior occurs. Continuing with the example of caring about school, a boy may care about school but may at the same time feel constrained in which strategies he can use if he believes that others may see some strategies as things boys do not do. Girls might have the same constraint for strategies they see as male. Finally, interpretations are the meaning one makes of experienced difficulty in engaging in school tasks, using strategies, or even imagining oneself succeeding in school. Difficulty can make the goal all the more attractive but it can also make it feel impossible, depending on which interpretation comes to mind.

Contextual Attunement. IBM theory focuses on contextual forces that influence these processes. In doing so, IBM theory makes a number of situated predictions. First, any particular context will cue some of a person's identities, strategies, and interpretations from memory and not others. Second, because people need to figure out how to act in context, contexts actually support and scaffold the creation of new identities, strategies, and interpretations to fit the current situation. Third, only those identities, strategies, and interpretations that are both *accessible* and *experienced as relevant* in context influence judgment and behavior. These three ways in which contexts matter make it difficult to predict how a person will act or think in one situation from the identities, strategies, and interpretations that came to mind (or that they described to a researcher) in another situation. Identities, strategies, and interpretations that are *available* in memory may not be *accessible* in the moment, and new identities, strategies, and interpretations can be dynamically constructed to fit the context. This sensitive attunement to contextual affordances and constraints is automatic and does not require conscious, systematic processing. Sensitive attunement also implies that small changes in context can have large effects on judgment and behavior via the spreading activation of associated knowledge networks.

Sensitive attunement and dynamic construction mean that people can come to see themselves in ways they had not before, to use strategies that previously might not have felt identity-congruent, and to interpret experienced difficulty in ways that might otherwise not have come to mind. A short intervention can set in motion a way of making sense of oneself that yields more productive engagement with school, and this productive engagement may change the environment with which one interacts, so that while remaining attuned to the environment, a positive spiral may ensue. Consider what happens when a student experiences the future as psychologically relevant to the present, strategies as identity-congruent, and difficulty as a signal of importance.

He[2] spends a little more time on homework than he otherwise would have, maybe learning more or understanding the classwork a bit better. He hands in the homework. Then he does it again. As his teacher begins to form a sense of the students who are really trying, she includes him in that image. Maybe she turns to him more or makes more eye contact with him in class. Because of that, she might notice if he seems to understand or to have a question. Little by little the immediate context to which he is attuned provides more opportunities for school-focused possible identities and strategies to come to mind and for experienced difficulty to be understood as signaling that school is important. Thus the core ideas of context sensitivity and dynamic construction imply that the STJ intervention can have lasting and even increasing effects over time as students engage their environment—as they seek out and respond to school-relevant cues.

---

2. In this paragraph I used the male pronoun "he" rather than "he or she" to denote the student and "she" rather than "he or she" to denote the teacher both because using both would be a mouthful but also because of the gendered reality. Boys are more likely to experience failure than girls in all societies in which girls are not explicitly held back, as reported by the Programme for International Student Assessment (PISA), teaching, at least in the United States, is a female-dominated profession.

Linking IBM to Particular School Outcomes. Because the goal was to develop a usable, scalable, feasible intervention, I wanted to be sure that I assessed the influence of STJ on the particular set of variables that have been most closely linked with school failure. As it turns out, these variables—grade-point average and school investment (e.g., attendance, time spent on homework)—are not only predictors of school failure but are also particularly important long-term predictors of future earnings and college performance—even more important than standardized test scores (Babcock & Marks, 2010; Farrington et al., 2012; Miller, 1998). Coming to class, doing homework, and engaging in class can all be considered self-regulatory behaviors, or actions taken to regulate and control oneself. They are all likely to promote learning as well as knowing when exams are and what material is to be covered. Thus the STJ process model, as detailed below, is to cue IBM, which should enlist self-regulatory behavior and improve academic engagement and attainment. Since school success is valued, students should also experience improved well-being (feeling fewer symptoms of depression, for example).

The STJ intervention focuses on making the future feel near and school-dependent in two ways: first by making adult identities feel near, or psychologically relevant to current choices, and second by widening the strategies children see as identity-congruent, things that people like them do in order to do well in school. STJ focuses on the meaning children make of their experienced difficulty in school in two ways: first by helping them to see experiences of difficulty as normative and part of the process of school (and life) for everyone and second by helping them to see experiences of difficulty in school tasks as signaling task importance rather than task impossibility.

IBM predicts that students will do better in school if schoolwork feels identity-congruent, feels like a path to attaining adult identities, and if they interpret experienced difficulty in schoolwork as implying that schoolwork is an important goal for them. If schoolwork feels identity-congruent and difficulties are interpreted as underscoring that point then students are more likely to spend time studying and doing homework, attending rather than skipping class, and taking initiative rather than disrupting others. As detailed in Chapter 1, we were successful in manipulating each of the components of IBM and were able to show effects on identity salience, time spent on schoolwork in class, likelihood of doing homework, and quality of performance on math and writing tasks, among others. The practical importance of STJ lies in the academic outcomes it targets: Students who study, go to class, ask questions, and accept that school is hard for everyone are students who don't misinterpret failure as meaning that school is not for them.

The proximal goal of STJ is to leverage students' IBM in three ways: (1) by making salient their images of who they may become, with particular emphasis on both the near future (the *student* they expect to become and are concerned they may become in the coming year—their academic possible identities) and the far future (the *adult* they expect to become and are concerned they may become); (2) by making *student* and *adult* possible identities feel connected to current strategies (e.g., studying) and congruent with other important identities (e.g., gender, race-ethnicity, social class); and (3) by framing *interpretation of difficulty* so that students are inoculated from

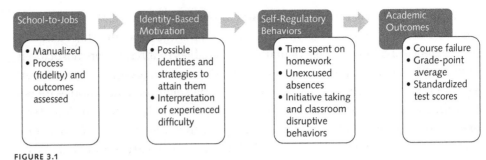

FIGURE 3.1

The general process model: IBM influences school-focused behavior, which yields better academic outcomes.

interpreting failures along the way as meaning that their possible student identities are impossible to attain.

Taken together, the goal is to make academic possible identities accessible, connect these possible identities with strategies to attain them, to create urgency to act now, and to help students interpret difficulties in school tasks as reminders of the importance of their possible selves rather than misinterpreting difficulties as meaning that their possible selves are impossible to attain. Change in IBM should yield change in self-regulatory behaviors, which should improve academic performance. Thus the targeted outcome of the STJ intervention is improved engagement and performance in school. This process model is outlined in Figure 3.1.

OUTLINING THE SCHOOL-TO-JOBS ACTIVITIES: A THUMBNAIL SKETCH

STJ was developed in two steps. First, with funding from the W. T. Grant Foundation and the National Institutes of Health, the activities were developed, piloted, and run as an after-school program with nine weekly sessions (P30MH38330, Oyserman project PI; Oyserman, Terry, & Bybee, 2002). As I developed each session, I manualized it. After each trial of a session, I revised the manual so that the final manual would fit the final round of the intervention. This round of tests included me, my graduate students, and the undergraduates we trained. Training involved first doing STJ as a participant (with materials in handouts relevant to the age group). Having experienced the intervention, we briefly discussed the topics outlined in Chapters 1 and 2, so that the trainers had a grasp of the process model and would not ad lib content that might undermine the active components of the program.

Then, also with funding from the National Institutes of Health, I was able to hire and train a group of trainers and observers and a training supervisor. Training was just as it had been before. Trainers were first participants. They did not pretend to be eighth graders; they participated as themselves (handouts were modified to fit their age group). Having a feel for the process is important (they feel STJ working and they see how it is imparted). Then we discussed active components and the theory, just as you have doing by reading until now. Our goal was to have trainers who were local and had an undergraduate degree. Thus trainers were an instantiation of the idea of STJ, local people getting through college. After initial training, I did not have further contact with trainers. Thus I could not influence trainers and we could see if the training and manual were sufficient to yield effects. As part of the development process,

I developed the fidelity measures that appear at the end of this book. To be sure that STJ would be feasible and scalable, I revised it from an after-school to an in-school program. To fit into regular school periods, I cut the length of each session, making some activities into two sessions. Thus the evaluated version of STJ was an in-school program with eleven in-school sessions and two follow-up parents-and-youths-together sessions (NIMH R01 MH58299 Oyserman PI; Oyserman, 2008; Oyserman, Bybee, & Terry 2006; Oyserman, Terry, & Bybee, 2002). Since these initial tests, we have provided STJ a number of times without an evaluation component. STJ is currently being used in schools and other settings in the United States and elsewhere, as gauged by feedback from users. STJ involves small-group activities typically presented twice a week in class over the first weeks of the school year.

In each STJ session, children engage in activities to link adult future images to school success, to make school success and strategies (e.g., studying) feel congruent with important social identities (e.g., race-ethnicity, gender, social class), and to inoculate them from misinterpreting difficulty as meaning that school-focused identities are impossible to attain. Each session involves an activity focused on a particular take-home point. Chapter 4 provides details of each activity and how to engage students in it.

Below is a brief thumbnail sketch of each of the sessions. Activities are simple, seemingly "easy." This was intentional, since ease and difficulty are used in meta-cognitive judgments of experience. If students found activities difficult, they would be at risk of interpreting this as meaning that thinking of the future is hard and "not for me." In the tested version, the "time line" sessions occurred as a single session and the parent and youth sessions were provided. Subsequent feedback from end users that they were unable to get through both parts of the session the timeline session in one class period suggests that this session can be divided in two.

Session 1, Setting the Stage: Students are paired up and briefly interview one another on the skills or ability they each have that will help them complete the school year successfully (e.g., "well organized," "positive attitude"). Then each student introduces his or her interview partner in terms of these skills. This provides an initial example of academic possible identities being compatible with important social identities because all youth engage in the task; the meta-message was, "We all care about school."

Session 2, Adult Images: Students pick photographs that fit their adult "visions" (their adult possible selves). Photographs include the four domains of adulthood: material lifestyle (e.g., a home, a lifestyle), job, relationships (e.g., family, friends), and community engagement. Photographs include both genders and match the racial-ethnic makeup of the school. Commonly most of the adult possible selves comprise images of material success, yielding the meta-message, "We all want a good future," which implies that important social identities situated in the room and in the school are compatible with a future orientation.

Session 3, Positive and Negative Forces: In session 3 students draw positive and negative forces—people or things that provide energy to work toward their possible identities and those that are draining or nay-saying.

The meta-message is, "Everyone faces obstacles and difficulties; this does not make a possible identity any less part of the 'true' self."

Sessions 4, Time Lines: In session 4 students draw time lines into the future, including forks in the road and obstacles. Then they examine them. Since students start with the present, all time lines involve school. The meta-message is, "Everyone has difficulties; failures and setbacks are a normal part of time lines and do not mean that academic possible identities are not true selves."

Session 5, Strategies: In session 5 students practice articulating specific strategies to attain their academic possible identities using an easy-to-recall formula ("because... I will... when..."), further highlighting the normativeness of difficulty in attaining academic possible identities. The meta-message is that difficulty is normative and academic possible identities can be attained with strategies.

Sessions 6 and 7, Pathways to the Future: In sessions 6 and 7 students build on previous sessions and use a different concrete medium—a poster board, stickers, and markers. First, students choose next-year's feared and to-be-expected possible identities and link them with strategies to attain them. Then students choose adult possible identities and link strategies to them, producing a concrete path from next-year's possible selves to adult possible selves via current actions (strategies). The meta-message is that one's adult future starts now.

Sessions 8, 9 and 10, Everyday Problems: Three sessions focus on the (mis) interpretation of difficulty. Students start with puzzles and then move on to academic problems and finally to high school graduation and college. In each case, the problem is difficult, and students practice breaking problems into smaller parts so that they can experience difficulty as meaning that effort can be increased because the problem is important rather than impossible to resolve. The meta-message is that all students care about doing well in school; difficulties along the way are normative and not self-defining.

Session 11, Wrapping Up and Moving Forward: The final in-school session cements students' new meta-cognitive interpretations by having them review the activities in order, critique them, and articulate in their own words each session's point.

Parent-Youth Sessions 1 and 2: *Building an Alliance, Active Listening and Having the Floor.* This is a double session that includes a parent or important adult in the student's life. Students bring the adults up to date on the activities they have participated in and what they mean, consider the transition to the next year, and then practice active listening and having the floor while discussing these topics. The meta-message is the core of IBM (the future starts now, strategies to get there, and interpreting difficulty).

Parent-Youth Sessions 3 and 4: Informational Interviewing. This double session includes a parent or important adult in the student's life as well as community members (people who have jobs). The first part of the session involves a discussion of the parent's own path from school to jobs, the training he or she had to have to get a job, and the difference between jobs and careers. The skill of informational interviewing is discussed—asking people who have a job you think you would want about the training needed to get there and the future prospects in such a job as a career path. Youths then informationally interview community members as parents watch. The meta-message is the core of IBM (the future starts now, strategies to get there, and interpreting difficulty).

STJ EMPIRICAL SUPPORT: TESTING OUTCOMES

Fidelity

An intervention, no matter how successful, can be repeated only if what was done is clear. Fidelity is a construct that focuses on this issue. An important aspect of documenting that effects are due to the intervention is to document that trainers delivered the intervention as expected. This is termed *delivery fidelity*, but it is only one of five forms of fidelity (design, training, delivery, receipt, and enactment fidelity). Design fidelity involves clarification of the dosage, number of sessions, length of each session, and content of each session. Training fidelity involves clarification of how trainers are to be trained and the skills they should have at successful completion of training. Delivery fidelity involves assessment of the extent to which the intervention is delivered as intended (e.g., use of observers to determine that the intervention was delivered following the manual). Receipt fidelity involves assessment of whether participants are doing what is expected of them in each session. Enactment fidelity involves assessment of whether participants apply skills learned in the intervention outside of sessions; this is also called *outcome evaluation*. I consider each of these in the sections below.

Snapshot of the Population and Procedure

I tested the effects of the STJ intervention on academic outcomes of children twice, once in a single school, following children for a year (Oyserman et al., 2002), and once in three schools, following children for two years after the intervention (Oyserman, 2008; Oyserman, Brickman, Rhodes, 2007; Oyserman, et al., 2006). In both cases, given the goal of demonstrating effectiveness in contexts in which achievement gaps are likely to be high, I went to schools serving predominantly minority and low-income students. Most students described themselves as African American (72 percent) or Latino (17 percent). Students lived in census tracts where 54 percent of households had an annual income below the poverty line, well above the U.S. Census Bureau's 40 percent cutoff for describing a tract as high poverty (Bishaw, 2005). Moreover, two thirds of students received free or reduced-price lunches.

In the first round of testing, STJ was provided as an after-school program. In the second round of testing, STJ was provided during the school day. The manual in Chapter 4 focuses on the in-school version of STJ. Results were parallel in both tests and I focus here on the in-school test of STJ because it provides long-term follow-up. Readers interested in details of methods, analyses, plan, and so forth should refer back to the original articles (Oyserman, 2008; Oyserman, Brickman, Rhodes, 2007; Oyserman, Bybee, Terry, 2006; Oyserman, Terry, Bybee, 2002).

To test STJ, all eighth-graders in three low-income middle schools were randomly assigned to receive or not receive the intervention twice a week, with the intervention concluding prior to the end of the first marking period. All children enrolled in regular classes who were on the school roster in the first weeks of school were included in the evaluation. Prior to randomization, all children filled out a baseline questionnaire in class in which they reported on their engagement with school and how they saw themselves now and in the future. Teachers filled out a parallel brief engagement-with-school set of items so that preintervention data included both child and teacher report. Both of these questionnaires are provided in Chapter 4. Data were collected again at the end of the school year and at the fall and spring of the subsequent school year. Each time, child and teacher reports were obtained. We also obtained school records of grades, attendance, and test scores. Students in STJ also provided ratings of their experience (see Chapter 4). Parents were included in two final sessions that occurred on the weekends. We did not find evidence that attending or not attending these sessions changed outcomes, and we chose receipt of five sessions as our theoretical cutoff for whether children had received enough sessions to be considered having received STJ. We ran all analyses twice, once with the full randomized sample, including those who moved, were suspended or otherwise missed the intervention. Results from these analyses are important because they reflect the real-world effects that can be expected by others using the intervention. We repeated the analyses with those who received at least five sessions of the intervention (compared with a parallel control group). This version of analysis is important as a test of the underlying theoretical process. Results are consistent across both of these analyses. Interested readers should refer to back to the original article for details on analyses, handling of missing data, and so forth (Oyserman et al., 2006).

Cost-Effectiveness

The significance of any intervention is increased by its cost-effectiveness. Cost-effectiveness analyses involve detecting control–experimental group differences in net benefits to health given reduced risk of school failure, these include lower initiation of substance use, and less likely engagement in risky sexual behavior. In the case of STJ, calculations revealed that the STJ intervention cost less than $200 or roughly $16 per session per youth. These figures are dwarfed by the costs of other interventions targeting at-risk youths. (For example, the costs of the Fast Track intervention exceed $60,000 *per youth* (Foster et al., 2005; Foster & Jones, 2006).

Effects on Academic Performance

STJ significantly improved academic performance as assessed by grade-point average, eighth-grade retention, and standardized test scores. At the beginning of eighth grade, children randomly assigned to STJ did not differ from children in the control group. By the end of eighth grade, however, intervention and control groups differed on IBM, self-regulatory behaviors, and academic performance. Thus, at the end of the first-year follow-up, more than twice as many control youths as intervention youths were retained in eighth grade, and they had more unexcused absences. The magnitude of the effect of intervention on unexcused absences was large, as measured in effect size or $d = .73$, which is a measure of the size of correlation between the outcome and the intervention. Standardized test scores were available only at the first-year follow-up; here too effects were significant and meaningfully large ($d = .36$). By the end of the second-year of follow-up, STJ students spent almost 70 percent more time on homework each week than control students.

Looking at the effects over the two-year period, we found that each semester, intervention youth averaged 2.25 more days in school than control youth, continuing the large intervention effect on attendance found at the end of the first year. With regard to grade point averages (GPAs) in core classes as assessed by school records, the children randomized to control and STJ groups continued to show divergent paths over time. Within-time models comparing intervention and control groups at each grading period showed that a significant difference in GPA emerged at the third quarter, and GPA between groups continued to diverge over time through the end of ninth grade (see Oyserman et al., 2006).

Thus this eighth-grade intervention administered early in the year fostered effects on critical predictors of on-time graduation (Allensworth & Easton, 2005, 2007). At two-year follow-up, effects were large for time spent doing homework ($d = .74$) and change in time spent doing homework ($d = 1.04$); they were significant (with small-to-moderate sized effects as defined by Cohen, 1992) for grades ($d = .30$), change in grades ($d = .35$), and unexcused absences taken from school records ($d = -.30$). STJ reduces the extent to which students' school grades drop over the transition to high school and improves attendance and engagement with homework.

Effects on In-Class Behavior

Turning to in-class effects, we found that STJ significantly reduces in-class behavior problems. The behavior problem measure included both student report of their behavior—"I annoy or interfere with my classmates' work" and the consequences of their behavior "How often does the teacher make you leave the classroom because of your behavior?" as well as parallel teacher reports. We found that STJ also significantly improves in-class initiative taking and effort. The initiative taking (e.g., "I do more than the work assigned.") and effort (e.g., "I actively participate in class discussions") measure also included both student and teacher reports on student behavior. Effects are meaningful, as can be seen by the effect sizes for in-class initiative taking ($d = .33$), change in initiative taking ($d = .43$), disruptiveness ($d = -.33$) and change in disruptiveness ($d = -.78$). That there were both differences between intervention and control groups and differences in change over time between the groups means that the size of the difference between the two groups was getting bigger over time. Students who had previously attended STJ were less likely to be rated in high school as a student who "annoys peers or interferes with peers' work," "is critical of peers who do well in school," "needs to be reprimanded or sent to the office," and "is verbally or physically abusive to the teacher." They were more likely to be rated as students who "do more than the work assigned," "persist when confronted with difficult problems," "actively participates in class discussions," and "engages me in conversation about subject matter before or after school or outside of class."

Effects on Well-Being

I wanted to obtain some measure of the effect of STJ on well-being, and the tight data-collection window (30 minutes for each wave) meant that obtaining an array of measures was not possible. When, by the spring of ninth grade, I reasoned that I would have a little time—both because students would be able to fill out the questionnaire more quickly, given that they were familiar with it, and because their reading skills might have improved—I chose to focus on depression. Depression is relatively common, with something like a quarter of adolescents reporting symptoms that warrant more careful attention. Being common does not imply that it is not a problem; depression is associated with an array of socioemotional, behavioral, and physical risk factors.

Therefore in the spring of ninth grade I added an assessment of youth-reported depression, using the standard twenty-item, four-point Center for Epidemiological Studies Depression Scale (Radloff, 1977). It is anchored at 0 = *not at all or less than one day in the past week* and 3 = *5 to 7 days in the past week*. Items include affective (e.g., "I felt depressed") and somatic (e.g., "I did not feel like eating; my appetite was poor") aspects of depression. The proportion of youths meeting the standardly used clinical threshold for depression (sum scores of at least 16) (Radloff & Locke, 2000) was 22.7 percent, comparable with the proportion of youth reaching the threshold for depression in national surveys (Costello, Mustillo, & Erkanli, 2003; Roberts, Attkisson, & Rosenblatt, 1998). Intervention effects on depression were significant; estimated mean Center for Epidemiological Studies Depression Scale scores were nearly two points lower for STJ than control youth at the end of ninth grade.

Schools and Other Programs Are Asking to Use STJ

STJ was adopted by the FASTTRACK preventive intervention group and is being used in a number of public and charter schools settings in the United States and abroad, including Singapore and England. I have sent copies of the manual to interested school personnel and researchers in South Africa, China, and Norway. The basic model and intervention structure is being used in English-language learning classes (Lamb, 2011; MacIntyre et al., 2009; Papi, 2010; Papi & Abdollahzadeh, 2012). While randomized clinical trials were not conducted, the spread of usage suggests that teachers and others find the manual and theory a good fit to their contexts and needs. Teacher identity formation has also been studied using the IBM framework (Hamman et al., 2013). This provides some indication that school personnel (teachers, counselors) find the program to be usable and feasible to implement. I hope that having this book will make the process of training and any needed revisions easier.

Summary

In summary, across measures of behavioral engagement and academic outcomes, STJ shows significant effects on the key academic outcomes predicting on-time graduation. While attaining and sustaining an intervention effect is notoriously difficult, we (Oyserman et al., 2006) also documented that effects were stable and even increasing over time. This sustained effect over two years is particularly impressive given the high-poverty neighborhoods in which the youth were embedded and the difficulty of improving academic outcomes while controlling for prior academic attainment. We also documented effects using two very different analytic strategies (structural equation modeling and longitudinal multilevel modeling) with different strengths and assumptions.

STJ EMPIRICAL SUPPORT: TESTING THE PROCESS MODEL

Having shown that children assigned to STJ got better grades and test scores than children who were not, we wanted to be sure that our process model could explain how that happened. That is, we wanted to show that STJ increased the number of school-focused identities and the strategies to attain them reported by the students. We also wanted to show that these identities felt congruent with the racial-ethnic identities of the STJ students.

The mediation model would be that children randomized to the STJ group and children in the control group would start out the same but show different trajectories of change, with children in the STJ group showing change in IBM factors and change in identity-based motivation predicting changes in self-regulation, which in turn predicts change in academic outcome. Statistical mediation analysis showed that the theorized process model was empirically validated (Oyserman et al., 2006). STJ changed IBM, which changed self-regulatory behaviors, including attendance (school records of unexcused absences), time spent on homework (child report), initiative taking in the classroom (teacher and child report), and classroom disruptive behaviors, which were reduced (teacher and child report). Effects on academic performance were mediated by effects on self-regulatory behavior. These significant effects were obtained two years after the intervention, at the end of ninth grade, which included the transition to high school.

Mediational analyses showed that the IBM variables significantly mediated the direct effect of STJ on homework, in-class behavior, grades, and test scores. We also showed that while racial identity and school-focused possible selves were not connected in the control group, in the STJ group they were. This means that while control group students were on average unsure whether their academic aspirations and strategies were identity-congruent, STJ students were sure that they were (Oyserman et al., 2006).

These results matter. First, they demonstrate the posited positive effect of IBM on academic outcomes. Second, because children were randomly assigned to the intervention or control group, effects cannot be attributed to other factors; therefore we know that core constructs are susceptible to influence from brief intervention. Third, effects are large enough to matter in real-world settings. For example, we found that being enrolled in STJ buffered students from the negative effects of low parent involvement with school, which undermined academic outcomes for control group children but not STJ children (Oyserman, Brickman, & Rhodes, 2007).

Even showing mediation does not yet show that each of the three elements of IBM was an active ingredient in the change process. To ensure that each IBM component matters, I conducted follow-up experiments with my students, each testing an aspect of the theory of change. We focused on demonstrating the effects on doing homework (Destin & Oyserman, 2009), doing science homework (Destin & Oyserman, 2010), persisting in challenging math assignments (Elmore & Oyserman, 2011) and successful performance on standardized writing and intelligence tasks (Oyserman, Novin, Smith, Elmore, & Nurra, 2014; Smith & Oyserman, 2014). Each of these studies is detailed in Chapter 1.

SUMMARY

In this chapter I have described decisions I made in developing STJ as well as the IBM rationale for these choices and for how activities were framed. I then summarized evidence supporting STJ and the process model on which it is based. In the next chapter, I provide the intervention manual used in the randomized clinical trials along with the fidelity checklists used for assessing whether the intervention was delivered as planned and whether the process of being in the intervention was experienced as planned (delivery and receipt fidelity). My goal in writing each of these sections was to concretize the process, so that those interested in using this intervention will have the translational skills to do so. This ability to translate with fidelity to a new context is the critical missing step between finding what appears to be an effective intervention and figuring out how to use the intervention in a given setting. I hope that I have made it easier to keep in mind what the core active intervention components are and how to think about the setting. Differences in participants, context, and dependent variables of interest (what a program wants to change) necessitate thinking carefully about how to translate the program without losing these core active components.

SCHOOL-TO-JOBS IMPLEMENTATION MANUAL

INCLUDING FIDELITY AND OUTCOME MEASURES

4

TABLE OF CONTENTS

4.1 OVERVIEW

4.1.1 An Outline of Pointers for All Sessions

1. Greet participants as they enter and take attendance in a notebook—noting if on time, late, or absent. This ensures that you will quickly learn all participants' names. Knowing names allows you to refer to participants by name, which is very positively reinforcing and increases engagement.

2. If you need help learning names, photograph participants in Session 1; make photo nametags with names large enough for you to read and have participants pick them up at the beginning of each session (and leave them behind). Repeat names each time a person participates. This enormously increases engagement.

3. Pay attention to the flow so that time will be adequate.

4. Stick to the session theme by eliciting discussion focused on theme and weaving focus back to theme. This is not counseling or therapy. Do not delve deeply into a student's life, problems, or issues. Do not go off on tangents about other information. This is not career counseling or academic guidance.

5. Positively reinforce both speakers and listeners. Positive reinforcement is task oriented. It is specific and helps participants behave in ways that will help them stay in school. Positive reinforcement is not simply saying "good" or "great job!" or "interesting comment." Positive reinforcement is specific; this means saying what was good or interesting about the job or comment. Examples would be (Session 1) "That was a good introduction; you gave a skill John has to succeed in next year in school." Or (Session 10) "Great! Your group came up with questions instead of jumping right in with a solution."

6. Use the outline agenda as a structure guide for participants. Hang the agenda prior to the start of each session.

7. Bring newsprint and writing material to each training session.

8. Write participant responses on newsprint so their work in the session is visible.

9. The newsprint serves to structure the flow and highlight themes. Responses that focus on themes relevant to the session should be organized physically on the page by placing content about a theme together without labeling and later labeling each theme as part of the connecting discussion. This helps reinforce the notion that the participants have something of worth to share, and it actively links responses to STJ concepts. For example, in Session 2, cluster adult image statements so that each newsprint sheet involves a one of the four themes of adulthood (e.g., jobs, lifestyle, relationships, community involvement). In Session 9, cluster questions about the math problem so that each sheet represents a way of doing it (as a timeline with stumbling block and fork, as an action goal, as a positive or negative model). This means that writing is more than documenting; it is also synthesizing so that students see their own competence.

10. Define concepts as you use them—write definitions on newsprint in advance and reveal them as you go along. This saves times and means students only watch you write what they said. The most fluent way to do this is to have the preprinted definitions in your newsprint pad for the session (count a few sheets for each of the youth-generated sections); in this way the preprint will come up naturally at the point that it should in the session.

11. Provide participants a preview of the next session, connecting the end of each session to the next session. This provides a sense of coherence often lacking in their other experiences.
12. Have a routine for passing out and picking up materials, evaluation forms, and snacks. Ask for help if it fits the flow; pick up as students finish, and have them help move desks to get the room back to its original condition. This reinforces their active participation.
13. If possible, take photographs of each session—both close-ups of participants and longer shots of the activities. You can use these in the final session, and participants enjoy seeing them.
14. Take time to talk with the other trainers and the site supervisor (if there is one) for a brief time immediately after each session, noting issues with specific participants and providing performance feedback to help organize issues to be raised at the future training sessions.

4.1.2 Time

To date, it appears that sessions may need to fit in school periods ranging from 45 to 70 minutes. To facilitate planning, each section provides a time range, such that the total minimum time fits a 45-minute session and the total maximum time fits a 70-minute session. Where needed, information on what can be cut is provided so that decisions can be made that do not undermine the core foci.

4.1.3 Materials

Each session involves use of specific materials, listed at the beginning of the session. Worksheets are located at the end of each session, as is the session evaluation form. The end-of-program evaluations are at the final youth session (Session 11). The exceptions are the images for the adult images activity in Session 2 and the graduation requirements for Session 10; you will need to obtain these locally. Be sure you have the required materials in sufficient quantity before you arrive.

4.1.3.1 MATERIALS FOR EVERY SESSION

Have a tubby for each of the groups you run that includes the following:

1. Agenda—written on newsprint prior to the beginning of the session
2. Snacks—may seem unnecessary but are important; no one concentrates when thirsty or hungry
3. Newsprint, tape, markers of sufficient width and dark enough to be read from the back of room
4. Camera
5. Attendance notebook
6. Ground rules developed in Session 1 written on newsprint.
7. Art supplies and session-specific materials (listed next)

4.1.3.2 MATERIALS TO PURCHASE

1. Colored marbles (one for each participant)
2. Newsprint, markers, and tape (for trainer use in each session)
3. Notebook (for marking attendance and participation and other notes)

4. Digital camera (or cellphone)
5. Art supplies (for each participant)
    a. Rulers
    b. Pencils
    c. Scratch paper
    d. Thin and thick markers, crayons and colored pencils (enough for all)
    e. Red, blue, black markers
    f. Two poster boards per participant (one for Session 4 and one for Sessions 6 and 7)
6. Food (juice box or water, granola or cracker packs)

4.1.3.3 SESSION-BY-SESSION GUIDE OF MATERIALS TO REPRODUCE

Writing takes time and is boring for participants unless it is about their own content. Therefore, write in advance or have preprinted newsprint sheets with the text that is boxed for each session. Write big enough and darkly enough that people in the back can read it—otherwise, it is a waste of time and you are communicating that this information is not for them. In addition, handouts are used in Sessions 3, 5, and 8–10. Make a copy of the handout for each student in the group; following are small versions so you know what to look for in the manual and what section it is in.

4.1.3.3.1 Session 1

1. Newsprint Sheet 1: AGENDA

1. *Introductions*
2. *Expectations and concerns*
3. *Aim*
4. *Naming the group*
5. *Games*
6. *Next session*

2. Newsprint Sheet 2: INTRODUCTIONS

Introductions are a way of saying who you are and what you can contribute.

3. Newsprint Sheet 3: STJ RULES

Participate
Share your ideas
Give others a chance to speak
Listen and ask questions
Be fair (no name calling)

4. Newsprint Sheet 4: STJ GOAL

School-to-Jobs:
Create a road map to success
Going from school to the world of work, by linking far and near goals,
working on strategies, and developing alternatives to get around obstacles

1. Newsprint Sheet 1: AGENDA

> 1. *Last session*
> 2. *Adult images*
> 3. *Common themes*
> 4. *Next session*

2. ADULT IMAGES

This needs to be prepared by you; you will need career, material lifestyle (homes, cars, vacations, leisure and sport), family and friendship relationships, and community participation photographs laminated to be adult images. The number is dependent on the number of participants in the group; the mix of gender and of race-ethnicity should balance that of the group and the images should be current. I use publically available images using an Internet search. Here is an example grid of matching image domain, race-ethnicity, and gender for a group of 25 mixed and predominantly Latino in origin.

Adult Domain	Photo Gender												Objects (e.g., Car, House)	TOTAL
	M				F				M+F					
	Photo Race-Ethnicity													
	L	B	W	A	L	B	W	A	L	B	W	A		
Job-Career	10	5	5	5	10	5	5	5						50
Family-Relationships									10	5	5	5		25
Lifestyle													30	30
Community Participation	2	1	1	1	2	1	1	1	2	1	1	1		15
TOTAL	12	6	6	6	12	6	6	6	12	6	6	6	30	120

1. Newsprint Sheet 1: AGENDA

> 1. *Last session*
> 2. *Far future adult images can become goals*
> 3. *Positive and negative forces*
> 4. *Next session*

2. Newsprint Sheet 2: POSITIVE FORCES

> *A positive force or role model is someone doing what you want to do. That person supports you and shows you the way to persist in spite of difficulties and obstacles.*

3. Newsprint Sheet 3: NEGATIVE FORCES

> *A negative force or model is someone who is doing the opposite of your goals. That person tells you it is impossible for you to succeed and that obstacles mean you should just quit.*

4. Handout 1: POSITIVE AND NEGATIVE FORCES

Located at 4.5.3.6.5.
This handout looks like the miniature version you see next.

JOB and CAREER FUTURE ME	RELATIONSHIP FUTURE ME
My Possible Self:	**My Possible Self:**
Positive Model or Force:	**Positive Model or Force:**
Negative Model or Force:	**Negative Model or Force:**

4.1.3.3.4 Session 4

1. How to Make a Timeline from Poster Board in Three Steps

Step 1: Start with poster board. Step 2: cut in half widthwise. Step 3: tape to make long line.

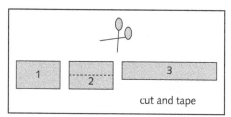

cut and tape

2. Newsprint Sheet 1: AGENDA

> 1. *Last session*
> 2. *Timelines*
> 3. *Discussion*
> 4. *Next session*

3. Newsprint Sheet 2: TIMELINES

> *A timeline is about something. It shows a series of events in order.*

4. Newsprint Sheet 3: TIMELINE INTO THE FUTURE

> *A timeline into the future is like a path; there are forks in the road* ⤙ *and obstacles* ⫰ *Choices matter by changing the path. Sometimes it is not your choice but things do not work out and you need to get around obstacles. All timelines into the future have at least one fork in the road. All timelines into the future have at least one obstacle.*

4.1.3.3.5 Session 5

1. Newsprint Sheet 1: AGENDA

> 1. *Last session*
> 2. *Action goals*
> 3. *Sharing action goals*
> 4. *Next session*

2. Newsprint Sheet 2: ACTION GOALS

> *An action goal is a specific statement that links a far future and a near future possible self by listing what actions you will take now and when and where you will take them.*

3. Handout 1: ACTION GOALS WORKSHEET
Located at 4.5.5.7

> **1. JOB or CAREER ACTION GOAL**
>
> Because I want (*adult job image*) _____
>
> _____
>
> I will (*nearer future possible self*) _____
>
> _____
>
> By doing (*what you can do TODAY or this week*) _____
>
> _____
>
> When (*after what activity and before what activity during the day*) _____
>
> _____

2. FAMILY or FRIENDSHIP ACTION GOAL

Because I want *(adult family or relationship image)* _____

_____

I will *(nearer future possible self)* _____

_____

By doing *(what you can do TODAY or this week)* _____

_____

When *(after what activity and before what activity during the day)* _____

_____

4.   Handout 2: ACTION GOALS WORKSHEET 2
Located at 4.5.5.8

My Action Goals

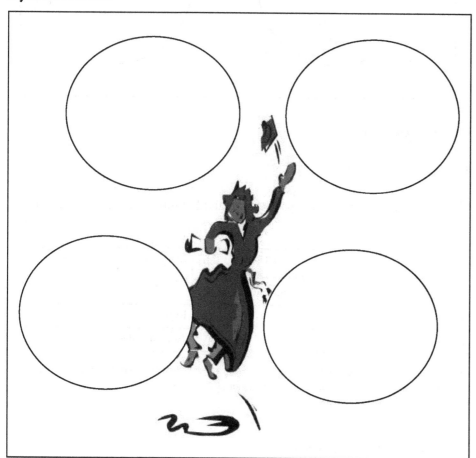

My Action Goals

4.1.3.3.6 Session 6

1. Create a Poster Board

Make a poster board for each participant divided into three horizontal sections and two vertical sections.

NEXT YEAR POSSIBLE SELVES	STRATEGIES Black = Doing now; White = Could do	ADULT POSSIBLE SELVES
Expected		Expected
To-be-avoided		To-be-avoided

NOTE: The key Black = I am doing this now *is written in red marker.* White = I could do this *is written in blue marker by the trainers as they make sure that participants know how to proceed with the task. Only the marker relevant to the task should be in the participants' hands.*

2. Newsprint Sheet 1: AGENDA

> 1. *Last session*
> 2. *Connecting next year and right now*
> 3. *Next session*

3. Newsprint Sheet 2: POSSIBLE SELVES

> *A possible self is a positive or negative image of what is possible for you to become in the future. It is energizing because it might really happen. Strategies turn that energy to action.*

4. Newsprint Sheet 3: STRATEGIES

> *Strategy—actions you are taking now or could take to become like or avoid being like a possible self*

4.1.3.3.7 Session 7

1. Newsprint Sheet 1: AGENDA

> *1. Last session*
> *2. Connecting next year and the future*
> *3. Sharing pathways*
> *4. Next session*

2. Newsprint Sheet 2: POSSIBLE SELVES from Session 6
3. Newsprint Sheet 3: STRATEGIES from Session 6

4.1.3.3.8 Session 8

1. Newsprint Sheet 1: AGENDA

> *1. Last session*
> *2. Solving puzzles*
> *3. Next session*

2. Newsprint Sheet 2: INOCULATION

> *Inoculation or vaccination is a way of thinking about a feeling of difficulty. Just because it is difficult does not mean it is impossible. Practicing can make you immune to getting infected with that idea and help you think of choices, obstacles, and ways to work around them.*

3. Handouts 1 and 2: PUZZLE 1 and PUZZLE 2

These handouts are found in 4.5.8.7.1 and 4.5.8.7.2 on pages 145 and 146.

4.1.3.3.9 Session 9

1. Newsprint Sheet 1: AGENDA

> *1. Last session*
> *2. Math problem*
> *3. Problems in a bag*
> *4. Next session*

2. Handout 1: EVERYDAY MATH PROBLEM

This handout is found in 4.5.9.7.4 on page 154.

4.1.3.3.10 Session 10
1. Newsprint Sheet 1: AGENDA

> 1. *Last session*
> 2. *Succeeding and moving to the next step*
> 3. *Next session*

2. Handouts 1 and 2: HIGH SCHOOL and COLLEGE HANDOUTS

You must prepare this handout prior to this session. Obtain and summarize high school graduation requirements, provide sample schedules from the high school schedules your students are likely to attend and college entry requirements for a number of colleges (local, those mentioned in class). This needs to be prepared by you since requirements are not standardized.

4.1.3.3.11 Session 11
1. Newsprint Sheet 1: AGENDA*

> 1. *Last session*
> 2. *What we did in STJ*
> 3. *Summary*
> 4. *Evaluation*

*AGENDA should add 5. *Next Sessions* and 6. *Getting Parent Contact Information* if the group is to include the next two parent and youth together sections.

4.1.3.3.12 Parent and Youth Together Sessions 1 and 2
1. Newsprint Sheet 1: AGENDA

> 1. *School-to-Jobs*
> 2. *Introductions*
> 3. *Concerns*
> 4. *Active listening and having the floor*
> 5. *Practice*
> 6. *Feedback and the future*

2. Newsprint INTRODUCTION from Session 1
3. Newsprint Sheet 2 STJ GOAL

> *School-To-Jobs GOAL:*
> *Helping create a road map from school to the world of work*
>
> *By*
> *Connecting the present to the near (next year) and far (adult) future and working on strategies that can be used to attain near and far goals.*

4. Handout 1: ACTIVE LISTENING AND HAVING THE FLOOR

This handout is found in 4.6.1.9

"The Floor"	
Rules for the Speaker	*Rules for the Listener*
• Don't go on and on.	• Listen for why things are important to the Speaker.
• Pause and let the Listener check out what he or she understood.	• Check out your understanding.
• Speak for yourself.	• Ask for examples and explanations.
	• Don't offer your own opinions or thoughts.
	• Concentrate on what the speaker is saying

4.1.3.3.13 Parent and Youth Together Sessions 3 and 4

1. Newsprint Sheet 1: AGENDA

> 1. *Last session*
> 2. *Getting a job or planning to get one*
> 3. *Informational interviewing—What is it?*
> 4. *Informational interviewing—Practice*
> 5. *Informational interviewing with community members*
> 6. *Feedback and the future*

2. Handout 1: INFORMATIONAL INTERVIEWING WORKSHEET

This handout is in section 4.6.2.7

> ### SCHOOL-TO-JOBS
> ### INFORMATIONAL INTERVIEWING WORKSHEET
>
> 1. I am interested in hearing about (name the client's type of work). Can you tell me a little about it here at (the place you are interviewing at)?
>
> 2. (If more than one job title is mentioned) I'd like to hear more about the job of _____.
>
> 3. What is it like to do this job? Is there some daily routine?
>
> 4. What kind of person fits in best? What personal characteristics are the best fits for this job?
>
> 5. What type of training and previous experiences does it require?

6. Is there any ongoing training? Can you describe it?

7. How would you describe the supervision received by a person in this position?

8. What equipment or machines, including computers and software, are used in this job?

9. Are there special requirements or skills needed to have this job?

10. What is the range of salary generally paid to a person in this field?

11. Could you describe the work conditions or job setting (is it in an office, is it noisy and so on)?

12. What do you predict will be happening in this field in 5 or 10 years?

13. What opportunities are there for promotion?

14. What poses the most problems for people who have interviewed for or tried to train for this job?

15. How did you come to this job; what types of jobs or training did you have before?

16. What are some of the satisfactions of this job?

17. What are some of the headaches of this job?

18. Are there other people or organizations you recommend I contact for more information about this job?

19. Is there anything else you think I should know about this job?

Thank the person for his or her time and help and leave.

3. Handout 2: THE STJ PROGRAM INFORMATIONAL INTERVIEWING FORM

This handout is in section 4.6.2.8

THE SCHOOL-TO-JOBS PROGRAM INFORMATIONAL INTERVIEWING

Informational interviewing is a way of learning about jobs that you may be interested in having in the future. By talking with someone who has a job or works in an area that you may be interested in, you can learn both more about the job and the training and skills needed on the job. Informational interviewing can help you come up with a plan for how to prepare for jobs you might be interested in pursuing in the future.

Informational interviews can be done by phone or in person. If you are setting up an in-person meeting, be sure you know how to get there and exactly when you are supposed to meet. Be sure you ask with whom you will be meeting. Ask how to spell the name so you are not confused when you arrive. When the interview is finished, thank the person for his or her time and help, and leave. When you get home, it is a good idea to follow up with a short thank-you letter.

1. Before you go, be sure to double-check:

   a) Appointment DATE: _____ TIME: _____

   b) Name of person you will interview _____
      (CHECK SPELLING WITH SECRETARY IF UNSURE)

   c) Name of company or organization: _____

   d) Address: _____

   _____

   e) Record information on how to get to the interview. If you did not get directions, call back and ask. You can ask these questions of a secretary, if there is one. Indicate whether you are coming by car or public transportation for better directions.

---

4. Handout 3: THE INTERVIEW

This handout is in section 4.6.2.9

THE INTERVIEW

1. Greet the person, express enthusiasm at being there, and begin the interview.

2. Say "I am interested in hearing about being a (name of job or area). Can you tell me a little about what it is like?"

3. What is it like to do your job? What is the daily routine?

4. What personal characteristics help make a good (name of job or area of interest)?

5. What previous experiences help to do well?

6. Do you get training while you are on the job?

7. How are you supervised?

8. What special requirements are there, and what skills are important?

9. What is it like to work here? Is it quiet or noisy? Do you work alone or with others?

10. What do you predict will be happening in this area of work in 5 or 10 years?

11. What are some of the satisfactions of having this job?

12. What are some of the headaches of having this job?

13. Is there anything else you think I should know about this job?

4.1.4 How to Read This Manual as a Trainer or Observer

The manual provides information about each session, structured in the following order:

1. An overview of the session.
2. A specific point to "take home." The take-home point is the content that the trainer should focus on in guiding discussion or making comments during the session.
3. A description of materials needed for the session.
4. A brief description of the room setup for the session.
5. An outline of the session in the form of an agenda. The agenda should be copied onto newsprint to be taken to the session so that youth can follow the process.
6. A description of the actual activities to take place. Activities are broken into approximate time sequences and contain both what the trainer should say (the text the trainer will use in the session) and also explanations to the trainer. Explanations provide background, suggest prompts, and connect activities to the rationale and take-home point of the session. Text does not need to be spoken verbatim but should be practiced so that the session runs smoothly. For ease of reading, text to be used by the trainer is presented in italics. It is also necessary to use your own words to do some of the activities written in the nonitalicized print, so it is important to know all of the material, not just the italicized text. The sequence of activities is listed in a numbered sequence. The last number of the heading corresponds to the agenda numbering.
7. A session succeeds to the extent that trainers elicit from participants their own knowledge and skills and observations and allows participants to learn through doing and helping others.
8. The final part of each session is debriefing—talking with your partner (if you are working in pairs) and the other trainers and supervisor about the session, how it went and what can be improved for the next session, as well as specific issues about participants.
9. In the initial tests, trainers came to school but were not the regular teachers; they were undergraduates, graduate students, and people with an undergraduate degree.

4.2.1 Session 1 at a Glance

• [Hang preprinted agenda] Greet/welcome participants/Greet latecomers • Trainer introduction (Name, from __, trait that helps me succeed at work) • Say: There is an observer in the room in order to observe the trainer (improve program not grade students)
• Ask what an **introduction** is: (a way of saying who you are and what you can contribute) (Write student def. on newsprint; show def. on preprinted newsprint) • Different goals for introductions (depends on context) • Ask about skills and abilities for succeeding in school (since this is School-to-Jobs) • Write examples of skills and abilities students give on newsprint
• Introduction activity (Pass out marbles/Pair up/Learn partner name and skill/ Ask for questions/Circulate, check for understanding) • Make big circle, partner introduction, repetition of names and skills, take attendance, start with the person to your right and go clockwise for names and counterclockwise for repetition
• **Expectation/Concern** task, explain concepts: what are expectations concerns • Use newsprint to write group expectations and concerns • Reinforce and repeat four basic themes: **seeing both my far and near future, developing strategies to work toward my future, seeing the path between now and my future, getting help (parents, community members, teachers)** • Elicit **group rules** (Write on newsprint)
• Say: Goal of program (Use prepared newsprint)
• Group Naming Activity: Explain activity (Give examples, elicit ideas, and vote)
• Explain session schedule/Provide contact information/Write on board
• Explain task, line up from youngest to oldest without talking (Encourage/When completed, ask month of birth) • Congratulate/Reinforce cooperation
• Explain task, stand in circle, cross arms in front and grab hands of two people across the circle, without letting go of hands, get them uncrossed so we are again in a circle • Trainers are part of the circle/Congratulate/Reinforce cooperation
• Review: Ask for names (take attendance as this happens) • Summary statement: We introduced each other with strengths to succeed next year. • Connecting statement: Next session will work on adult images • Pass out snacks (elicit help doing so) • Pass out session evaluation form (elicit help doing so) • Ask for help rearranging the room • Good-byes/Collect evaluation/Check attendance/Rate participation/Label newsprint

4.2.2 Session 2 at a Glance

- [Hang preprinted agenda] Greet participants by name/take attendance/ Say: Pick up nametag/greet latecomers by name
- Say: Today is Session 2, **Adult Images**
- Ask: what happened last session (introduced our **skills for succeeding next year**, STJ rules—**in STJ everyone participates**, games)

- Say: This is the **Adult images** task
  - Choose pictures that represent visions of yourself as an adult.
  - Pick 3–5 pictures
  - Will be asked: What does this mean for you? When will it be true of you?
  - Afterwards we will share 1 image from each
- Pass out snacks if people are finishing at different times
- Mingle—check for understanding
- Have everyone rejoin circle
- Sharing adult images task—show 1 picture and explain to group, while group listens to common themes that emerge

---

- While students are speaking, write key words on newsprint—1 per adult domain.
- Time permitting, ask students what's similar across descriptions
  - Likely will be a dominant theme (e.g., lifestyle).
  - If so, give this theme its name (lifestyle)
  - Ask: how do adults get the things they want? (jobs)
  - If no dominant theme, circle the themes that occurred and name them

---

- Summary statement: Today we picked adult images. People described lifestyles they wanted; this is a domain of adulthood (if other themes, repeat them—divide into jobs, family and friends, community). If not present, do not say
- Connecting statement: Next session we will identify positive and negative forces and models
- Pass out session evaluation form (elicit help doing so)
- Ask for help rearranging the room
- Good-byes/Collect evaluation/Check attendance/Rate participation/Label newsprint

- [Hang preprinted agenda] Greet participants by name/take attendance/ nametags/greet latecomers by name
- Say: Today is Session 3, **Positive and Negative Forces and Models**
- Ask: What happened last session (adult visions, when they would happen)?
- Ask for domains of adulthood and examples (**lifestyle**, **career**); add if not noted **relationships with family and friends**, **community involvement** (write on newspaper)
- Reinforce participation (use participation book)
- Ask for ideas: what are positive and negative forces or role models?
- Write on newsprint then circle core ideas (show preprinted positive and negative force definitions)
- **Positive force or model**—can be model for an adult image or sooner, or can support attaining adult or sooner image
- **Negative force or model**—can be model of what do not want for adult image or sooner, or undermines effort
- Say: Today we will talk more about future self-images and connect them to both positive and negative forces and adult domains

- Use newsprint to explain task
- Explain task (for job domain, write or draw the adult image and identify a role model and a negative force)
- Could be an adult image you picked last week or a different one showing something about the kind of job or career you want to have
- Could be a specific job or just a kind of job (e.g., a job I enjoy)
- Hand out worksheets; students work alone
- Pass out snacks (elicit help doing so)
- Mingle—check for understanding, help individually as needed
- Have students make a big circle
- Get examples of role models by starting with a person who hasn't participated yet and say you will go around the circle, write on newsprint
- At halfway point get examples of negative forces, write on newsprint
- Cluster similar content/themes while writing
- Read through positive forces list, note common themes, repeat for negative themes

- Summary statement: Adult images can be about careers, relationships, lifestyle, and community involvement. Today, we worked on role models and negative forces
- Connecting statement: Next session, we'll try personal timelines into the future
- Pass out session evaluation form
- Good-byes/Collect evaluation/Check attendance/Rate participation/Label newsprint

- [Hang preprinted agenda] Greet participants by name/take attendance/ nametags/greet latecomers by name
- Say: Today is Session 4, **Timelines**
- Ask: What happened last session (drew **adult image**, **positive** and **negative force**)
- Reinforce key concepts (**positive and negative forces, domains of adulthood**)
- Say: Today we will begin to map out how to get from now to the future

---

- Ask: What are **timelines (timelines show the order of events in time)**
- Write **timeline** ideas on newsprint (reveal preprinted newsprint)
- Ask what about timelines into the future (**not for sure,** have to have **choices, and things can go wrong**) (reveal preprinted newsprint, forks in the road and roadblocks)
- Every timeline into the future has to have at least one fork (a choice) that leads to different outcomes
- Every timeline into the future has to have at least one roadblock (something that went wrong)
  - Sometimes we do not choose, but our plan does not work. That is an obstacle. No one sits down on the path of life; people get around obstacles.
- Explain the task. Start now and go as far as you can into the future, with at least one fork, and at least one obstacle to get around. No one has a timeline in her head. So do a rough draft of things that will happen, get that in order, then do timeline
- Pass out materials (long sheet of paper, ruler, markers)
- Pass out snacks (elicit help doing so)
- Repeat instructions while circulating; everyone has to have fork and stumbling block
- Provide help to make sure all have fork and stumbling block

---

- Regroup students; have them move into a circle
- Have everyone hold up their timelines; point out the fork and the stumbling block
- Have 1 or 2 students state their own fork or stumbling block
- Time permitting, have participants suggest an additional step in the timeline of the participant next to the YOUTH SESSIONS AT A GLANCE m.
- Reinforce participation (check participation book)

- Summary statement: Today we did timelines with forks in the road and obstacles
- Connecting statement: Next session we will work on action goals
- Pass out session evaluation form
- Ask for help rearranging the room
- Good-byes/Collect evaluation/Check attendance/Rate participation/Label newsprint

- [Hang preprinted agenda] Greet participants by name/Take attendance/ nametags/greet latecomers by name
- Say: Today is Session 5, **Action Goals**
- Ask: What happened last session (**Timelines, obstacles, forks in road)**
- Say: What domains of adulthood were on timelines (jobs, relationships, community service, lifestyle). Timelines usually have jobs and relationships only.
- Say: Today we will work on action goals

- Say: We talked about adult images, positive and negative role models, obstacles and forks in our timelines. Some adult images are hopes or dreams and others may be possible selves.
- Ask: What is a possible self? Use newsprint to record responses (Hopes and dreams are good but possible selves are possible because we actually work on them)
- Reveal preprinted newsprint definitions (**Action Goal**: An action goal **has an adult possible self, a closer possible self, a strategy, when and where actions occur**)
- Say: This takes the form of a sentence: Because I want (adult positive self), I will (nearer possible self), by (a specific strategy), when and where during the day (get specific or it will not happen)
- Explain task—write specific action goal for one or two domains of adulthood
- Pass out handouts/ask to spread out/Circulate and provide help
- Pass out snacks (elicit help doing so)
- Move back to circle
- Have students read their action goals (pick a student who hasn't participated yet and say you will move counterclockwise)/Write response on newsprint, cluster similar themes by "I will" statements (if a student can't say when during the day, pick a different goal)

- Summary statement: Today we worked on action goals
- Connecting statement: Next session we will work on poster boards and strategies
- Pass out session evaluation form
- Ask for help rearranging the room
- Good-byes/Collect evaluation/Check attendance/Rate participation/Label newsprint

• [Hang preprinted agenda] Greet participants by name/Take attendance/ nametags if needed/Greet latecomers   • Say: This is Session 6, **Possible Selves and Strategies**
• Ask: What happened last session (**Action goals—Because, I will, by, when**)   • Reinforce **action goals** as specific goals linking more distal goals to closer ones with activities to be done in certain contexts.   • Say: Last session we linked adult images to closer goals with strategies and specific actions that we would take that day or week in specific situations   • Say: This session we will focus on the close future, next year possible selves   • Say: Adult images can be dreams or hopes. This session we will focus on futures you see as possible for yourself; they could be what you are now and expect to continue being, what you are becoming or want to avoid   • Reveal preprinted newsprint for possible self and strategy definitions
• Show example poster board. Say: now we are working only on the left side   • Distribute boards with **next year possible self stickers** bag. Point to left of board   • Say: Use your bag of stickers to find 5 next year expected, 5 next year to be avoided possible selves. Put the rest of the stickers in your bag. You can also write your own. Don't peel the stickers until you've picked everything   • Circulate, clarify instructions out loud and in person, reinforce, help   • As students finish their first bag say: Now look at each next year possible self. Ask yourself: Am I doing anything now to be that way or to avoid being that way?   • Say: I will give you a bag of **strategies**. For each possible self, if you are doing something about it, find a sticker that says what you are doing; place it on the board under strategies near that possible self (hand out **strategy stickers bags)**   • Pass out snacks (elicit help doing so)   • Say: Raise your hand for a red marker when you are done. Then draw a red line connecting that strategy to the possible self   • As students finish, say: Raise your hand as you finish. I will give you a blue marker. Look in the bag, and if there is a strategy you could use for a possible self that does not have one, take it. Draw a blue line between it and the possible self it connects to   • Circulate, clarify instructions out loud and in person, reinforce, help
• Summary statement: Today we did possible selves and strategies boards   • Say: Some possible selves have strategies and some do not. Sometimes we have possible selves but are not doing anything about it   • Connecting statement: Next session is connecting strategies to adult possible selves   • Pass out session evaluation form/Check attendance/Rate participation   • Ask for help rearranging the room/Good-byes/Collect evaluation/Label newsprint

• [Hang preprinted agenda] Greet participants by name/Take attendance/Greet latecomers by name/nametags • Say: This is Session 7, **Pathways to the Future**
• Ask: What happened last session (next year expected/to-be-avoided possible selves) • Put up the preprinted newsprint definitions for possible selves and strategies • Reinforce concepts (**possible selves** expected and to be avoided, **strategies** as the things we do or can do to make them happen). • Say: Last session we mapped next year possible selves and strategies. This session we will connect those strategies to adult possible selves
• Pass out boards. Say: Now we are using the right side. Point: Adult Selves • Pass out **adult stickers**. Say: Read the stickers; pick 5 expected, 5 to-be-avoided • Say: Remember, adult possible selves are possible, not for sure, that could be positive outcomes we expect or negative ones we prefer to avoid but are possible • Circulate, clarify instructions out loud and in person, reinforce, help • Pass out snacks (elicit help doing so) • Say: When you have your 5 expected and 5 to-be-avoided stickers, raise your hand. Put the rest back, and I will give you a red marker • As you hand out markers, say: For each adult possible self look at red line strategies and ask yourself if it helps you get to an adult expected possible self or avoid an adult to-be-avoided possible self. If so, draw a line from that strategy to that possible self • Circulate. Repeat instructions out loud and individually. Look at boards. Reinforce
• Say: Draw your red lines, then raise your hand. I will trade your red for a blue marker • As you hand out markers, say: For each strategy with a blue line, ask yourself if that strategy could help you get to an expected adult self or avoid a to-be-avoided adult self; if so, draw the line • Say: Let's move back to the group (get circle so students can see each other's work)
• Ask each student to show his or her poster board (Just raise up so all can see) • Define pathway/Look for pathways. Say: Some of you have pathways; strategies make connections between next year and adult futures. Some are strategies you are using now (red). Some are strategies you could use but are not yet (blue). Some possible selves are not part of pathways. We are not doing anything to get them • Point to examples. Ask: Show a pathway (start opposite you, work around the circle)
• Summary statement: Today we looked for pathways • Connecting statement: Next session will be difficult puzzles • Pass out session evaluation form/Check attendance/Rate participation • Ask for help rearranging the room/Good-byes/Collect evaluation/Label newsprint

• [Hang preprinted agenda] Greet participants by name/Take attendance/ Greet latecomers by name/nametags • Say: Today is Session 8, **Puzzles**
• Ask: What happened last session (**Adult possible selves and pathways to the future, some red lines that we are doing now, some blue lines that we could do, and some possible selves we are not doing anything about**) • Say: Sometimes a possible self, using a strategy, hitting an obstacle, feels difficult. Today we are working on that feeling of difficulty. • Say: To inoculate ourselves from believing that if it is difficult, it is impossible. It is like getting a vaccination so difficulty won't infect us with giving up. • Ask: What is **inoculation/vaccination**? Like getting a shot, a bit painful, to prevent disease. Write responses on newsprint, reveal preprinted newsprint
• Pass out **Puzzle 1** • Read puzzle out loud, tell people to work in groups to solve • Have students say how they are trying to solve and write their descriptions on newsprint or have the groups write on newsprint (a grid is the easiest way to solve this problem, but students may have other ways) • Reinforce cooperative behavior • Reinforce responses that move toward problem solution • Reorient group to trainer, walk through solution, reinforce how impossible it seems before trying (at least one student usually says this right away)
• Pass out snacks (elicit help doing so) • Pass out **Puzzle 2** • Read puzzle out loud, tell people to work in groups to solve • Have students say how they are trying to solve and write their descriptions on newsprint (a grid is the easiest way to solve this problem, but students may have other ways) • Reinforce cooperative behavior • Reinforce responses that move toward problem solution • Reorient group to trainer, walk through solution, reinforce how impossible it seems before trying (at least one student usually says this right away)
• Summary statement: Today we had puzzles that seemed impossible but could be solved. The first had all the information, and the second required some trial and error • Connecting statement: Next session we will work on everyday problems • Pass out session evaluation form • Good-byes/Collect evaluation/Check attendance/Rate participation/Label newsprint

- [Hang preprinted agenda] Greet participants by name/Take attendance/Greet latecomers by name/nametags
- Say: Today is Session 9, **Solving Everyday Problems**

- Ask: What happened last session (puzzles, seemed impossible but could solve if started, had a plan, did not give up, like inoculation from illness)
- Say: We did puzzles but now we are going to try solving everyday problems
- Have students move desks into groups

- Pass out math problem
- Read math problem out loud
- Remind students that their job is to figure out what are the questions to ask
- Have students write their questions on newsprint (or paper)
- As soon as students begin to flag, turn to large group
- Have students say their questions
- Group questions to fit format of action goals (Because, I will, by, when) or format of timeline (is math class a fork in the road, an obstacle, what happens if fail or if transfer out, can you get to goals anyway) or positive and negative forces; that is, some questions are about pragmatics (by doing what) or context (when during the day); while some questions are about the next year possible self (I will), and other questions are about adult images (Because)
- Reinforce participation and use of questions

- Pass out snacks (elicit help doing so)
- Say: Now we are going to try this again. Everyone write down a problem they have or have had in school. Write it down briefly. Crumple it up and throw it on the floor
- Push crumpled paper to middle of the room, have students circle
- Read four or so of the problems. Ask which the group should work on
- Have the group do the same process of asking which questions to ask
- Write on newsprint, cluster questions into STJ concepts (action goals, timelines, etc.)
- Repeat by reading another four or so problems time permitting
- Reinforce participation/Reinforce asking: Obstacles, forks, action goals, strategies

---

- Summary statement: Today we worked on everyday problems
- Connecting statement: Next session we will do more inoculation by looking at what you need to finish high school and get more training, such as college
- Pass out session evaluation form/Check attendance/Rate participation
- Good-byes/Collect evaluation/Label newsprint

- [Hang preprinted agenda] Greet participants by name/Take attendance/Greet latecomers by name
- Say: This is Session 10, **Solving Everyday Problems and Graduating**

- Ask: What happened last session (solving everyday problems, inoculation from difficulty, asking questions/applying STJ concepts, not thinking difficult problems are impossible)
- Say: Today we are going to work on another everyday problem, graduating high school

---

- If possible, divide into groups. Otherwise, turn chairs to large circle
- Ask students, what does it take to graduate high school?
- Are there classes you need to take? Other things you need to do?
- Circulate and check on groups' progress, encourage
- Have each group write responses on newsprint (or trainers do this in front of room)
- Reinforce knowledge
- Pass out **high school graduation requirements**
- Facilitate student understanding of course names, content for sequential offerings in science, math
- Connect graduation requirements to what students know
- Pass out and read out loud **high school course sequence samples**
- Connect high school course selection to graduation requirements

---

- Pass out snacks (elicit help doing so)
- Pass out **college entry worksheets**
- Ask students, what does it take to get into college?
- Are there classes you need to take in high school? Other things you need to do?
- Circulate and check on groups' progress, encourage
- Have each group write responses on newsprint (or trainers do this in front of room)
- Reinforce knowledge
- Pass out a local 4-year college's entry requirements.
- Connect high school course selection and high school graduation requirements to college entry.
- Pass out another 4-year or community college students mentioned, repeat connection.

- Summary statement: Worked on what you need to finish high school, get to college
- Connecting statement: We will have a wrap-up session and talk about inviting parents and community members)
- Next session we will review all sessions and have a party
- Pass out session evaluation form/Check attendance/Rate participation
- Ask for help rearranging the room/Good-byes/Collect evaluation/Label newsprint

- [Hang preprinted agenda] Greet participants by name/Take attendance/Greet latecomers by name

- Say: This is Session 11, **Wrapping Up and Moving Forward**. There are a few parts, a party, remembering what we did, and considering inviting parents/other grownups
- Ask: What happened last session: getting through high school, graduating, to college

- Provide food and other party materials

- Say: Can someone say what we did in each session? Say what you remember.
- Use newsprint, elicit all the sessions, get them in order using multiple participants
- Ask: What did we do in each session?
- Ask: Which one did you like best? Why? (Write on newsprint)
- Ask: Which one did you like least? Why? (Write on newsprint)
- Ask: Looking back, how do the sessions connect? (Ex: we worked on adult images, linked them to role models/negative forces, action goals and strategies. We drew the process to get there with forks in the road and obstacles. We used puzzles to think about difficulties along the way; mapped getting through high school and to college)

- Say: After today there will be two more STJ sessions in order to invite community members to talk about their pathway to their job. These sessions will not be during the school day
- Ask: Why do you think we are doing that? How will that change STJ?
- Use Newsprint to capture and chunk responses to connect to STJ sessions/themes
- Point to where these are on the newsprint and Say: We talked about obstacles and everyday problems, positive and negative forces; the idea is to get a person who is a positive force to know about STJ. Often people talked about parents or other adults in their life that way. We talked about obstacles and inoculation from difficulty and asking questions to solve everyday problems. We will use community members to learn "informational interviewing."
- Say: We want you to come. (Pass out contact sheets) tell us who to contact
- Summary statement: We started with skills to succeed in school and adult images, connected them to positive models and negative forces, made timelines with forks in the road and roadblocks, linked adult images to doing something with action goals, made pathways from current strategies to next year and adult possible selves, solved impossible problems, and mapped getting through high school and to college
- Pass out session evaluation form
- Ask for help rearranging the room
- Good-byes/Collect evaluation/Check attendance/Rate participation/Label newsprint

4.3 PARENT AND YOUTH TOGETHER SESSIONS AT A GLANCE

4.3.1 Parent and Youth Sessions 1 and 2 at a Glance

• Greet student participants/Greet parents/Hand out nametags/Circulate attendance list • **Introduce selves and program** (names/program/program aim/observer/ observer role to help improve program)
• Elicit a **review of activities** (Review each session/in correct order/rationale for activities)/Reinforce student participation • Provide **summary description and aim of program**
• Ask for students to tell what an **introduction** is/Define introduction/Model by introducing one another (skill or ability to do well in school or as a parent) • Pair students and parents/Provide instructions for **introducing partner**
• Split parents and youth into two separate groups to discuss concerns for the coming school year • Elicit **concerns for the coming year** from each group • Reconvene groups/Tape up concerns from each group • Read concerns/Highlight differences (lack of overlap) • **Highlight similarities in concerns/**Reinforce group participation • Provide break for group/Provide food

• Elicit from parents and students best **ways to communicate concerns** to one another
• Write responses on newsprint
• Note that group possesses a lot of knowledge about communicating
• Role-play skit using only way to communicate brought up by group
• Elicit responses from group about role play/How was it?/What should we add?
• Pass out **rules for listener and speaker**
  • Separate parent and child pairs to practice using communication rules to discuss one of their concerns
  • Circulate, help pairs to stick to rules when communicating

• Reconvene group/Ask group **how it went to use the rules** when communicating • Encourage parents and students to use this method of communicating at home and with others • Summary statement: Today we reviewed STJ, discussed concerns for the coming year, having the floor and active listening • Connecting statement: Next session, we will work on how to find information about the kind of jobs you want in the future. It will be our last STJ meeting. I hope you can come • Provide session evaluation forms, thank everyone for participation, good-byes • Pick up evaluation forms, rate participation

- Greet student participants by name/Greet parents by name/Circulate attendance list

---

- Say: This is our last STJ session, informational interviewing.
- Ask: What happened last session? (STJ sessions, concerns for next year, active listening, having the floor).
- Reinforce: Participating, remembering
- Say: Last session we reviewed STJ so far, discussed common concerns of parents and students, practiced communicating
- Ask: Did anyone try active listening and having the floor at home? How did it go? Say: This session we will **figure out how to get information about the jobs and careers we want and learn a helpful skill to get information**

- Elicit responses from **parents** about **how do people find jobs**
- Write responses on newsprint. Reinforce that most parents have this knowledge
- Elicit responses from students about **how people find out about the kind of jobs they want**. Write responses on newsprint
- Ask **difference between job and career**. Write responses on newsprint

---

- Introduce the concept of **informational interviewing**/Generate some of the questions that would be asked/Pass out list of informational interviewing questions
- Use marbles to pair each parent with a youth partner (not their own) to practice interviewing techniques/Circulate to insure each partner practices interviewing
- Reconvene all pairs and discuss interviewing process
- Provide a break/Provide food/Reconvene group
- Facilitate discussion about how it went

- Introduce **community members**
- Describe activity/Provide separate interview rooms for each community member
- Parent-youth pairs move from room to room doing informational interviews
- 5-minute break
- Reconvene parents and youth in one room and community members in another
- Elicit responses about the interviewing process (What went well?/What is hard about this/obstacles?/What can be added?)
- Join all participants for final discussion
- Encourage students to ask community members about **doing informational interviewing in the real world**

- Encourage students to use informational interviewing technique in the future
- Pass out session evaluation forms, Thank everyone for their participation, good-byes
- Pick up evaluation forms, rate participation, label newsprint

4.4 FREQUENTLY ASKED QUESTIONS

1. **How can I present instructions clearly and make sure group members are listening and understand what I mean?**

   - Use the newsprint outline so that all instructions are easy for students to see as they are working.

   - Say instructions out loud a piece at a time so that students can start working step by step. More than one step at a time is confusing.

   - Use the same phrase each time you are giving an instruction so that students know that this is useful. Show the material. Give one instruction. Say something clear such as "There are three steps, the first one is. . ." so that students know to pay extra attention. Circulate and repeat.

   - Repeat key concepts that link to instructions.

   - Ask the group simple response and "yes-no" questions as you are teaching key concepts and allow the group to call out responses. Assume that everything is repeated. Be cheerful about it.

   - Leave your sentences unfinished so that the group can finish them for you, supplying key ideas themselves.

   - Instructions should be at the needed level of detail.

   - Once students move their desks into groups, instructions have to be provided to each group separately.

   - Always instruct prior to providing the writing materials (show the worksheet, point to what needs to be done, then hand out the writing supplies).

   - Too many directions at once results in confusion.

   - Split directions into manageably small pieces.

   - Ask students to repeat instructions back to you, both as a group and individually as you are handing each student his or her supplies. E.g.: Give bag of stickers and ask—what are you supposed to do now?

2. **How can I engage group members and encourage them to participate?**

   - School-to-Jobs is set up to start with fun and easy to engage with activities, to have lots of different activities, and to not go on and on or in too much depth on any topic. If something feels fun and easy, students are more likely to engage.

   - School-to-Jobs is not counseling or career guidance or academic planning. That means it is not likely to induce reactance (saying no, refusing to participate). If something feels like it is limiting choices or options, it is likely to produce the opposite effect. Instead of preaching, School to Jobs consists of fun activities engaged in at a developmentally appropriate and culturally sensitive level. Students should not feel you are trying to change them or trying to convince them of anything.

   - Learn the names of your students. Students are much more likely to engage if you call on them by name. Play the name game with the students. Make nametags with the students' pictures and study them before coming to class. Call out names as students enter and learn from your mistakes. Tell students that you are working on this and will be saying their names and ask them to do the same. Everyone feels more accountable when engaged by name. Students often enjoy being given special jobs or responsibilities—this helps to remind them that they are important and needed members of the group. Choose participants who are especially quiet or shy to hand out or put away supplies or to help you move desks or hang up newsprint. Always have multiple people doing each job and be careful and keep track of who you asked each session. Everyone should be participating. This is both a group ethos and a chance to show all students that you care about them—this strategy only works if students do not feel you are keeping favorites. If this is too chaotic, at least have everyone move desks back at the end of each session.

- Allowing students to write on newsprint can also be extremely reinforcing. Almost all of the activities that involve summarizing can have students come to the front of the room to write on newsprint. This is something that many students love to do because it shows that they are important and at the front, commanding attention. In activities in which the trainers write on the newsprint, students can do at least some of the writing. This is a good strategy if you'd like to encourage more responses—just announce that whoever has an idea can come up and write it on the newsprint. Give the student a marker to do so and then turn to the rest of the class for further ideas. Remind the students that they must return to their seats immediately after they finish writing. Be aware that this approach, while often inspiring great enthusiasm from students, also means that a task may end up taking significantly longer than it would if you simply wrote their ideas on the newsprint yourself. This approach can boomerang if the students have difficulties writing and you are putting them up for embarrassment. If this is a concern, do not go down this path. Have a look if students can write on worksheets or on newsprint in their smaller groups. If you cannot have the students write, at least be sure that students see that you are writing their responses; repeat what the student said using the student's name so that the student's contribution is marked and honored.

3. **What should I do if students identify goals or possible selves that probably aren't realistic, because few people attain these (like playing professional sports or being a rapper) or are too humble (like doing hair at home or being a clerk)?**
   - Don't worry.
   - School-to-Jobs activities are designed to help students to see that everyone wants to be successful adults (including the four domains of doing meaningful work, having family connections, having a pleasant life, and serving community), that this future is close and connected to the present, and that failures and difficulties along the way are normative and just mean that these goals are important, not impossible to attain. Whether a goal is realistic is not an issue. Activities draw out the experience of a near future, no matter what the particular adult goals. Indeed, trainers should not get too focused on what the actual goals are as these are unlikely to be fixed. The important focus of activities is the process of developing current strategies, since strategies all have in common an academic focus regardless of adult goals. Whether students are aiming to be the president or a pro basketball player, it's a good idea to learn math

skills (if simply to keep track of one's earnings!) and to graduate from middle school and high school.

- On a similar note, there is no need to discourage goals that might seem humble, such as doing hair at home or being a clerk in a clothing store. Rather, students with such plans should be reinforced for having goals that are relatively independent of luck and possess concrete pathways for achievement. Just as always, focus is on the ways in which current engagement can improve chances for success.

4. **I want to add more (artwork, expressive movement, teaching aids such as studying, career aids such as providing information on training needed for particular careers).**

- This is probably not a good idea.
- Each session is very full as it is; adding more effort (e.g., making a collage of adult images instead of just picking images) can completely change the tenor of the activity from an easy, fun "we all have a future" message that encourages participation to a difficult, painful art project (looking through magazines, cutting pasting, being annoyed that one's future does not look as appealing as imagined) that actually robs the activity of its main point. Participants may not know what their future as an adult is in detail; by making this hard, you actually encourage nonparticipation and reactance. The same is true for various aids and additional information. The point of School-to-Jobs is that everyone has a future, that school is the path, that there will be difficulties and obstacles along the way. Students can succeed even if they do not know what they want to be or keep changing their mind; getting in depth with specific paths is not the point. STJ does not replace the school guidance or counseling facilities and is not meant as a tutoring tool. The active ingredient is turning on identity-based motivation so that students will see schoolwork as relevant, the future as close, and experienced difficulties and failures along the way as normal and part of the path to their adult possible selves.

4.5 YOUTH SESSIONS

4.5.1 Session 1: Creating a Group

4.5.1.1 OVERVIEW

This session uses games to introduce participants to each other and to set up a positive sense of ownership of the group and belief in the group's ability to do things and solve problems. This session sets the stage. It allows youth to begin to notice that school and the future matter for themselves and for their peers; that others can be helpful; and that being good at school is valued in their community. The first game involves introducing one another in terms of each person's skills and abilities to succeed in the coming school year and to make it to high school. Trainers begin to model and reinforce active listening techniques. After the introduction game, participants are asked to express their expectations and develop rules for the group, gaining a sense of ownership of the process and feeling they have some choice. Two final games end the session. These are nonverbal, involve lots of movement, are engaging, and help participants gain a positive perspective on the group's ability to handle problems and provide a positive sense of connection. Throughout, trainers model and reinforce a focus on competence. As students participate, one trainer should go around the room and take headshots. These will be used to make participant nametags to ensure that trainers learn participant names.

4.5.1.2 TAKE-HOME POINT

STJ is a place where your concerns and expectations will be heard; you will have some say in the rules. STJ will teach you about yourself; you have some skills. In STJ we work together.

4.5.1.3 MATERIALS

- Agenda
- Colored marbles
- Newsprint, markers, and tape
- Aim written on newsprint
- Paper and pencil for each participant
- Notebook for trainer note taking
- Attendance and participation notebook
- Digital camera

4.5.1.4 ROOM SETUP

Chairs should be arranged in a semicircle facing the board or surface where newsprint will be taped.

4.5.1.5 POINTS FOR REINFORCEMENT

1. Everyone has some skills that can help him or her succeed in school.
2. Everyone can be a valued member of the group; each of us knows things that can help others.
3. The group norm is to participate and share.
4. Everyone will learn and everyone will be heard.

4.5.1.6 AGENDA

1. Introductions
2. Expectations and concerns
3. Aim
4. Naming the group
5. Games
6. Next session

4.5.1.6.1 Introductions (17–28 minutes: 2–5 minutes introduce activity, 5–8 minutes marble-match partnering, 10–15 minutes naming plus skills)

Greet participants as they enter

This is the School-to-Jobs program. We are part of your school and come here from _____ (name of your organization). We will be meeting _____ (give days, times, and room number) until close to Thanksgiving. We'll be working on ways to turn your hopes and dreams into reachable goals. We will meet in this classroom but School-to-Jobs is not like a regular class. You will take part in activities and talk about things that are important to you and reaching your goals.

My name is (first and last name) *and this is* (first and last name); *this is* (first and last name). (Introduce yourself, your co-trainer, and then the observer by first and last name. If you are a student, say so and which university). *The observer (videographer, camera in room) is just here to watch what we are doing and make sure we do all the activities we are supposed to do. The observer/camera is not grading any students. It's really more like grading the trainers. He/she (the camera) may move around a little bit so he/she (the camera) can see and hear better, but he/she is not going to be participating.*

The first thing we are going to do is make sure that we all know one another by doing a kind of introduction. Can anyone say what an introduction is? (Write participants' comments on newsprint entitled "Introduction." Reinforce the following points: An introduction is a way of letting others know who you are. Introductions can be short or long. Introductions begin with the person's name, but they are not all alike because introductions can have different goals.) Uncover the following short description of the concept on the newsprint.

> *Introductions are a way of saying who you are and what you can contribute.*

Introduce STJ as success oriented. *So, we know that there are different kinds of introductions. Since this is School-to-Jobs, and we're going to be working on reaching goals and being successful, what do you think our introductions should focus on?*
(Write participants' comments on newsprint entitled "School to Jobs Introduction." Reinforce the following points: skills and abilities for succeeding at school.)
Good, so our introductions should focus on skills and abilities each of you have for succeeding this year and moving on to the ___th grade (or to the next level of schooling)

So now (name of other trainer) and I are going to introduce ourselves to you again. Trainers introduce each other: This is (name) and he is good at (ability).

(If only one trainer, introduce yourself with a skill or ability. Pick something that highlights a STJ construct like "I don't give up easily" or "I can come up with alternatives if the first plan does not work.")

Activity (5–8 minutes working in pairs, 10–15 minutes presenting)
Each of you will introduce someone in the group to the rest of us. The way we are going to do that is to have each of you choose a marble from this bag. Your partner will be the person with the same color marble. You'll interview each other, making sure that you write down your partner's name, and also one or two things about him or her that will make him or her succeed at school this year and move on to the __th grade. We will pass out pencils and paper so that you can write everything down. If the person you are interviewing says things that do not seem to be skills and abilities, ask him or her to explain. Try and figure out what skills your partner has that help him or her do well or overcome problems in school.
For example, what if your partner says, "I like pizza"? Is that a skill or ability that will help him or her succeed? No? What should you say to your partner? (Elicit responses—i.e., how is that going to help you succeed in school this year?)

(Pass out colored marbles). *Who has the same color as yours? That is your partner. Find your partner. When you have your partner, you can start. Pull your chairs apart so that you can talk to the person you are interviewing without bothering everyone else. While you're working today, (name of trainer) is going to go around and take your picture. We're going to use these pictures to make nametags.* (Trainers should circulate to make sure that some skills and abilities are being written down, not just something about the person—use positive reinforcement to move participants toward appropriate focus.)
Okay, we'll take just a minute or so more. When you are ready, start moving your chairs back together to make a big circle.

Okay. Now each pair will introduce themselves, starting at this end of the circle (the person to your right) and going around (clockwise). Pay attention because you will have to be able to say their names and at least one thing you remember about the skills and abilities described. Let's start here—pick the person closest to you and then move clockwise. (First pair introduces themselves. *Who wants to say the names and at least one skill from this pair? Let's start here.* Introductions are going clockwise, so go counterclockwise to call on people.) *If the person gets it right, we'll go on to the next pair. If not, I'll ask the next person to try.* First person repeats names and at least one skill. Then go on, continuing until all have been introduced and all have said everyone's name and a skill for each. The last ones to take a turn should be the trainers. Each should say the other's name again and a skill or ability (decided in advance) that will help him or her to succeed in college. The trainers should have their chairs in the circle.

This can be a good time to get names into the attendance book.

4.5.1.6.2 Expectations and Concerns (8–10 minutes)

Now that we have met each other, we would like to hear about your expectations. What do you think will be covered in School-to-Jobs? What would you like to cover in School-to-Jobs? How would you like people in the group to behave? What are you not interested in? What topics or knowledge do you want to get and what don't you want to cover or do? (The trainer should write these on the newsprint on separate sheets—one entitled "+"; another "–"; and a third "Rules for STJ." The purpose of the expectations activity is to find out what participants thought that the group would be about and what they would like to do (+) or not do (–). By getting this information out, it can be dealt with directly. For example, for youth who thought that the group would help them get a summer job—that is not what we are doing and so on. Getting information about what youth don't want has the same goal—for example, they don't want tests and homework in STJ—good! There aren't any and so on. By asking participants to generate rules, they have a greater stake in the group and some control, which is important for adolescents. Rules are usually stated as negations—don't swear, don't make fun of each other, don't interrupt. Trainers should ask youth what they want participants to do as well as not do—then youth should be able to come up with rules such as participate, be helpful to other participants, and share your ideas. Trainers help youth reformulate negatives into positives as needed. This is the beginning of formation of a sense of group identity and joint purpose. Trainers should reinforce everyone's participation, reflect questions back to the group to get feedback where possible, and model active listening and having the floor (see Parent-Youth Session 2). After youth have generated ideas, those that will be the focus should be highlighted in yellow marker. Youth may suggest having food; the trainer should say, "Yes, we will have snacks." Youth may suggest a party at the end; the trainer should say, "Yes, we can do that."

Let's look over all of the ideas. I highlighted the ones we will be working on in the group:

> *Seeing both my far and near future*
> *Developing strategies to work toward my future*
> *Seeing the path between now and my future*

The trainer should say something about any other ideas youth have come up with—either by explicitly connecting them to the actual group goals or saying, "We won't work on this."

Just like the process of highlighting group goals, the trainer needs to elicit and highlight group rules. The way to do this is to return to the group rules newsprint and circle or highlight the STJ group rules and end with the preprinted ones, which are listed next.

> *Participate*
> *Share your ideas*
> *Give others a chance to speak*
> *Listen and ask questions*
> *Be fair (no name calling)*

We ask that each of you participate in the group, share your comments with the group, and listen to give others a chance to speak as well. It is great if you can give feedback to one another. That means that you check that you understood what the other person said and then comment on things that could be helpful for that person, given what he or she said. Every one will have a chance to speak each session. We will have different activities each session. This is a school program so we will be taking attendance just like any other class. If you know you'll be absent, let us know in advance.

4.5.1.6.3 Goal (1 minute)

Put up the newsprint sheet with this goal written on it. *We are going to use as many of your suggestions as possible while we're focusing on this goal:*

> *School-to-Jobs:*
> *Create a road map to success*
> *Going from school to the world of work, by linking far and near goals*

To create a road map to success, you will need to:
Think about your goals for next year and farther into the future.
Work on strategies you can use to obtain these goals.
Take difficulty as routine; get around obstacles and create alternatives.

Our goal is that you will finish the program with a clearer and more detailed sense of what you need to do and how to do it. Because nothing is for sure and difficulty is normal, we want to make sure that you have had a chance to think about alternatives and likely obstacles. Each session we will do something different. Each session builds on the previous session, so it is very important not to miss a session.

4.5.1.6.4 Naming the Group (5–10 minutes)

Now that we have been introduced, have talked about expectations, aims, and rules, it is time to name our group. How would you like to be called? For example, this could be the (School Name) School-to-Jobs Group, the (School Name) Pathway group—any name you want so we can talk about the group using a name we agreed on. I will write these names on newsprint and then we can take a vote. The trainer elicits nominations, then a vote—using raising hands and tallying. Prior group name ideas have been Nonstop Achievers, Reaching for the Stars, Unlimited Goals, Future Achievers, Dwell in Your Goals, Spain Successes.

So our group name is _____. If we need to send out information or contact you, we will use this name.

4.5.1.6.5 Games (Learning to Work as a Group) (15–25 minutes)
Go directly to circle activity if time is running short:

Name review *Before we move to the next activity, can someone go around the circle and say each member's name and skill to succeed?* (Go through a few rounds to make sure that the members and trainers are familiar with one another's name.) *Good! Now, the last things we will do today do not involve talking.*

Line up task *First, what we want you to do is to line up from youngest person to oldest person—but without talking. You need to figure out a way to signal to the other group members so that you are all in the right order.*

Once the youth are in a final order, ask each to say his or her age and month born to check whether the line is in the right order. Congratulate the group—it is tricky to figure out how to get started. This exercise shows the group that together they can work on problems that they cannot solve alone; it connects members and gives youth a sense of competence.

Great! What did you do to figure out how to stand—what worked? Trainers should positively reinforce specific instances of being attuned to others and working to make information known.

Human knot *Now we are going to try something else. This is what we call the human knot. Everyone stand in a circle. Cross your arms in front of you. Grab hold of a hand of one person who is across from you and then grab hold of a hand of another person who is across from you.* The trainer should help make sure that everyone understands the crossing of the hands and that everyone is in the end holding two other people's hands. Trainers should join the circle. *Once everyone is holding hands, it looks like a knot. What you need to do is try to get back to a circle, without letting go of the hands you are holding. In the end, no one's hands should be crossed. Again, we'll use communication besides talking.* (Trainers and members struggle and finally succeed.)

Great, the group really works well together. Trainer, allow participants to share their strategies. *Each of you really focused on paying attention to the task and kept trying until the circle worked.*

4.5.1.6.6 Next Session (1 minute)

Pass out snacks at this point. Pass out evaluation sheets. *This is an evaluation sheet. Each week we will ask you to check off your opinions of the session. We use your opinions when we think about how to improve the program for the future.* As students finish: *Next session we will be working on our adult images. Can everyone help move the chairs back into place and clean up? Thank you for coming and we will see you next session. Remember, next session we will be working on adult images.* (Say good-bye to students as they leave.)

Trainers rate each member's participation by scoring a "+" (good participation), "0" (moderate participation), "–" (lack of or inappropriate participation), or "absent" next to his or her name on the class list provided. Add comments as needed. Make sure to score participants separately because the trainers may have different perceptions based on their own activities.

4.5.1.7 SESSION 1: CREATING A GROUP EVALUATION

Thank you for participating in the School-to-Jobs program. We would like your feedback. Please rate this session by marking the number that fits your opinion and give you ideas for improvement.

To what extent was this session											
Boring	1	2	3	4	5	6	7	8	9	10	Interesting
Difficult	1	2	3	4	5	6	7	8	9	10	Easy
Not useful	1	2	3	4	5	6	7	8	9	10	Useful
To what extent did this session											
Provide no new way of thinking	1	2	3	4	5	6	7	8	9	10	Provide a new way of thinking
Provide no new information	1	2	3	4	5	6	7	8	9	10	Provide new information

We want to improve this session. What would make it better?

_____

_____

_____

4.5.2 Session 2: Adult Images

4.5.2.1 OVERVIEW

In Session 1, youth gained a sense that everyone has some skills related to school success and that they could work as a group. In this session, youth have a chance to imagine themselves as adults.

Youths choose among pictures portraying adults in the domains of career, family and friendship relationships, material lifestyle, and c service. Pictures should reflect the racial-ethnic and gender mix of Each youth is asked to choose pictures that remind him or her of the she wants to become. The number of pictures per participant depends of the group. Ten pictures per participant drives home the idea that e many adult images, but the number of pictures needed, the time it w choose and to describe each picture are too much for larger groups. lowing guideline: 10 pictures per participant for groups of 10–14 an per participant for groups of 25. Having picked pictures is really the To drive the point home, each youth is asked to show one (or more ting) of his or her pictures and what adult image they represent. Er positive reinforcement of good listening. The pictures and descrip stage for working on one's own timeline into the future in subseque

Note: If participants are already adults (for example, completing general equivalency rather than middle school), then throughout rather than label the session adult images, the session can be called "distal future images" and throughout replace far future for adult.

4.5.2.2 TAKE-HOME POINT

Everyone has an image of himself or herself in the far future as an adult

4.5.2.3 MATERIALS

- Agenda
- Laminated pictures, approximately 6 per participant (male/female, in the four life domains, of varying adult ages)
- Newsprint, tape, and markers
- Notebook for trainer note taking
- Attendance and participation notebook
- Digital camera
- Nametags with pictures taken last session
- Ground rules on newsprint

4.5.2.4 ROOM SETUP

Arrange desks around the periphery of the classroom for the placement of pictures. Pictures can also be placed on the floor along the walls of the classroom if desks are limited. Chairs (and some tables) should be arranged in a semicircle facing a blackboard or newsprint surface.

4.5.2.5 POINTS FOR REINFORCEMENT

1. Everyone has some vision or image of himself or herself in the far future as an adult.

2. These images are in a number of domains: everyone needs to figure out how to earn a living, how to make and keep relationships with family and friends, how to be part of a community, and how to have a particular lifestyle.

4.5.2.6 AGENDA

1. Last session
2. Adult images
3. Common themes
4. Next session

4.5.2.6.1 Last Session (2–3 minutes)

(Greet participants by name as they enter and take attendance, greet latecomers by name, tell participants to pick their nametag as they enter.) *Hi. Welcome back. Today is session two, adult images, but first, can someone tell the group what we did last session?* Ask for a volunteer to tell about last session's activities and session. Elicit two pieces of knowledge. First, what the group did; and second, why—what youth thought the activities meant or were for. Youth should be able to say that they introduced one another with a skill or ability to do well in school, talked about expectations and concerns, rules, goal of STJ, and describe the games they played (i.e., age line and human knot). Positively reinforce participation and trying. Make sure that the introduction is talked about and that youth say that the point was to see that people have lots of different skills that will help them succeed in school. Note nametags if trainer needs them: *I made nametags; please wear them so I can practice every week until I am perfect with everyone's name.*

4.5.2.6.2 Adult Images (15–25 minutes)

Good. Now let me explain what we will do next. Look around the room. There are a lot of pictures, and you will choose the pictures that represent for you the images of the adult you want to become. Choose only [10 for small group, 3 for large group]. *Take them back to your seat. For each picture think about what it represents for you and how old you'll be or how many years in the future that will be. Everyone will have a chance to share an adult image and talk about it.*

Trainers can pass out snacks if people are finishing at different times to keep everyone busy.

4.5.2.6.3 Common Themes (15–40 minutes)

Set up four sheets of newsprint (untitled) on the blackboard. The four sheets correspond to the four domains of adulthood, which are work, family and relationships, lifestyle, and community service. The goal of the activity is that the domains emerge as themes of adulthood from what participants are saying, so do not label the pieces of newsprint beforehand.

Trainer: You may be tempted to have volunteers write on each piece of newsprint. This is typically not a good idea because you will either have no organization or you will need to direct where statements should be written without revealing the theme, and this will be unwieldy.

Now, we will go around the circle. Each person will show one of the images he or she has chosen and tell us about his or her image. For each picture, hold it up; say something about why you chose it and how old you will be when you will be this way. Make sure you listen really closely to what each person says so you can see what is similar between people. (Each person presents for approximately 1 minute; use fewer images for shorter sessions.)

If there are two trainers, one trainer should be directing the activity while the other trainer writes down what youth are saying on the newsprint. Otherwise the trainer does both. Once the group has all presented, point to newsprint, read some of the responses that are on a newsprint cluster because they fit a theme of adulthood (jobs, relationships, lifestyle, community involvement), and say, *What is similar across these answers?* Reinforce participation, which may well be concrete; if so, move up to a higher order (e.g., they are all jobs, or all are about lifestyles people want to have).

Youth are likely to mostly mention lifestyle. That is fine. If there are jobs, note that jobs finance lifestyle; if no jobs are mentioned, ask youth how people get the things listed on the lifestyle sheet. Someone should say jobs. No need for further commentary or trainer opinion at this point. The point is that all participants have a future in mind.

If relationships are mentioned, make the same links (supporting a family requires a job). If community involvement is mentioned, make the same links (people want to live in a safe place with clean streets and nice public areas, how do you get these—by participating in your community). If these are not brought up, do not mention—it is more than participants can absorb at this point. The point of adult images is that everyone has them.

4.5.2.6.4 Next Session (1 minute)

This session we focused on our images of the far future as adults. Next session we will think about where these images come from, both positive and negative models and forces. (PASS OUT EVALUATION FORM.) (PICK UP EVALUATION FORM. Say good-bye to students as they leave.)

Trainers rate each member's participation by scoring a "+" (good participation), "0" (moderate participation), "–" (lack of or inappropriate participation), or "absent" next to his or her name on the class list provided. Add comments as needed. Make sure to score participants separately because the trainers may have different perceptions based on their own activities.

4.5.2.7 SESSION 2: ADULT IMAGES 1 EVALUATION

Thank you for participating in the School-to-Jobs program. We would like your feedback. Please rate this session by marking the number that fits your opinion and give you ideas for improvement.

To what extent was this session											
Boring	1	2	3	4	5	6	7	8	9	10	Interesting
Difficult	1	2	3	4	5	6	7	8	9	10	Easy
Not useful	1	2	3	4	5	6	7	8	9	10	Useful
To what extent did this session											
Provide no new way of thinking	1	2	3	4	5	6	7	8	9	10	Provide a new way of thinking
Provide no new information	1	2	3	4	5	6	7	8	9	10	Provide new information

We want to improve this session. What would make it better?

_____

_____

_____

4.5.3 Session 3: Positive and Negative Forces

4.5.3.1 OVERVIEW

In Session 2, youth imagined their far future adult images and began to consider this future in terms of four adult domains (work, relationships, lifestyle, and community). In Session 3, youth will consider bolstering and undermining influences on these far future images called positive role models (positive forces) and negative models (negative forces). The session starts with a recap of the prior session. Cued by this, trainers highlight jobs and elicit a br[ief con]nection between jobs and each of the other domains of a[dulthood ...]draw or write about their job, relationship, community inv[olvement ...]future adult images and choose a positive and a negative [force for]two domains (job and relationship). To do so, youth are as[ked ... someone]in their life or someone in the media or something else lik[e ...]that gives them a positive role model or support to wo[rk ...]image—making it a real goal and not just a hope or d[ream ...]think of someone else or a movie, song, or book that [gives an]example of what not to become or makes them feel th[at ...]and that the goal won't be reached anyway. This nega[tive force is]someone they know personally or people that they se[e ...]lating what these positive and negative models actua[lly do ...]motivation, persistence—as well as specific strategi[es ... partici]pants have a chance to begin noticing the influences [... an]opportunity to talk about working on goals and obstacles, handling se[tbacks,]seeing difficulties as normal. Important things are difficult.

The agenda is posted so that participants can see what the structure is and the names of each part of the session.

Handwritten note:
- Obstacles are normal
  - exist for everyone
- stray away from counseling
  → ask for negative forces

4.5.3.2 TAKE-HOME POINT

Positive forces lay out paths for success and handling difficulties and setbacks. Setbacks are part of life. Negative forces do the opposite. They lay out paths for failure and make difficulties and setbacks seem like signs that the goal is impossible to attain.

4.5.3.3 MATERIALS

- Agenda (write in advance)
- Newsprint and markers
- Newsprints with four areas of adulthood from Session 2
- A worksheet for each participant labeled JOB on left and RELATIONSHIPS on right. Each worksheet should have an outline of a stick figure, labeled FUTURE ME with a thought bubble labeled MY GOAL. Beneath the stick figure should be lines labeled POSITIVE FORCE and NEGATIVE FORCE (an example is provided at the end of the session)
- Papers
- Rulers, pencils, and drawing implements for participants
- Attendance and participation notebook
- Digital camera

4.5.3.4 ROOM SETUP

Tables spread around the room so each participant has some personal space.

4.5.3.5 POINTS FOR REINFORCEMENT

1. Everyone can have future self-goals.
2. Role models help in developing these goals, in seeing a path to success.
3. Everyone faces obstacles; difficulties are normal.
4. Negative role models help you see paths to failure.
5. Both positive and negative models can increase your own motivation.

4.5.3.6 AGENDA

1. Last session
2. Far future adult images can become goals
3. Positive and negative role models
4. Next session

4.5.3.6.1 Last Session (4 minutes)

(Greet participants by name as they enter and take attendance, point to nametags if using, and greet latecomers by name.) *Hi, welcome back, this is session three, positive and negative forces. Can someone tell us what we did last session?* (Trainers should try to get new participation. Check which members were the ones who participated last session—use the participation book to refresh your memory and try to draw in others. Participants should be able to say what was done—picked pictures—and what was talked about.) *Okay, so last session we looked at pictures and used them to see our own far future adult images. We separated these images into domains. What were the domains?*

(Have students identify the domains they heard. Add to make the four domains—Career, Relationships, Community, and Lifestyle.)

Good. You remembered the domains we talked about last week. There are a few more, four all together, Career, Relationships, Community, and Lifestyles. Today, we will talk more about far future self-images and connect them to both positive forces that propel us forward and negative forces that pull us off-track.

4.5.3.6.2 Adult Images and Possible Selves (1 minute)

Some adult images are sort of dreams. They would be nice, but we are not really expecting them. Others feel really possible and other people can be models for how to get there or for what not to do. Those are possible selves.

4.5.3.6.3 Positive and Negative Models (5–15 minute discussion, 15–20 minute student work time, 10-minute wrap-up discussion—length depends on session length)

Who can tell me about positive or negative models and forces? I am going to write down what you say on these sheets labeled positive and negative forces.

Write responses on newsprint. End with the following:

> A positive model or force is someone who shows the way, someone who supports you or shows you the way to persist in spite of difficulties and how to get around obstacles.

A positive role model can be someone you know, like a family member or friend, or someone famous or someone that you've heard about from TV or a book or movie.

A negative model or force is someone who shows examples that you don't want to copy or who tells you it is impossible for you to succeed, that obstacles mean you should just quit.

Now we're going to pass out worksheets. You will see two domains of adulthood—career and relationships. Start with career. Write or draw your job or career adult image and identify a positive and a negative force for it. Your job or career could be an adult image you picked last week or a different one showing something about the kind of job or career you want to have. It could be a specific job or just a kind of job—like "a job I enjoy." When you have written or drawn your job possible self, think about someone who is a positive force or role model for you to get this possible self. Write down who that person is under POSITIVE MODEL, then think of someone who is a negative force or model for you in terms of your job possible self and write that in the NEGATIVE MODEL space. If you have time, do the same thing again for your relationship possible self. The POSITIVE and NEGATIVE MODELs can be the same or different in each domain of adulthood.

Trainers should pass out the worksheets that are printed at the end of this session along with snacks.

Trainers, circle around as participants are working. By mingling, you can read what each participant is writing and help him or her formulate specific positive and negative models or forces for each domain. The idea is that participants will be able to come up with a job or career possible self and also someone who is a positive model or positive force (builds up their chances of success in the domain) and someone who is a negative model or negative force (tears down their chances of success in this domain). If a part is blank, help the student think of a response with questions to focus his or her attention on the task. This facilitates later discussion because students will feel confident that they did what they were supposed to do. If the student has time, he or she can go on to the second part (relationship possible self).

As students are finishing, trainers should move from individual to group time. Have students make a big circle. *Let's move our chairs into a circle.* Start with a student who has not yet participated in the discussion so far. Point to him or her and say, *We will start with you and work around the circle. Name your positive model for your career possible self.* Time permitting, all should participate. If there is not enough time, at the halfway point, say, *Now I want you to start listing negative forces.*

While students are talking, the trainer should be listing the positive models and clustering the ones that are similar (for example, all the family members). Repeat for negative models. Use a sheet labeled "Positive or + Models and Forces" and a sheet labeled "Negative or – Models and Forces." Ask students why they chose who they did if they have not already said so. Typically participants say things like "They support my choices" or "They answer my questions."

Read through positive model list. Repeat the kinds of things that positive models and forces do to build up chances of success.

Read through negative model list. Repeat the kinds of things that negative models and forces do to undermine confidence or suggest misturns.

Note that everyone has both positive and negative forces in his or her life. Both positive and negative models can be motivating, just in different ways. A negative model shows how not to do it—for example, a negative model loses his or her temper and is not patient.

Reinforce that possible forces and models remind us that important things are difficult. Negative forces or models misinform us that difficulty means that you can just quit trying.

4.5.3.6.4 Next Session (1 minute)

This week we thought about positive and negative forces on the way to attain our adult possible selves. (Pass out evaluation form.) *Next week we will draw time lines into the future and think about obstacles and ways around them.* (Say good-bye to students as they leave.)

Trainers rate each member's participation by scoring a "+" (good participation), "0" (moderate participation), "–" (lack of or inappropriate participation), or "absent" next to his or her name on the class list provided. Add comments as needed. Make sure to score participants separately because the trainers may have different perceptions based on their own activities.

JOB and CAREER FUTURE ME	RELATIONSHIP FUTURE ME
My Possible Self:	My Possible Self:
_____	_____
_____	_____
_____	_____
Positive Model/Force in My Life:	Positive Model/Force in My Life:
_____	_____
_____	_____
Negative Model/Force in My Life:	Negative Model/Force in My Life:
_____	_____
_____	_____

4.5.3.8 SESSION 3: POSITIVE AND NEGATIVE FORCES EVALUATION

Thank you for participating in the School-to-Jobs program. We would like your feedback. Please rate this session by marking the number that fits your opinion and give you ideas for improvement.

To what extent was this session											
Boring	1	2	3	4	5	6	7	8	9	10	Interesting
Difficult	1	2	3	4	5	6	7	8	9	10	Easy
Not useful	1	2	3	4	5	6	7	8	9	10	Useful
To what extent did this session											
Provide no new way of thinking	1	2	3	4	5	6	7	8	9	10	Provide a new way of thinking
Provide no new information	1	2	3	4	5	6	7	8	9	10	Provide new information

We want to improve this session. What would make it better?

_____

_____

_____

4.5.4 Session 4: Timelines

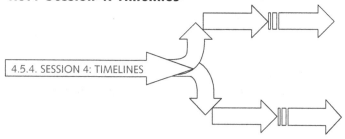

4.5.4. SESSION 4: TIMELINES

4.5.4.1 OVERVIEW

In Session 2, youth imagined their far future adult selves; in Session 3, youth considered their positive and negative models and how they make a difference. In Session 4, youths begin to work on their future timeline. The t[...] opportunity for students to begin to consider temporal order choo[...] options (forks in the road and stumbling blocks). In Session 3, pos[...] ative forces were described as differing in how they helped stude[...] difficulties and obstacles along the way. In Session 4, difficulties ar[...] sented as normal parts of life. Part of what makes a future self-goa[...] that it is hard to attain. Youths draw a personal timeline starting wi[...] and going as far into the future as they can. Timelines are linear p[...] should also have at least one "fork in the road" and at least one "roa[...] figure on the top, the stumbling blocks appear after the forks in th[...] order is fine. Forks in the road are choice points at which point you[...] one way or another and show how the timeline would proceed de[...] choice. Forks show opportunity costs because taking one option [...] ing another option. Forks can be choosing one college major over a[...] also occur less mindfully, such as when a student gets so involved [...] ity that other parts of life get neglected; for example, skipping class to hang out [...] may result in not getting the grades one needs to get into an advanced class the next year. Obstacles are not personal choices but roadblocks. They require coming up with back-up plans or alternatives—and address situations in everyday life that happen to everyone (for example, you studied for the exam but failed to get the grade you needed to go on to the next level—now what?). [...] ent their timelines so all the forks and obstacles can be seen; [...] participants will be asked to help their neighbor by adding a p[...] path (verbally, not by drawing in). This session has youth begi[...] domains of adulthood integrate with one another. Timelines [...] on school, jobs, or relationships but some include material att[...] or a house. Trainers support the process of beginning to think [...] nections among domains of adulthood, and to begin to see f[...] This is enough. Do not try to teach participants about wha[...] their goals or try to make timelines realistic—what they [...] large step forward and too much becomes too difficult to in[...] group process, trainers should provide positive reinforce[...] to develop a plan, to think about time and options, and t[...] However, trainers should not direct youth to do so. The t[...] current capacities. Getting the idea of order, choice, and[...] this session.

This session can be divided into two. The first session will only involve making timelines; the second session will involve discussing them.

4.5.4.2 TAKE-HOME POINT

The future is like a path. Difficulties along the way are normal; obstacles can be planned for. The far future choices we can have are constructed by the near future choices we make now.

4.5.4.3 MATERIALS

- Agenda
- Newsprint and markers
- Long sheets of paper 3 x 1 feet (one per participant)
- Scratch paper for all
- Thin and thick markers, crayons and colored pencils (enough for all)
- Rulers and pencils (one per participant)
- Attendance and participation notebook
- Digital camera

4.5.4.4 ROOM SETUP

Tables should be spread around the room so each participant has some personal space.

4.5.4.5 POINTS FOR REINFORCEMENT

1. Everyone can make a plan.
2. Forks in the road come from choices.
3. Difficulties are part of life. Everyone faces obstacles and unfair treatment; making alternative plans helps.

4.5.4.6 AGENDA

1. Last session
2. Timelines
3. Discussion
4. Summary
5. Next session

4.5.4.6.1 Last Session (2 minutes)

(Greet participants by name as they enter and take attendance; greet latecomers by name and use nametags if still needed.) *Hi, welcome back; this is session four, timelines. Can someone tell us what we did last session?* (Trainers should try to get new participation. Check which members have participated last session—use the participation book to refresh your memory. Try to elicit both what was done and why.). *Okay, so last session we talked about positive and negative models and forces. What are four domains of adulthood again?* (jobs, relationships, community participation, and lifestyle) *We discussed how positive and negative forces matter. They can help us remember that difficulties along the way are normal and come from working on things that are important to us. Today, we will begin to map out how to get from now to the future. We are going to do this by drawing personal timelines.*

4.5.4.6.2 Timelines (3–5 minutes participatory exploration of the construct, 30–40 minutes student work)

The trainer should be ready to write what students say on newsprint. *Can anyone say what a timeline is?* The trainer elicits possibilities, positively reinforcing participation and youth knowledge. *Okay, so a timeline is about something; it shows a series of events in order over time.* Reveal preprinted newsprint now.

> *A timeline is about something; it shows a series of events in order over time.*

Ask for and provide examples; timelines from history classes could be examples.

Timelines are often about what happened in the past. But you are going to draw a timeline into the future.

Of course, timelines about the past involve events that already happened. What about a timeline into the future?

Trainers elicit possibilities, reinforce participation, and repeat the idea of uncertainty in the future.

A future timeline is not certain because we don't know what will happen. So things might change. It is not for sure, so there has to be a chance to make choices and things can go wrong. Choices are like forks in the road; things will turn out differently depending on what we choose. So the timeline will go a different way depending on the choice. Everyone has forks in the road because everyone makes choices even if we do not always think about it that way, doing one thing means not doing something else at the same time. So your timeline has to have at least one fork in it.

Besides forks in the road, there are also roadblocks. These are not choices but obstacles; they are problems that get in the way of your plan. Roadblocks can be out of your control, like the economy or something about you that you cannot change like a height requirement for the job you want that you do not meet. But no one just stands still on the path of life, so your timeline cannot just end when there is a roadblock. You need to get around it. Every timeline has at least one roadblock and how you get around it.

Reveal Preprinted Newsprint

> *A timeline into the future is like a path; there are forks in the road —⟨ and obstacles. —|||Choices matter by changing the path. Sometimes it is not your choice but things do not work out and you need to get around obstacles. All timelines into the future have at least one fork in the road. All timelines into the future have at least one obstacle.*

Remember, because you cannot know for sure what will happen in the future, you need to show at least one obstacle and alternative plan and one fork in the road. No one has a timeline in his or her head. We will start with a rough draft; switch to your timeline when you feel you have your ideas in order.

Since it is not yet for sure, before you draw your timeline, just write a list of all the things you think will happen and when. No one already has a timeline in his or her head. Just start; this is a draft. You can go back and add things as you think of them.

Pass out paper and pencils so that students can start writing and then pass out snacks. [Circulate to make sure students are starting to write]

Pass out timeline boards, rulers, and markers once students already have rough draft lists going. The trainer should remember the goal is not that the timelines include all steps or be realistic. The goal is just to begin to try to order one's own future and to think about a fork and a roadblock as normative. Choices now matter for later. No one stands still on the road of life.

The trainer should circulate and repeat instructions—asking for the fork and the stumbling block. Hand out snacks. The instructions to repeat are as follows:

Everyone has to have a fork in the road, a choice point that changes what comes next. Everyone has to have a stumbling block, something that is not your choice but does not work so you have to get around it.

4.5.4.6.3 Discussion (10–25 minutes)

Okay! I know you are not done yet, but let's all turn to the center and hold up our timelines.

This is very fast paced. If there is only one trainer and a larger number of participants, each participant will only be able to have about a minute to point to one part of his or her timeline. The goal is that everyone sees that everyone else has a timeline too and that everyone has a fork and a roadblock. Obstacles are normal. Choices matter.

Everyone point to his or her fork. Great! Now everyone point to his or her stumbling block. Great! Now let's hear some examples of forks. Ask the student directly across from you to read the fork. Get the next two forks. *Now let's hear a stumbling block* Ask the student to your left to read his or her stumbling block, and get the next two blocks. *So now everyone has a fork and stumbling block.*

Time permitting; it is great to actually have each person show his or her timeline, say what is there, the fork, and stumbling block. However, with a group of 25 this is not possible.

Time permitting, it is great to have students see that they can think and contribute to others. To do this, say we have time for one person's timeline (call someone who has not yet participated to describe his or her timeline, either all the way or up to the fork or stumbling block). Say to the others that they will have a job of thinking about a step that would be added to help that person think about his or her timeline. For example, perhaps a person's timeline includes "become a band director" but he or she has no prior job or training to attain this skill. The step could be getting trained or interviewing. If the step is getting married, but there is no step of dating or meeting people, those could be the prior step.

Okay! Time for one more look at a timeline. This time I'll ask someone who did not yet participate to show his or her timeline and we'll listen with the job of saying something to help along the way. Name one person if no one makes eye contact suggesting he or she wants to be picked. *Can you start? Go until your* (trainer pick a point like fork or obstacle). *Then* (name person to participant's left) *we'll start with an idea of something to add, a step between two points on the timeline.*

4.5.4.6.4 Next Session (2 minutes)

This session we talked about our timeline into the future. No one had a timeline already in his or her head, but everyone drew a timeline into the future. Timelines show that there are steps along the way, including forks and stumbling blocks. Next week we will think about action goals. Taking the timeline and linking adult possible selves to things we are doing now.

Trainers note participation and comments in attendance book.

4.5.4.7 SESSION 4: TIMELINE SESSION EVALUATION

Thank you for participating in the School-to-Jobs program. We would like your feedback. Please rate this session by marking the number that fits your opinion and give you ideas for improvement.

To what extent was this session											
Boring	1	2	3	4	5	6	7	8	9	10	Interesting
Difficult	1	2	3	4	5	6	7	8	9	10	Easy
Not useful	1	2	3	4	5	6	7	8	9	10	Useful
To what extent did this session											
Provide no new way of thinking	1	2	3	4	5	6	7	8	9	10	Provide a new way of thinking
Provide no new information	1	2	3	4	5	6	7	8	9	10	Provide new information

We want to improve this session. What would make it better?

_____

_____

_____

4.5.5 Session 5: Action Goals

4.5.5.1 OVERVIEW

In Session 4, youths drew their personal timelines into the future, including forks in the road and obstacles. In Session 5, youths will begin to separate out possible selves from hopes and dreams and practice articulating actions to attain their possible selves.

As part of the group process, trainers should provide positive reinforcement of youth efforts to develop a plan and consider alternatives, and their efforts to think about time.

Unlike dreams, possible selves feel possible to attain because they can be linked to behavioral strategies. These possible selves can be part of "action goals." Action goals include an adult possible self, a closer possible self, strategies to attain that possible self, and where and when these strategies will be used.

For example, "I will get good grades" is a possible self but without strategies. "I will get good grades by doing my homework every night" is a specific possible self with strategies that are not quite specifically cued (when every night is not clear). To make this possible self and strategy actionable, it is necessary to really be able to visualize doing the activities. "I will get good grades by doing my homework every night after I eat a snack and before my favorite evening TV show" does just that. This is an action goal because it is clear [when to] stop the activity. Finally, "because I want to afford a nice hou[se...] grades by doing my homework every night after my snack and [before my TV] show" is an action goal that links adult and next possible sel[ves and] context. Having the full link makes the near possible self have [more] of force.

In this session, youth practice going from future self to futu[re strate]gies to action goals using an action goal worksheet.

4.5.5.2 TAKE-HOME POINT

Linking adult images to nearer possible selves with specific st[rategies to hap]pen at particular times makes it more likely to actually work o[n them.] Trying to do this highlights what stumbling blocks there are a[nd the informa]tion on choices. People cannot work on all their possible selves [at once.]

4.5.5.3 MATERIALS

- Agenda
- Newsprint and markers
- Worksheet 1: Action goal sheets—two for each participant
- Worksheet 2: Graduate and bubbles sheets
- Scratch paper for all
- Thin and thick markers, crayons, colored and regular pencils (enough for all)
- Attendance and participation notebook
- Digital camera

4.5.5.4 ROOM SETUP

Students should spread out to do their worksheets alone and then move to circle (or two if there are two trainers)

[handwritten note: - Education dependent identity — specific goals — use far away example for personal example (not similar to std)]

4.5.5.5 POINTS FOR REINFORCEMENT

1. A strategy is something that the student can work on NOW.
2. Taking action now makes the far future come closer and become more certain.

4.5.5.6 AGENDA

1. Last session
2. Action goals
3. Sharing action goals
4. Next session

4.5.5.6.1 Last Session (2 minutes)

Greet participants by name as they enter and take attendance, greeting latecomers by name and using nametags if still needed.

> *Hi, welcome back, this is Session 5, Action Goals. Can someone tell us what we did last session?*

Trainers should try to get new participation. Check which members have participated last session—use the participation book to refresh your memory. Elicit what timelines are for; they organize the future, set things in order, and there are forks and obstacles.

> *Okay, so last session we discussed our timelines, including roadblocks and forks in the road. Timelines showed the order that things happened from next year until adult possible selves.*

> *Today we will link far future and near future possible selves to current action.*

4.5.5.6.2 Action Goals (20–30 minutes)

> *In our timelines, there were things that would happen in the far future—some were adult images that were like hopes and desires but others might feel like possible selves—possible because we actually work on them. Today we are going to focus on action goals. Action goals link far future possible selves and near future possible selves through specific actions we are taking right now.*

> *What is the difference between a dream and a possible self? For dreams, we don't really believe it will happen anyway so it would be great if it came true but not bad if it did not. Possible selves are something that we have control over.*

> *Some possible selves become action goals.*

> *An action goal links far future and near future possible selves by listing what actions you will take now and when and where you'll take these actions. So action goals take the form of a sentence: "Because I want (adult possible self), I will (nearer possible self) by (action)(where and when these actions occur)."*

Reveal preprinted newsprint on action goals.

> *I will pass out worksheets. Let's do an example together "because I want (choose an adult image or ask students for ones), I will (ask students or give an example from timeline) by (ask students or give an example from timeline) during class (or whatever makes sense).*

An example could be "Because I want a good job, I will finish high school by attending all my classes everyday" or "Because I want to be a band director, I will play in my high school band by practicing half an hour every weekday, after dinner cleanup is done."

Pass out worksheet. Pass out snacks.

Circulate. Check each participant's action goal sequence, and repeat instructions out loud.

4.5.5.6.3 Sharing Action Goals (20–30 minutes)

Okay. Let's turn to the center and share action goals. Trainer, ask students to orient their bodies to the center so that they can see each other and what is being written. Write the near possible selves, the "I will" statements on newsprint; clustering the school-focused ones together.

Read your action goals, starting with (say a participant's name and point to him or her) *and then each one in turn* (go counterclockwise if you went clockwise in the past weeks). All should have a "Because_____, I will_____, by_____, when _____statements. Help those who need help. It may be difficult for participants to say when during the day they will act because they believe they'll act later. This is actually the point of the action goals idea. Without being forced to say when they will act, people end up with too many vague hopes and act on none of them. Say *that's okay. Let's pick an adult image and nearer possible self you can act on now.* Elicit ideas so each participant succeeds in creating a link from an adult possible self to a near self to a strategy to a time during the day.

4.5.5.6.4 Next Session (1 minute)

Last session was timelines; this session was action goals; next session we will be doing something new, poster boards. Pass out evaluation form. Get help to clean up and reset the room. Say good-bye to students as they leave.

Trainers note participation and comments in attendance book.

1. JOB or CAREER

Because I want (*adult possible image*) _____

_____

I will (*nearer possible self*) _____

_____

By doing (*what you can do TODAY or the week*)_____

_____

When (*during the day or week*) _____

_____

2. FAMILY and RELATIONSHIPS

Because I want (*adult image*) _____

_____

I will (*nearer possible self*) _____

_____

By doing (*what you can do TODAY or this week*)_____

_____

When (*during the day or week*) _____

_____

My Action Goals

My Action Goals

PATHWAYS TO SUCCESS THROUGH IDENTITY-BASED MOTIVATION

4.5.5.9 Session 5: Action Goals Session Evaluation

Thank you for participating in the School-to-Jobs program. We would like your feedback. Please rate this session by marking the number that fits your opinion and give you ideas for improvement.

To what extent was this session											
Boring	1	2	3	4	5	6	7	8	9	10	Interesting
Difficult	1	2	3	4	5	6	7	8	9	10	Easy
Not useful	1	2	3	4	5	6	7	8	9	10	Useful
To what extent did this session											
Provide no new way of thinking	1	2	3	4	5	6	7	8	9	10	Provide a new way of thinking
Provide no new information	1	2	3	4	5	6	7	8	9	10	Provide new information

We want to improve this session. What would make it better?

_____

_____

_____

4.5.6 Session 6: Possible Selves and Strategies (Poster Boards)

4.5.6.1 OVERVIEW

In Session 2, youth picked adult images and in Session 3 youth discussed positive and negative forces. Positive forces show the way to desired adult future selves. Negative forces highlight undesired adult future selves to be avoided or paths one should avoid so as not to be derailed on the way to a desired adult self. However, sessions have largely focused on positive future selves. In Session 4, youth created timelines. Through the timelines, youth could begin to concretize how their goals connect in temporal order and also begin to consider obstacles and choices.

Youth often feel that there is nothing they could be doing *now* to attain their adult images because the future is too far away. This does not mean that youth do not know how to plan; it is that they have never thought through the connection between long-term goals or visions of the future and current activities. This session builds on Session 5 action goals by helping youth make the connection between their adult images nearer possible selves, next year and now. This session involves next year possible selves and strategies they are using now or could use now to attain them. The final product (after Session 7) is a "pathways" poster board that links next year and adult possible selves through the strategies used to attain them. This activity makes concrete the youth's pathway to the future.

Prep time for this session is longer than for others because there are poster boards to prepare and sticker bags to make (see materials). Having students prep their poster board themselves is only an option for small groups with two trainers and longer sessions.

4.5.6.2 TAKE-HOME POINT

What you do now matters for next year. Sometimes we forget to do things now for ourselves next year.

4.5.6.3 SUMMARY OF THE ACTION

Using poster board, youths map out their next year possible selves (their expectations and concerns for next year) by sticking stickers representing each of these selves on the left side of the poster board. They then look at their next year pos-

[handwritten note: - Even if far future is NOT realistic, not the time to discuss]

... kers that represent what they are doing now (or ... avoid negative possible selves next year. These ... y stickers are put in the middle section of the ... t possible selves with strategies by drawing lines ... eir next year possible selves and the actions they ... itive and avoid negative possible selves. Red lines ... this strategy now. Blue lines mean that this is a ... try but is not using now. Having mapped out next ... t strategies, youth are ready for Session 7 when ... e of the poster board.

... s not divided because the same strategy can be ... pectation and move away from a negative or to-be- ... h youth can make their own poster board setup, in ... roups and/or with one trainer, it is important that ... made as youth may take so long making the setup that they do not ... time to think about their next year possible selves.

Instructions focus on the step currently being taken. Hand out the sticker bag for possible selves and trade this for the strategies sticker bag. After students choose their strategies, have them put all remaining stickers back in the bag but keep the strategy sticker bag when they receive a red marker (because they will need it again). Trade red markers for blue markers. Explain before you give each supply. Repeat instructions before you hand out supplies and again as students are working.

There is no need for an example unless participants are quite young. If your participants are in sixth grade, you can do an example on the board. Show your own poster board with possible selves that are relevant for *you* for next year. Pick some strategies and draw the red line. Do one expected and one to-be-avoided possible self. This clarifies HOW to do the poster board and a model of which part of the poster board to be using. Trainers should use possible selves that are relevant to their own lives—not use the possible selves in the sticker bag; this is both less confusing and also avoids having students just copy what the trainer did [e.g., *I will show you an example. I am using possible selves that make sense for me*]. By eighth grade, participants can do this without an example.

Each youth should put his or her name on the board he or she works on so that it can be collected and returned the next session.

4.5.6.4 MATERIALS

- Prepared-in-advance poster boards (see sample on p. 68)
- Bags of stickers for each person (labeled "Next Year Possible Selves" and "Next Year Strategies")
  - Next year: 48 stickers with "expected" and "to-be-avoided" selves (prepared labels from prior studies with eighth graders) which are on pp. 129–130.
  - Strategies: 30 stickers with strategies to attain or avoid possible selves (prepared labels from prior studies with eighth graders) which are on p. 131.
  - Xerox these onto stickers and cut and place into baggies
  - Use one bag for possible selves; the student picks what is to be avoided and what is expected
  - Use a second baggie for strategies. The same strategy can work for an expected or to-be-avoided possible self
- Red and blue markers for each participant
- Black markers, pencils
- Newsprint and prepared-in-advance possible selves and strategies newsprint sheets
- Agenda
- Attendance and participation notebook
- Digital camera

4.5.6.5 ROOM SETUP

Youth need to have space to work so desks should be pushed together to form a working space large enough for the poster board. Youth should work on their own so working spaces should be set up around the room.

4.5.6.6 POINTS FOR REINFORCEMENT

1. Everyone has images of what he or she wants to be like and avoids being like for next year.
2. Everyone can do something to make attaining these selves more likely.

3. Working on a possible self is likely to involve overcoming obstacles and barriers.

4.5.6.7 AGENDA
1. Last session
2. Connecting next year and right now
3. Next session

4.5.6.7.1 Last Session (5 minutes)

Greet participants by name as they enter and take attendance. *Hi, this is Session 6, Possible Selves and Strategies Poster Boards. Can someone tell us what we did last session?* (Elicit what was done and why). *Good. We worked on action goals—linking adult and nearer possible selves with action we can take now today and saying where and when we will do it. We talked about the difference between adult images that are hopes or dreams and possible selves; these are images that are possible and linked to action.*

This week we are going to focus on next year possible selves and what we are doing or can do now; these are called strategies.

Reveal and read out loud preprinted possible selves newsprint:

> *A possible self is a positive or negative image of what is possible for you to become in the future. It is energizing because it might really happen. Strategies turn that energy to action.*

Reveal and read out loud preprinted strategies newsprint:

> *Strategy—actions you are taking now or could take to become like or avoid being like a possible self.*

4.5.6.7.2 Connecting Next Year and Strategies to Get There (25–45 minutes)

Look at this poster board. See that it is divided into three sections and labeled with

NEXT YEAR POSSIBLE SELVES	STRATEGIES Red = Doing now; Blue = Could do	ADULT POSSIBLE SELVES
Expected		Expected
To be avoided		To be avoided

Next Year Possible Selves, Strategies, and Adult Possible Selves. Within the Next Year Possible Selves column, the top half is labeled "Expected" and the bottom half "To Be Avoided"; that is also how the Adult Possible Selves part is set up. We will do the Adult Possible Selves part in the next session. This session we will be mapping out next year possible selves.

You will get a poster board and a bag of stickers with possible selves. Make sure you have enough room to spread your poster board out on your desk; you can sit on the floor if it is easier. Pass out and get help passing out boards, by bringing a stack to a few students and asking them to pass them out.

Now that you have a board, you are going to get a bag of stickers. Do not pull off the backings until you hear all the instructions. The bag is full of Next Year possible selves; selves you expect to be like and selves you want to avoid being like next year. Go through all these stickers and pick no more than five that describe your most important expectations for next year—the way you expect to be, and no more than five that describe your most important to-be-avoided possible selves—what you don't want to be like.

Hand out possible selves bags as you are continuing to give instructions. As you give each student a bag of next year possible selves stickers, point to the boxes for the "next year possible selves" stickers.

Put the rest of the stickers back in the bag so you only have ten stickers out: the five expected possible selves and the five to-be-avoided possible selves. If your expected or to-be avoided possible self is not included in the stickers, you can write it in on the blank stickers provided.

Do not pull off the backings as you go. You may change your mind. Lay out the ones you choose on your poster board. Put your expected possible selves in the top left box and your to-be-avoided possible selves in the bottom left box.

Make sure you have no more than five expected and no more than five to-be-avoided possible selves. Before you pull off the backings, be sure you put them one below the other and not in a row because these stickers might connect to stickers you will put in the strategies column next.

When you are sure you have five expected and five to be-be-avoided next year possible selves, put the rest in the baggie and pull off the backing. When you are done, raise your hand and I will trade you for a strategies baggie.

Trainers circulate. As students work, stop at each participant's desk; ask how he or she is doing and make sure they understand. As students begin to finish putting their stickers on their poster boards, bring their attention back to the front of the room.

Okay, I was looking and I see people getting their next year possible selves stickers in place. That is great! Now we're ready for the second part. Strategies are things that you can use to become your expected next year possible selves and to avoid becoming your to-be-avoided possible selves.

Point back to preprinted strategies newsprint. *When you finish, raise your hand and I will trade you your possible selves baggie for a strategies baggie.*

To use this baggie, read each of your possible selves. Ask yourself. Am I doing something now to work on this? If so, look through your strategies baggie and find the strategy that fits. If not, that is okay. Some possible selves are not linked to current action. A strategy can be used for more than one possible self. If you have a strategy like that, put it opposite one possible self and later you will be able to draw a connection to the other possible selves for which you use that strategy.

As you are giving these instructions out loud, pass out the strategies stickers bag with a snack.

Do the same thing for each possible self. You might have a strategy for each possible self. It might be that the same strategy works for more than one possible self. It might be that some possible selves have no strategies.

When you have picked all the strategies you are using now, put the rest of the stickers back in the bag.

Do not pull the backings off until you are done. For each strategy you put down, you will then need to draw a red line to the possible self it relates to, so make sure there is space. This line shows that you are using this strategy NOW. Once you arranged your strategies so you can draw the line connecting the strategy and the possible self, you can pull off the backing and put it on.

Trainer, pause while students are working and wait to begin the next set of instructions until students begin to have strategies arranged on their poster board.

When you are done with your strategy stickers, put them in the bag, keep your bag, raise your hand, and I will give you a red marker.

Sometimes we have possible selves that we are not doing anything about. Those possible selves have no red line linking them to a strategy.

Trainers circulate. Point to the strategies column as you give each student a bag of stickers. When the students have finished putting their stickers on their poster boards, give them red markers. The flow is at the pace of the student.

Trainers should continue to circulate. As students finish the first task, give them instructions on the second task, which is a repeat of the first one but allowing students to add in strategies they could use but are not using now.

When you have finished drawing all of the red lines between possible selves and the strategies you are using now, you are done. Raise your hand and I will trade your red marker for a blue marker.

I will tell you what to do with the blue marker.

Look at your possible selves again. Ask yourself if there are possible selves without a strategy. For those possible selves, you can look back at the sticker bag and find strategies you could start using. If so, go through your sticker bag and take out a strategy that you could use but are not using now for that possible self. Put it in the strategies column. Then draw a blue line from that possible self to the "could be using it" strategy.

4.5.6.7.3 Next Session (11 minutes)

Ask students to help summarize what was done today. Something such as *Today we did poster boards. We picked possible selves for next year and linked them with strategies we are using now. The color of the line says if it is something we are doing now or could be doing in the future. More red lines means doing more things now. More blue lines means strategies are not yet being used but could be. No lines means that next year possible self is not yet part of an action goal.*

Pass out evaluation form.

Next session, we will finish our poster boards by adding in adult possible selves. We will see pathways to the future through strategies, things we are doing now. Say good-bye to students as they leave.

Trainers note participation and comments in attendance book.

4.5.6.8 NEXT YEAR EXPECTED AND TO-BE-AVOIDED POSSIBLE SELVES STICKERS

Following on pages 129–130 are the common next year possible selves that students in our prior studies have generated. Xerox these onto sticker forms, cut them, and put them into a baggie. Provide some blank stickers so if students do not find what they want, they can write in their own text. The reason to use printed stickers is that it makes it a fun activity rather than a difficult writing task. It also provides a sense that one's own expectations and concerns are normative: tell students that the stickers are from what others have said (which is true). The stickers mix positive and negative since expectations can be either and to-be-avoided possible selves are always negative. Typically students' main focus for the coming year is on school and relationships. Relatively few possible selves focus on material lifestyle and almost none on community involvement. Since the main focus of STJ is on the pathway to adulthood through school, these other domains are not included.

Being a great student	Getting good grades	Being in high school
Learning more and new things	Being good at sports and activities	Playing in the band
Being popular	Making new friends	Having a boyfriend/girlfriend
Having a part-time job	Being well liked, having friends	Being smarter
Having people think I am cool	Having fun/doing fun things	Being a nicer person
Having a good relationship with teachers	Having a good relationship with my parents	Being a more mature person
Having a bad relationship with teachers	Still in the same grade	Failing in school
Being a dropout	Being kicked out of school	Being in trouble at school

Being in a gang	Being a "dummy"	Being lazy
Being a drug dealer	Getting into fights	Being bad
Getting talked about	Doing drugs	Having social problems
Being a bully	Being picked on	Being lonely
Become pregnant/ Fathering a child	Being excluded from activities	Being lonely
Being disliked by teachers	Being shy	Being unattractive
Being a class clown	Feeling confused in class	Getting bad grades
	Having problems with parents	Fighting with parents

4.5.6.9 STRATEGIES TO ATTAIN POSITIVE AND AVOID NEGATIVE POSSIBLE SELVES STICKERS

Page 131 provides strategies stickers. Xerox these onto sticker paper and cut to separate so that each student has a sticker bag. Again, these are strategies other students have written. The student just needs to find one he or she is using or could use. Some possible selves have no strategies. That is okay.

Ask parents for advice	Get an education	Learn about possibilities
Trying to talk with my parents	Listen to my parents	Talk with others
Reminding myself of my abilities	Watching and learning from others	Staying away from the wrong people
Respecting myself and others	Taking on responsibility	Not getting in trouble with the law
Learning and practicing healthy habits	Studying	Doing my homework
Participating in class	Coming to class on time	Putting in all my effort (not just getting by)
Going to after school programs	Practicing my sport/ music/art	Paying attention in class
Listening to teachers	Not talking back to teachers	Going to the library to read/check out books
Following directions in class	Having a regular schedule (mapping out my schedule)	Not staying up too late
Eating regular meals, not a lot of junk food	Budgeting my time	Not watching too much TV/ not spending too much time on computer/video

4.5.6.10 SESSION 6: POSSIBLE SELVES AND STRATEGIES SESSION EVALUATION

Thank you for participating in the School-to-Jobs program. We would like your feedback. Please rate this session by marking the number that fits your opinion and give you ideas for improvement.

To what extent was this session											
Boring	1	2	3	4	5	6	7	8	9	10	Interesting
Difficult	1	2	3	4	5	6	7	8	9	10	Easy
Not useful	1	2	3	4	5	6	7	8	9	10	Useful
To what extent did this session											
Provide no new way of thinking	1	2	3	4	5	6	7	8	9	10	Provide a new way of thinking
Provide no new information	1	2	3	4	5	6	7	8	9	10	Provide new information

We want to improve this session. What would make it better?

_____

_____

_____

4.5.7 Session 7: Pathways to the Future

4.5.7.1 OVERVIEW

In Session 4 youth created timelines and began to see possible selves over time. In Session 5 youth began to practice writing action goals; in Session 6 youth mapped out possible selves and strategies for next year. Session 7 completes the poster boards to concretize the link between current action, next year possible selves, and far future possible selves. Thus, this session is the third time that participants have worked on ways of connecting the distal future to the near future through current action.

Youth often feel that there is nothing the~~y~~ ~~attain their~~ adult images because the future is ~~that youth do~~ not know how to plan ~~connection~~ between long-term vis~~ ~~on helps youth make the conne~~ ~~them-~~ selves moving from thi~~ ~~7 is a poster board that links n~~ ~~tegies~~ used to attain them. Thi~~ ~~their future selves.

4.5.7.2 TAKE-HOME POIN~~

What you do now matters fo~~

4.5.7.3 SUMMARY OF THE A~~

Using the possible selves poster~~ adult possible selves, including b~~ ers representing each of these se~~ then look at the strategies they c~~ could do to attain expected possibl~~ possible selves. Youth then connect~~ adult possible selves. These are th~~ expected and avoid to-be-avoided a~~ youth is using this strategy now. Blu~~ is willing to try but is not using now~~

Instructions about strategy lines~~ to do this part. Trainers pass out mat~~ tions as necessary. Trainers wander through the room, checking that students are working and understand what do to.

[Handwritten notes: - can ask them to break pathways into connection colors & talk abt that ... paths across all 3 columns]

4.5.7.4 MATERIALS

- Participants' poster boards from last session
- Preprinted newsprint with possible selves and strategies from the last session
- Bag for each participant labeled "Adult" with the 48 "expected" and "to-be-avoided" stickers printed from the end of this session on sticker sheets on pages 138–139.
- Red and blue markers for each participant
- Black markers and pencils
- Agenda
- Attendance and participation notebook
- Digital camera

4.5.7.5 ROOM SETUP

Youth need to have space to work. Desks should be pushed together to form a working space large enough for the poster board. Youth should work on their own so working spaces should be set up around the room.

4.5.7.6 POINTS FOR REINFORCEMENT

1. Everyone has images of what he or she wants to be like and avoid being like for next year and as an adult.
2. Everyone can do something to make attaining these selves more likely.
3. By working on a next year self, participants can make their adult images more likely. This is called a pathway.

4.5.7.7 AGENDA

1. Last session
2. Connecting next year and the future
3. Sharing pathways
4. Next session

4.5.7.7.1 Last Session (2 minutes)

Greet participants by name as they enter, take attendance, and greet latecomers by name. *Hi, this is session 7, Pathways to the Future. Can someone tell us what we did last session?* (First establish what was done, then see if youth can talk about why they think they did this.) *Good. We worked on possible selves for next year expected and to-be-avoided possible selves and strategies to attain them. Strategies are the things we do or can do to make possible selves happen. Not all possible selves had strategies. Last session we connected next year possible selves to strategies. This time we are going to work on adult possible selves and connect strategies to them. Adult possible selves came up in action goals; they were the "because" part of the action goal.*

4.5.7.7.2 Connecting Next Year and the Future (20–30 minutes)

The trainer shows a poster board; points to the right hand column labeled, adult possible selves. *Remember adult possible selves are possible, not for sure, adult possible selves could be positive ones we expect to become or negative ones we prefer to avoid becoming but they are possible nonetheless. We are passing back your poster boards. We will also give you a baggie of stickers with adult possible selves—selves you expect to be like and selves you want to avoid being like as an adult.* (The trainer holds up the bag and passes out boards and sticker bags while talking; point to the right column on the board as you hand board and bag to each participant.)

Read through the stickers and pick the five that describe your expected selves for when you're an adult and five that describe your to-be-avoided adult possible selves— what you don't want to be like as an adult. Even if you can think of more, just take the five most important to you. We also have blank stickers if you do not find your adult selves in the stickers.

Pick your five expected adult possible selves and put them on the top right of your poster board. Put your five to-be-avoided adult possible selves on the bottom right of your poster board. Do not take off the backs until all are arranged and you like what you see. Remember to put them one under the other so that you can draw strategy lines. When you are ready, pull off the back of the sticker. Stick on your possible selves stickers, then read each possible self and look at the strategies you have. Ask yourself, "Is this strategy helping me with this possible self?"

When they are finished putting on their adult possible selves stickers, repeat marker instructions (see following) and pass out snacks.

When you are finished putting your adult possible selves stickers on, raise your hand and I will give you a red marker. Read each adult possible self you've pasted on your board. Then look at the strategies in your strategy section that have red lines. If you are using a strategy right now, it has a red line already. For each strategy with a red line, ask yourself, does this strategy help me with this adult possible self? Then connect the strategy with the adult possible self with a red line. Then read the next possible self and ask the same question. Some strategies will help get to an adult possible self, but not all will. When you are done, raise your hand and I will trade you for a blue marker.

Circulate and repeat instructions. Reinforce that not all possible selves have strategies. Reassure students that their poster boards are going well. As students complete their red lines, say:

As you finish with your red marker, raise your hand and I will trade you for a blue marker. Blue markers are for strategies you could use. If you aren't using the strategy right now, but you could use it, it has a blue line already. If you could use that strategy for an adult possible self, draw a blue line between it and the adult possible self. Remember, you could be using more than one strategy for an adult possible self, or you could be using none.

4.5.7.7.3 Sharing Pathways (20–35 minutes)

Have students move to a circle with their chairs (reorienting so they all see each other). *Let's move back to a circle.*

Can everyone show his or her poster boards? Raise them up so everyone can see.

Strategies are things we are doing now to work toward possible selves. Sometimes a strategy can be used to work on more than one possible self and sometimes a strategy to work on a next year possible self also helps us get to a farther future possible self. When a strategy or a bunch of strategies links a next year self to an adult self, we can call this a pathway.

I am going to ask everyone to share a pathway from a next year possible self to an adult possible self through a strategy.

[Look for pathways, point to examples and say names of participants who have red pathways; start opposite you and work around the circle.]

Can you read me your next year possible self and strategy in red that is linked to it and the adult possible self at the end? [Do reds, then if there are a lot at the halfway point, switch to blues so that time does not run out.]

Okay, we heard pathways through strategies people are doing now. Let's hear some pathways through strategies people could use.

If there are no or few pathways, ask for next year possible selves and linking strategies. Either continue the circle or start again if completed. Time permitting, ask for domains of adulthood and which of these were part of pathways. Reinforce the fact that all the adult selves actually pass through school—they needed to get a good job, which supports a lifestyle and allows for raising a family and giving to a community.

4.5.7.7.4 Next Session (2 minutes)

(Pass out evaluation form) *Next session, we will start working on ways to use strategies to solve impossible puzzles.* Say good-bye to students as they leave. Pick up forms and rearrange room.

Trainers note participation and comments in attendance book.

4.5.7.8 ADULT EXPECTED AND TO-BE-AVOIDED
POSSIBLE SELVES STICKERS

On pages 138–139 are the common adult possible selves that students in our prior studies have generated. Xerox these onto sticker forms, cut them, and put them into a baggie. Provide some blank stickers so if students do not find what they want, they can write in their own text. The reason to use printed stickers is that it makes it a fun activity rather than a difficult writing task. It also provides a sense that one's own expectations and concerns are normative: tell students that the stickers are from what others have said (which is true). The stickers mix positive and negative because expectations can be either and to-be-avoided possible selves are always negative. The stickers do not cover specific careers because students often are not sure what specific career they want. The main focus of STJ is on the pathway to adulthood through school and does not require that students get worried about what exactly they will do; this is fine.

Having a good job	Have a profession	Earning a living
Getting paid/Being able to pay bills	Being a provider for my family	A hard-working person
Going to college	Being a responsible person	Being a good/moral person
Being an independent person	Belonging to community organizations	Being a volunteer
Being a good husband or wife	Being a good mother or father	Being a member of my church
Being a parent	Having a good relationship with my family	Having friends
Being involved in crime	Being in jail	Being on drugs

Selling drugs	Having problematic family relations	Being an abusive parent or spouse
Getting certified or licensed in my chosen field	Still living at home with my parents	Lonely not having friends
Being homeless	Being poor, not earning a living	Being jobless
Being an alcoholic	Being on welfare	Not being able to provide for my family
Not being able to have the things I want	Looking old	Becoming unattractive
Being sick		

4.5.7.9 SESSION 7: PATHWAYS TO THE FUTURE SESSION EVALUATION

Thank you for participating in the School-to-Jobs program. We would like your feedback. Please rate this session by marking the number that fits your opinion and give you ideas for improvement.

To what extent was this session											
Boring	1	2	3	4	5	6	7	8	9	10	Interesting
Difficult	1	2	3	4	5	6	7	8	9	10	Easy
Not useful	1	2	3	4	5	6	7	8	9	10	Useful
To what extent did this session											
Provide no new way of thinking	1	2	3	4	5	6	7	8	9	10	Provide a new way of thinking
Provide no new information	1	2	3	4	5	6	7	8	9	10	Provide new information

We want to improve this session. What would make it better?

_____

_____

_____

4.5.8 Session 8: Puzzles

4.5.8.1 OVERVIEW

In Session 2, youth imagined far future adult selves; in Sessi[on]
these far future selves to current positive and neg[ative]
model how to stay on track or become derai[led]
personal timelines, considering roadbl[ocks]
and 4 helped students begin to articulat[e]
meaning that the tasks at hand were imp[ortant]
and 7 youth began to think of strategies th[at]
and far future possible selves, linking curre[nt]
next year possible selves and strategies to at[tain]
future closer by highlighting what can be done
possible selves. In Sessions 8 and 9, focus cont[inues]
interpretation of difficulty with emphasis on dif[ficulty]
relevant to each of the domains of adulthood an[d]
to each participant no matter his or her gender, so[cial]
background.

In this session, the process of making a plan is ma[de]

The puzzles seem impossible, but they turn out t[o]
start, keep trying alternatives, and use the gro[up]
provides a sense that things that f[eel]
to work on. Sometimes getting ther[e]
for alternatives. The goal of the puzz[le]
and resourcefulness rather than di[scouragement]
face of a seemingly impossible task. [The]
components to make possible a task t[hat]
groups to solve story problems. Ther[e]
session. The task seems unsolvable, b[ut]
can work through the problem and solv[e]
group competence in, problem solving. [The]
into component parts and dealt with rat[ionally]
progress.

4.5.8.2 TAKE-HOME POINT

Things can seem impossible and difficult, [but breaking down] problems and looking for alternative ways to set up what the problem is shows a different way of
thinking—difficulty can be part of making progress on important goals.

4.5.8.3 SUMMARY OF THE ACTION

How this activity is structured depends on the number of trainers and the participants themselves. It can be something participants do in groups alone and then
discuss in the larger group or something that they do together with the trainer.
The trainer should switch to a larger format as soon as groups begin to flag.

If there are two trainers, divide participants into two groups; otherwise have
groups of three or four participants working without a trainer. Have groups turn
their tables together. At first, the puzzle seems impossible to solve. Have youth
talk through how to proceed. Groups that are working should be allowed to work.
As groups solve the problem, have them write their steps on newsprint. As groups
flag or if the problem seems unsolvable, turn the groups to the center to work as

a larger group. Work through the puzzle as a group. Each step of the way should be talked about. The trainer should structure discussion of how to proceed so that students discover the idea of a template (see solution at end of session) that makes sure that nothing is forgotten.

Highlight that part of writing down what is known in a grid helps in figuring out which information is relevant and which is irrelevant; working step by step, the puzzle suddenly becomes easy. Solving the puzzle is fun as a group task and almost impossible alone. Working together provides a sense of competence and an active understanding of thinking about problems with contingencies (like the students' adult visions). Working together highlights that achievement is valued by the group and by members of one's racial-ethnic community, and it provides a way of making sense of obstacles and barriers and dealing with them.

4.5.8.4 MATERIALS
- Pencils, paper, markers, and newsprint
- Two puzzles
- Attendance and participation notebook
- Digital camera

4.5.8.5 ROOM SETUP
This session uses tables or desks set up in small groups and then separated as needed.

4.5.8.6 POINTS FOR REINFORCEMENT
1. Keep trying; persistence often pays off.
2. First solutions may not work, that is to be expected.
3. Others are likely to have similar difficulties and eliciting help can be useful.

4.5.8.7 AGENDA
1. Last session
2. Solving puzzles
3. Next session

4.5.8.7.1 Last Session (5–10 minutes)
Trainers greet participants by name as they enter. Take attendance in notebook. Greet latecomers by name. *Hi everyone—this is Session 8, Puzzles. We are going to do something a little different today. But first, can anyone say what we did last session?* Trainers should elicit responses focused on poster boards. *Okay, we did poster boards about adult possible selves and strategies. What was that activity about?* Points to be reinforced are connecting the present with the future and connecting current school tasks to strategies that lead to attaining adult possible selves. *Okay, so last session we talked about strategies that make pathways from now, to next year, to adult possible selves. Some strategies were in red, used now. Some were in blue, the one's we could try. Working on strategies can feel difficult. In those cases people sometimes do not have a strategy at all, just a possible self. Today we are working on that feeling of difficulty. Important things are often difficult. Today we will inoculate*

ourselves from believing that if it's difficult, it is impossible. Like getting an inoculation, so difficulty does not infect us with giving up.

Have you ever heard of the word inoculation or vaccination? The trainer writes guesses as to what these mean on the board. *It has something to do with shots; that is right, but what does it do?* Get more guesses. *It protects against diseases. Today we are going to work difficult puzzles that seem impossible. If you have a vaccination for the measles, it can protect you from getting sick, and we are getting inoculated from believing that if it is difficult, it is not worth one's time or is impossible.* Reveal the preprinted newsprint.

> *Inoculation or vaccination is a way of thinking about school difficulties to remind you that school is difficult because it is important. It reduces the chance that every-day problems in school will feel like too much.*

Here is the first puzzle (get help passing out). The trainer should read the puzzle out loud. *You should get into groups to work on solving the puzzle. As you are trying to solve it, write down each of the steps that you take to figure out the answers. We're going to talk about these steps, so make sure you remember to write them down.*

4.5.8.7.2 Solving Puzzles (15–25 minutes)

Let's move into groups.

The trainer circulates. If groups are solving, have them write their steps so they can share them. If groups are stuck, orient them to the center to walk through the steps of solving.

Trainers elicit responses from students and demonstrate how to make a grid to solve the problem on newsprint if no group has used this method.

Okay, so we've figured it out! Let me ask you an important question—how did you feel when you first got this problem? Did it seem easy or hard? It seemed pretty hard and confusing because there was so much information in there, right? What did we do then? We kept working and it got easier. What made it easier? Emphasize responses involving working together, making a grid or a list.

Great, so you worked together with your group members and you figured out a way to organize all that information so that it made sense. Starting, being willing to start again, and organizing things are really good strategies. Sometimes when things seem really difficult and confusing, it helps a lot to organize what you need to do and take steps. Being willing to start again and again can make a problem that seems impossible become possible and important. Want to try a second puzzle?

The benefit of Puzzle 2 is that youth see that sometimes getting organized and doing each step in order is not enough and they have to add trial and error as a strategy.

Let us now try again with a new problem.

Hand out Puzzle 2 and snacks. Read out loud again.

You can work with your group again (solution is at the end of the session).

Have groups work until they flag; then reorient to a larger group. Have students say their steps. While in Puzzle 1 it was sufficient to have a grid and work step by step until the answers emerged, in Puzzle 2, there is not quite enough information and youth have to just start and try something and see if it works; trial and error is a strategy.

> *So in this case, after getting organized, you just had to start trying—that can be a strategy, too—just start!*

> *Trial and error is a strategy, but we have to remember that error is in the name; that means that sometimes trying will lead to errors. It is important not to get discouraged if the trial leads to a dead end (error) because it is always okay to just retrace steps to the error part and start again; that is like the obstacles in the timeline activity.*

4.5.8.7.3 Next Session (10 minutes)

Can anyone tell us what we did today? Participants should mention puzzles that seem impossible but then could be solved. *So today we did puzzles that seemed impossible at first, but getting started working in a group writing things down and having a plan made them possible. Sometimes the plan was clear like using a grid, and sometimes the plan was that if it doesn't work try again.*

Pass out evaluation forms. *Next session we will work on inoculation from difficulty, but we will work on everyday problems in school like getting bad grades and having to figure out what to do next.*

Trainer says good-byes, picks up evaluations, and rates participation.

4.5.8.8 PUZZLES AND EVERYDAY OBSTACLES
4.5.8.8.1 Puzzle 1

Ms. Smith, Ms. Garcia, and Ms. O'Leary all teach at St. Andrew Junior High School. One of the women is a mathematics teacher, one is an art teacher, and one is a science teacher. The art teacher, an only child, has taught the least number of years. Ms. Garcia, who married Ms. Smith's brother, has taught more years than the mathematics teacher. Name the subject each woman teaches.

4.5.8.8.2 Puzzle 2

George, Isaiah, Andrew, and Julio each had four dates to four different Parish Center Dances with four different girls, named Cher, Connie, Melissa, and Kendra. On the second date, George dated Connie and Julio dated Kendra. On the third date Andrew went out with Melissa, and Isaiah went out with Connie. Melissa went out with George and Cher went out with Isaiah on the fourth date. What couples went out together on the first date if no pairs went out more than once?

4.5.8.8.3 Procedures and Solutions to Puzzles

Puzzle 1

First, one should write out the three names and then put known characteristics about each as they come out of the puzzle. The key is to write out what subject each could not possibly be teaching and then the solution is discovered.

	Math	Art	Science
Smith			
Garcia			
O'Leary			

The art teacher is an only child and taught the least years (write it in; maybe it will help)

	Math	Art (only child, taught least years)	Science
Smith			
Garcia			
O'Leary			

Ms. Garcia is married, but this piece of information is actually irrelevant to solving the problem. What is relevant is that Ms. Smith has a brother, so that means she cannot be the art teacher since we already learned that the art teacher is an only child (mark N for Art for Smith). Ms. Garcia taught more years than the math teacher, so she is not the math teacher and cannot be the art teacher either (since the art teacher taught the least years); mark N for Art and for Math for Garcia, so she must be the science teacher (mark Y).

	Math	Art (only child, taught least years)	Science
Smith (has a brother)		N	
Garcia (taught more years than math teacher)	N	N	Y
O'Leary			

If Ms. Garcia and Ms. Smith do not teach art, the art teacher must be Ms. O'Leary and then the math teacher must be Ms. Smith.

	Math	Art (only child, taught least)	Science
Smith (has a brother)	Y	N	N
Garcia (taught more years than math teacher) so cannot be art either	N	N	Y
O'Leary	N	Y	

Puzzle 2

This requires a very similar solving method as the first puzzle but more characters are involved. First, chart out the names and fill in the known information. Second, use a system of trial and error to figure out the missing information, keeping in mind the rules stated within the problem.

Know this and also know each only dated each other once.

	George	Isaiah	Andrew	Julio
Cher		4		
Melissa	4		3	
Connie	2	3		
Kendra				2

After filling in what is known, there is still missing information, so it is necessary to start with a guess and see if it works. I start by putting in Cher as George's first date and Kendra as his third.

	George	Isaiah	Andrew	Julio
Cher	*1*	4		
Melissa	4		3	
Connie	2	3		
Kendra	*3*			2

Kendra cannot be Isaiah's fourth date (that is Cher) and she already has a second date (that is Julio); therefore, she could be Isaiah's first date and Andrew's fourth date, which would make Melissa his second date.

	George	Isaiah	Andrew	Julio
Cher	*1*	4		
Melissa	4	*2*	3	
Connie	2	*3*		
Kendra	*3*	*1*	*4*	2

That would make Julio Melissa's first date.

	George	Isaiah	Andrew	Julio
Cher	**1**	4		
Melissa	4	**2**	3	**1**
Connie	2	**3**		
Kendra	**3**	**1**	**4**	2

This makes Connie and Andrew the final first date pair (the rest of the dates do not matter since you only need to provide first dates for each couple)

	George	Isaiah	Andrew	Julio
Cher	**1**	4		
Melissa	4	**2**	3	**1**
Connie	2	**3**	**1**	
Kendra	**3**	**1**	**4**	2

Thank you for participating in the School-to-Jobs program. We would like your feedback. Please rate this session by marking the number that fits your opinion and give you ideas for improvement.

To what extent was this session											
Boring	1	2	3	4	5	6	7	8	9	10	Interesting
Difficult	1	2	3	4	5	6	7	8	9	10	Easy
Not useful	1	2	3	4	5	6	7	8	9	10	Useful
To what extent did this session											
Provide no new way of thinking	1	2	3	4	5	6	7	8	9	10	Provide a new way of thinking
Provide no new information	1	2	3	4	5	6	7	8	9	10	Provide new information

We want to improve this session. What would make it better?

_____

_____

_____

4.5.9 Session 9: Solving Everyday Problems

4.5.9.1 OVERVIEW

This session continues the logic of Session 8. Session 8 focused youth on breaking down problems that seemed impossible and using strategies like "get a grid," "break it into parts," "try again," and "get help" to solve what seemed impossible. In Session 9 they learn to see e[...] the farther future self, the nearer fu[...] do now is easier if each part is c[...] the long run, what do I need to g[...] the path? As in the timetable ac[...] (roadblocks) that one needs to [...] everyday problems in school. [...] from others is made explicit. B[...] of school to their own adult p[...] between school successes and [...] identity as African American, [...] The same holds for children of [...]

This session highlights al[...]ded achievement, connectedn[...] is valued by, and part of being [...] in school is a positive reflection on one's racial-ethnic group [...] nd others may or may not see things that way so that obstacles and roadblocks may include others' misperceptions of what a person from a particular background can do or achieve. The goal is to promote active engagement and resourcefulness rather than disengagement and a sense of futility in the face of obstacles and difficulties along the way. Youths work in small groups to ask themselves how to handle problems in math class. For long sessions with small groups of participants and two trainers there is more time to work on the second task, which is everyday problems. Everyday problems can be set up like the timelines, poster board, or action goal activities. Positive and negative forces should be considered. There are choice points and difficulties that are obstacles to navigate.

[handwritten note: Solving sooner rather than later]

4.5.9.2 TAKE-HOME POINT

Everyday situations involve current action linked to near and far possible selves; there are choice points and difficulties that are obstacles to navigate.

4.5.9.3 MATERIALS

- Pencils, paper, markers, and newsprint
- Problem sheets (History class)
- Attendance and participation notebook
- Digital camera

4.5.9.4 ROOM SETUP

This session uses tables or desks. These should be set up in small groups at first and then moved into a large circle as the session ends.

4.5.9.5 POINTS FOR REINFORCEMENT

1. Keep trying. Persistence often pays off.
2. First solutions may not work; that is to be expected.

3. Others are likely to have similar difficulties and eliciting help can be useful.
4. Start right away; problems at school get harder to solve when they are put off.

4.5.9.6 AGENDA
1. Last session
2. Math class
3. Problems in a bag
4. Next session

4.5.9.6.1 Last Session (2 minutes)
Trainers greet participants by name as they enter. Take attendance in notebook. Greet latecomers by name. *Hi, everyone. This is Session 9, Everyday Problems. Can anyone say what we did last session? What did you learn last session—can someone say?* Points to be reinforced include the following: puzzles seem impossible but can be solved with a strategy like breaking it down or using a grid or try again, and we worked on inoculation from difficulty feeling like impossibility.

Today we are going to work on everyday problems at school. We will use the same strategy as last session. Work with a partner. Ask what question do I need to ask to decide what to do. Trainers should have participants push their desks together.

Now we are going to do another puzzle. This time it is a real-life one.

4.5.9.6.2 Difficulties in Math Class (15–25 minutes)
Trainer, pass out the math class problem with student help and read it out loud using a narrative voice so the problem is engaging. *Remember your job is to figure out what are the questions that need to be asked in order to solve this problem.*

Imagine it is October, right before Halloween. In School to Jobs last year you learned that there are different levels of math classes and that math skills are one of the keys to better career opportunities. So you are taking the hardest math class you could get in. But you are having problems in the class and need to figure out what to do. You got a C on the first quiz, a C- on the second quiz, and a D on the third quiz. Things have been getting worse, but you've really been trying. You've been doing your homework as best you can and you've been calling a friend to ask how to do the homework problems and to check your answers. The next quiz is coming up. The teacher says that anybody who doesn't get a B or above on it should transfer to a lower math class. The way things are going you need to figure out how you can pass this class, let alone get a B on the next quiz. What should you do? What questions do you need to ask yourself?

Students can work in their groups to come up with questions. Have students write their question on newsprint or read in groups. This is a group effort so if there are 25 students, have no more than 6 groups or this will take too long. Circulate, keep on task, and reinforce instructions.

As the groups finish or begin to flag, have the students reorient to the larger circle and read their questions aloud. Questions are likely to be specific, but the trainer should write them down in clusters so that emerging from these specific questions are a cluster of adult possible selves, a cluster of next year possible selves, a cluster of strategies, and a cluster of contexts. In the end, the trainer will be able to have some clusters that look like action goals: "Because" (adult possible self) "I will" (next year possible self) "by" (action goal) when and where during the day (context). Some students might ask questions that look like the timeline constructs. *Is this an obstacle or a fork? For example, can I solve the homework, can my friend, or does working with my friend not help. Do I know what is happening to others besides my friend; am I the only one getting bad grades?* Some questions can be clustered as role models and negative forces (*Is the friend a positive or negative force?*).

Passing the class is obviously a near future goal and maybe going to college or getting a good job is a far future goal. Studying and getting help from a friend are strategies. Breaking things down this [way] and far future possible selves make se[nse] possible selves need to be changed.

So the math class problem can be thought [of in] the way we talked about timelines. The m[ath is the] way we talked about positive and negativ[e forces. Is it] helping you or do you need to find someon[e else?]

4.5.9.6.3 Problems in a Bag (25–35 min[utes])

Now we are going to try something else. (H[and out pieces] of paper and write down a problem you ha[ve. It can be the] problem we just did or something else. Cru[mble it into a] circle and then put the problem onto the flo[or.] [This might feel like things are] getting crazy, but having a chance to "t[hink" is important. To the] Trainer, your job is to brush the problem[s around by your feet. Use cau]tion so problems remain anonymous. *Everyone has a problem. Now they are crumbled up.* Once all the problems are there, open and read four. As you read, edit as needed so problems remain anonymous. This is School-to-Jobs, not counseling, and problems are supposed to be about school. Read out loud four (or, if need be, five). Have students say which one to work on, then do the same process as the math problem. *Okay, what questions do we have to ask to solve this one?* Cluster responses into STJ concepts so that students practice action goals (Because I will by when) or practice asking for adult possible self, next year possible self, and strategies. Strategies can include getting other people involved, and that other person can be a role model or a positive force. Strategies can include getting rid of a negative force. Having tried one problem, say *Want to try another problem?* Then read the next four to five problems in the same way and edit as needed and go through the same process. Longer sessions allow for more rounds, but there is no need to do all problems out loud.

4.5.9.6.4 Next Session (3 minutes)

Can anyone tell us what we did today? (Make sure everyone knows that the session was about solving everyday school problems.) *What did you learn? We talked about dealing with school problems and breaking them down into questions using our School-to-Jobs skills. This is like an inoculation of difficulty because it has us thinking about forks in the road and obstacles. We used the strategy of thinking about adult and next year possible selves and action plans.*

Pass out evaluation forms. *Next session we are going to keep working on inoculations by looking at what you need to finish high school and get more training—like going to college or something else.* (Say good-bye to students as they leave.)

Trainers rate each member's participation and add comments as needed.

[Handwritten note: Cluster responses into STJ concepts (possible selves, strategies, forks, etc.)]

4.5.9.7 MATH CLASS

Imagine it is October, right before Halloween. In School-to-Jobs last year you learned that there are different levels of math classes and that math skills are one of the keys to better career opportunities. So you are taking the hardest math class you could get in. But you are having problems in the class and need to figure out what to do. You got a C on the first quiz, a C– on the second quiz, and a D on the third quiz. Things have been getting worse, but you've really been trying. You've been doing your homework as best you can and you've been calling a friend to ask how to do the homework problems and to check your answers. The next quiz is coming up. The teacher says that anybody who doesn't get a B or above on it should transfer to a lower math class. The way things are going you need to figure out how you can pass this class, let alone get a B on the next quiz. What should you do? What questions do you need to ask yourself?

4.5.9.8 EXAMPLES OF QUESTIONS STUDENTS MIGHT WRITE

- Does it matter what grade you get in a class or only that you pass?
- Is it important for you to stay in this class? Why or why not?
- What do you think is best for your grades now?
- What do you think is best for your future after high school?
- What are you going to do to improve, if you decide that you want to stay in the class?
- Is there someone you should talk with about this? Why or why not?
- Should you discuss this problem with your teacher, your school counselor? Why or why not?
- Should you let your parents know? Why or why not?
- Decision: What should you do?

4.5.9.9 SESSION 9: SOLVING EVERYDAY PROBLEMS: SESSION EVALUATION
Thank you for participating in the School-to-Jobs program. We would like your feedback. Please rate this session by marking the number that fits your opinion and give you ideas for improvement.

To what extent was this session											
Boring	1	2	3	4	5	6	7	8	9	10	Interesting
Difficult	1	2	3	4	5	6	7	8	9	10	Easy
Not useful	1	2	3	4	5	6	7	8	9	10	Useful
To what extent did this session											
Provide no new way of thinking	1	2	3	4	5	6	7	8	9	10	Provide a new way of thinking
Provide no new information	1	2	3	4	5	6	7	8	9	10	Provide new information

We want to improve this session. What would make it better?

_____

_____

_____

4.5.10 Session 10: Solving Everyday Problems II: Graduation

4.5.10.1 OVERVIEW

In Session 2 youth imagined far future adult images; in Session 3 youth connected these far future possible selves to current positive and negative forces that model how to stay on track or become derailed. In Session 4 students worked on personal timelines and learned about roadblocks and forks in the road. Thus, Sessions 3 and 4 helped students begin to articulate difficulties along the way as normal—meaning that the tasks at hand were important, not impossible. In Sessions 5, 6, and 7 youth began to think of strategies they can use to work toward near and far future possible selves, linking current action to adult possible selves via next year possible selves and strategies to attain them. These sessions bring the future closer by highlighting what can be done now to move toward far future possible selves. Sessions 8, 9, and 10 all focus on thinking about the present as connected to the near and farther future, to youth's possible selves, through action plans and strategies. Youth practiced ways of thinking about obstacles and getting help so that current situations do not become forks in the road—choice points that lead to a future different from the aspired future, without even noticing it. In Session 10, the focus is squarely on finishing high school and transitioning to college. If the group is not in a regular school program but instead is in an equivalency program, focus should be on getting from the equivalency program to passing the test and from passing the test to the next level of training (e.g., 2- or 4-year college). Youths work in dyads on their guesses about requirements for high school graduation (or the process of completing equivalency certification). Youth then document their guesses on newsprint or say them out loud. Requirements are then passed out and read through. The content of classes that fulfill requirements is explained. The exercise is repeated for prerequisites/skills needed for college and other training.

4.5.10.2 TAKE-HOME POINT

It is possible to know the steps to get from the present to the future. Some of these steps can be hard. That is okay; important steps are often hard.

4.5.10.3 MATERIALS

- **Needed but not included at the back of the session because they are specific to the setting in which you are working**
  - High school requirements handout (graduation course and attendance requirements, standardized tests, organized by year of high school)
  - Local college entry requirements (high school course, credit, standardized test score, letters of reference, deadlines to apply)
- Pencils, paper, markers, and newsprint
- Attendance and participation notebook
- Digital camera

4.5.10.4 ROOM SETUP

Tables or desks to accommodate whole group; desks may be shifted into smaller work groups.

4.5.10.5 POINTS FOR REINFORCEMENT

1. You already know a lot about what is needed to graduate high school and go to college.
2. Each school year builds on the one before, and it is important to revisit your plan as you move along.
3. Even if you fail or don't do well in a class you need, you can still work toward your goal but you need to work on backup or alternative paths.
4. Careers, colleges, and majors all differ in required coursework; you can find out what they are.

4.5.10.6 AGENDA

1. Last session
2. Succeeding and moving to the next step
3. Next session

4.5.10.6.1 Last Session (2–5 minutes)

Greet each participant by name as he or she enters and mark attendance. Greet latecomers. *Hi, this is Session 10, Everyday Problems II. I am glad to see everyone. So what did we work on last session?* The trainer should elicit comments like math class, problems on the floor (or in the bag), and asking questions to solve problems. Everyone is likely to experience some problems at school and everyone has skills to work on these. Responses should be written on newsprint as main points: ask yourself questions about the problem; how will what you do make a difference now, next year, and farther down the road; what do I need to learn to figure out my action plan; and who can help me?

Last session we began to think about everyday problems and practiced thinking about them so that we are inoculated from thinking of problems as meaning that we should give up. Instead, we thought of problems as signaling that we should check in with our action plan.

4.5.10.6.2 Succeeding and Moving to the Next Step (40–65 minutes)

Today we are going to work on another part of taking steps now for the future: Succeeding in getting from now through high school, graduating, and getting to the next step. We will start with what schools require. What does it take to graduate? What does it take to get to the next step? So the first thing we are going to do is to divide up into groups. Depending on the group, this could be pairs or larger groups or even two subgroups with a trainer at each. *Take paper and work with your partner. Write down what you need to graduate high school (or whatever level is relevant for your group). Can anyone give me some ideas of what kinds of things you'll be writing down? How many years are there of middle school? What about high school? In middle school, are there certain classes you have to take? How do you know if you passed each grade? What about high school—are there certain classes you have to take? What about grades— does it matter what grades you get? What about attendance—is there some attendance requirement? In middle school, should you be applying for more competitive high schools? When do you do this? Anything else you need for high school?* Trainers circulate or stay one per group if there are two trainers and two groups. This activity can be done as a full group calling ideas out. The idea of the smaller groups is that everyone has a chance to think first and maybe notice that this information is actually needed. Trainers should not simply provide information, participants should or no one will be listening. When the groups are done, they can write or say out loud their ideas so that the trainer can write it at the front of the room. The trainer should make sure to cluster responses into domains so that the result provides students with a sense that they know something about each of the target areas: which classes, for how much credit, and what credit entails. Each group will know parts of the information needed in each cluster; together, they may well know everything. At this point organize; do not add. This allows students see that they have some knowledge about Class Topics (math, science, history, and English are core classes), Class credits (to count for credit, grades must be above a threshold), Class distribution (how many of each kind of class is needed), and Attendance (too many absences will bar graduation). Trainers should reinforce students' knowledge. The trainer then passes out actual requirements. *Can someone help pass out the requirements?*

Read your state's requirements for high school aloud. Handouts should have courses needed: how many math, science, history, English, and other credits needed. They should also say what level is needed, attendance requirements (unexcused absences are the opposite of attendance), GPA requirement, state and national exams, and deadlines and procedures for applying to competitive high schools. Translate these into common terms and connect these to the newsprint list of requirements that students have already generated.

Now I am handing out sample course sequences from a high school. Some high schools make it easier than other high schools to meet requirements to graduate. If you know what you need, you can have a plan from the ninth grade on no matter which high school you attend. The trainer reads course sequences out loud. *Now I will read the course sequences for another high school.* The idea is to show that they are not the same so that choices matter. The goal is to provide structure to what students already know, to give them a sense that they have a path and know the steps. Say a few words about what is covered in each class. Ask students if they know *what is in algebra?* Solving for x. *What is in geometry?* Working with shapes. *What is in trigonometry?* Working with angles. *What is in biology?* It is about the body and living things. *What is in chemistry?* It is about elements and how they are combined. *What is in physics?* It is about gravity, magnetism, and other features of the natural environment. By articulating what the courses are, trainers provide participants a sense of how things fit. This reduces the sense that the future is chaotic or random.

Okay. So we have a sense of what courses are needed to graduate high school. How do you get from high school to the next point? What is needed? Anything other than graduating from high school? Can anyone give examples of what you need?

Are there certain courses you need to take in high school? Does it matter what grades you get? What else do you need besides courses and grades? What about sports or extracurricular activities? Are there tests you take? Anything else? When do you do these things?

This can be done as a large group or in pairs as before. Students write or say out loud their ideas on newsprint. These are organized by the trainer so that what comes out is a clear summary in terms of students' guesses about courses and other requirements. The trainer then passes out Xeroxes of admissions for a local college or university that might be a reasonable choice. These are again read aloud and teased apart—what is required, which course is that? Is it the same as graduating high school or are there other specific requirements. Time permitting, do this again for a college of university mentioned by students in prior sessions or for another college or university that has different requirements, if none mentioned, though usually some are. If someone has wanted engineering, look at the requirements and see if they differ by program within a university. They often do.

[Pass out snacks.]

Finishing middle school and high school, graduating, and getting to the next step are part of getting to your future goals. There also can be other requirements. So working on your plan is a good idea. Each class builds on the one before—especially math and science courses.

Laying out the sequence will be surprising to students who had been simply showing up at school and assuming that there was no particular order to schooling. There is no need to focus negatively on specifics (e.g., avoid saying, "If you want to be a doctor, you better get really good science and math grades"). STJ is not career planning. It is helping students see the future as close, school as a way to get to their future, and obstacles along the way as normal.

Note: The focus of School-to-Jobs is school; hence, the focus is on getting education as the step to future goals. Parent and Youth Sessions are devoted to the job versus career issue and to the skills employers want. For groups in which students may be questioning whether high school graduation is in the cards (e.g., children aging out of foster care), following are school-to-work issues that can be raised if the session is taking place in a longer format.

Say you want to go from school to employment. What do people do at their jobs? What skills do you need to do these things? Start by telling me what people do. Trainers should help participants to think of the concrete tasks that make up most jobs and then write these tasks on newsprint. The domains that should be covered are as follows: (1) talking with customers/clients/people; (2) reading and writing about a paragraph's worth of text; (3) doing some math, solving some calculations; (4) computer skills, including word processing, data entry, and using a cash register or inventory monitoring system. These skills come from descriptions of new hires in a recent national survey of employers.

Say you want to convince someone to hire you, what do employers ask to see before hiring? Trainers should help participants to think about what is needed for jobs they can get now versus jobs they would want as adults. A high school degree is pretty much required and students should know that. Skills should be written on newsprint. The skills that should be covered are as follows: (1) high school diploma, (2) related experience, (3) vocational training, and (4) references. These are taken from a recent national survey of employers.

4.5.10.6.3 Next Session (3–6 minutes)

We are nearing the end of the session. What did we do today? Get responses. Students should be able to say that they figured out about requirements to get from their current year in school through high school and college. *What was new?* Get responses. Students should be able to say that they learned about the specific courses needed to graduate high school and that these courses build on one other and that one's goals should take into account the plan to get there.

Next session is the last session of STJ in school. We will celebrate, go over where we have been, and get your opinions on each session [if parents sessions are included, say *and we will think about next steps.*] *We are also going to have our party.* (Get votes as to what to have among choices that you can provide—pizza?)

Trainers rate each member's participation and add comments as needed.

Thank you for participating in the School-to-Jobs program. We would like your feedback. Please rate this session by marking the number that fits your opinion and give you ideas for improvement.

To what extent was this session											
Boring	1	2	3	4	5	6	7	8	9	10	Interesting
Difficult	1	2	3	4	5	6	7	8	9	10	Easy
Not useful	1	2	3	4	5	6	7	8	9	10	Useful
To what extent did this session											
Provide no new way of thinking	1	2	3	4	5	6	7	8	9	10	Provide a new way of thinking
Provide no new information	1	2	3	4	5	6	7	8	9	10	Provide new information

We want to improve this session. What would make it better?

_____

_____

_____

4.5.11 Session 11: Wrapping Up and Looking Forward

4.5.11.1 OVERVIEW

Youth join a circle to go over each of the sessions. Have students say what each session was by focusing on the main activity. As they state an activity, ask them what they learned. This can be like Session 1—Introductions, everyone has a skill to help him or her succeed this year in school and get to the next year. By repeating each session activity and take-home point, students get a coherent sense of what STJ is about. Making connections across sessions clarifies to students that they now have a set of tools for the future. Youth help us improve the program—they tell us what they liked and disliked about the program so far. If you are including parents and community member sessions next, talk about expectations and concerns for the second part of the program. Discussion should then move to issues of contact with and communication with adults who can help in the issues that were raised until now.

4.5.11.2 TAKE-HOME POINT

What I do now makes a big difference for attaining my possible selves for next year, for the next few years, and farther as an adult. Possible selves that are linked to strategies and to time and place of action become action goals. There are forks (choices) and roadblocks (failures) along the way. It will be difficult and may feel impossible, but asking questions helps break down what I need to find out and helps me connect to others—positive forces and models—as well as to learn from negative forces and models of what not to do.

4.5.11.3 MATERIALS

- Party supplies
- Pencils, paper, markers, and newsprint
- Attendance and participation notebook
- Digital camera
- STJ goal newsprint from Session 1

4.5.11.4 ROOM SETUP

Tables or desks to accommodate all, circular positioning

4.5.11.5 POINTS FOR REINFORCEMENT

1. Recalling sessions and linking them to the core STJ message
   a. Current choices matter; the link to the future starts now.
   b. Everyone can connect present and future, and current actions with future selves.
   c. Adult future selves feel close when linked to near future selves through school-focused strategies.
   d. Difficulty can mean importance.

4.5.11.6 AGENDA

1. Last session
2. What did we do at STJ?
3. Summary
4. Evaluation
*5. Next session
*6. Getting parent contact information

* These items are for groups that include parents and community member sessions.

4.5.11.6.1 Last Session

Greet participants by name and take attendance. Greet latecomers by name. *Today is our last in-class session of School-to-Jobs. What did we do last session?* Youth should be able to describe the main issues; see overview. *How does that connect to the sessions before? How does that connect to the program overall?* Youth should be able to talk about how the last session tied to other sessions, including adult images, timelines, strategies, asking questions to solve problems, and working together as a group.

This is our last session of STJ. Or for groups that continue on: *This is our last session of STJ that includes only students. The next part of the program will include parents and other adults.*

So we decided to have a party.

4.5.11.6.2 What Did We Do at STJ?

Snacks and so on should be available, and the group should move their chairs so that they are all sitting in a circle.

While having our party, we want to go over all of the sessions and learn from you what you liked and did not like, which sessions were helpful, and what you thought the main point was. Can anyone start? What was the first session? The trainer should get as many comments as possible on each session. Going in order helps connect the concepts to each other. So if a student skips a session, turn to others to get that session on the newsprint. For each session, participants should name the activity, specify the point of it, indicated what they learned, say whether it was, and indicate what could be done to make it better in the future. Get everyone's opinion at the end of the best and worst sessions and what he or she might change. Make sure to write responses down. Student responses matter. Reinforce this. Prior students have improved the program. Use feedback from students to reinforce core STJ points, and repeat the STJ goal from Session 1.

Here is an overview of all the sessions. In Session 1, youth learned school-skill-focused introductions, named the group, played human knot, and set ground rules. In Session 2, youth chose pictures of their adult selves. Domains of adulthood (jobs, lifestyle, relationships, and community involvement) were introduced. In Session 3, youth connected adult far future selves to current positive and negative forces that model how to stay on track or become derailed. In Session 4, students worked on personal timelines with roadblocks and forks in the road. Thus, Sessions 3 and 4 helped students begin to articulate difficulties along the way as normal and meaning that the tasks at hand were important, not impossible. In Session 5, participants completed worksheets to link far and near future to current action (i.e., because, I will, by, when during the day). In Sessions 6 and 7, youth put stickers of next year expected and to-be avoided possible selves on their posters and drew red lines to strategies they are using now and blue lines to strategies they could use. Then they put in adult possible selves (career, relationships, lifestyle, and community participation) and considered which strategies they are using now that actually help attain adult possible selves. Session 8 was the impossible-at-first puzzles. Session 9 was the math class problem and everyday problems crumpled on the floor solved with questions. Session 10 was graduating and going to the next phase. So the last three sessions all involved translating a future self into current action, handling difficulties by asking questions, trial and error, and considering positive and negative forces.

4.5.11.6.3 Summary

So we worked on adult images, positive and negative forces, near and far possible selves strategies and action plans, forks in the road, overcoming obstacles, puzzles, and learning about requirements to get to next steps. (For groups ending now), *Here is the STJ goal: How did we do at accomplishing this? Now we need your evaluation—here are the forms.* For groups continuing to the next two sessions, continue after this to the next section.

4.5.11.6.4 Evaluation

Pass out evaluation sheets for both *this session* and the *overall program evaluation*.

4.5.11.6.5 Next Session

This is a section for groups having next meetings.

In STJ we talked about obstacles and everyday problems, positive and negative forces; the idea is to get a person who is a positive force to know about STJ. Often people talked about parents or other adults in their life that way. Having positive forces and communicating with them helps work on action goals. In the next two sessions we will bring in parents or other adults who are positive forces in your lives as well as other community members to learn "informational interviewing." Elicit from students opinions about how adding parents will change/influence group. Trainers should encourage students to participate in second phase. Ask youth for numbers to reach their parents and ask them to be sure to let them know about the program. *We want you to come. Give us your contact information so we can reach a parent or the family member in your life who is your positive force.*

Trainers should thank participants for coming and participating. Trainers should be sure that they have contact information for the participants.

4.5.11.6.6 Getting Parent Contact Information

Trainers rate each member's participation and add comments as needed.

4.5.11.7 SESSION 11: WRAPPING UP, LOOKING FORWARD: SESSION EVAULATION

Thank you for participating in the School-to-Jobs program. We would like your feedback. Please rate this session by marking the number that fits your opinion and give you ideas for improvement.

To what extent was this session											
Boring	1	2	3	4	5	6	7	8	9	10	Interesting
Difficult	1	2	3	4	5	6	7	8	9	10	Easy
Not useful	1	2	3	4	5	6	7	8	9	10	Useful
To what extent did this session											
Provide no new way of thinking	1	2	3	4	5	6	7	8	9	10	Provide a new way of thinking
Provide no new information	1	2	3	4	5	6	7	8	9	10	Provide new information

We want to improve this session. What would make it better?

_____

_____

_____

ID: _____

What is today's date? _____/_____/_____
MONTH   DAY   YEAR

Thank you for participating. We would like your feedback.

These are questions about the program.

To what extent was **this program**											
Boring	1	2	3	4	5	6	7	8	9	10	Interesting
Difficult	1	2	3	4	5	6	7	8	9	10	Easy
Not useful	1	2	3	4	5	6	7	8	9	10	Useful
To what extent did **this program**											
Provide no new way of thinking	1	2	3	4	5	6	7	8	9	10	Provide a new way of thinking
Provide no new information	1	2	3	4	5	6	7	8	9	10	Provide new information

These questions are about your trainer

To what extent was **my trainer**											
Boring	1	2	3	4	5	6	7	8	9	10	Interesting
Unknowledgeable	1	2	3	4	5	6	7	8	9	10	Knowledgeable
Confusing	1	2	3	4	5	6	7	8	9	10	Clear
Critical of my ideas	1	2	3	4	5	6	7	8	9	10	Interested in my ideas

How much did **my trainer**					
	Not at all	A little	Some	Pretty Much	A great Deal
Seem to understand the problems I face in trying to succeed at school and in the future?	1	2	3	4	5
Listen closely to comments made by participants?	1	2	3	4	5
Respond to people by using specific examples?	1	2	3	4	5
Criticize participants' ideas?	1	2	3	4	5
Provide equal opportunities for people to share their ideas?					

In general **my trainer** was							
	Very	Somewhat	A Little	Neither or Neutral	A Little	Somewhat	Very	
Unenthusiastic	1	2	3	4	5	6	7	Enthusiastic
Unknowledgeable	1	2	3	4	5	6	7	Knowledgable
Cold	1	2	3	4	5	6	7	Warm
Confusing	1	2	3	4	5	6	7	Communicating clearly

ID:_____

These are questions about how you felt in the sessions.

During the sessions **I felt**	Not at All	A Little	Some	Pretty Much	A Great Deal
. . . comfortable participating and asking questions	1	2	3	4	5
. . . that I could trust others in the group to listen to what I had to say	1	2	3	4	5
. . . that the other participants shared their experiences and concerns about the future	1	2	3	4	5
. . . that other participants have the same problems that I do	1	2	3	4	5
. . . that the material and the discussion were relevant to my situation	1	2	3	4	5
. . . that my ideas would be criticized by another group member	1	2	3	4	5

These are questions about what **the group** felt like to you. The **group felt**. . .

	Very	Somewhat	A Little	Neither or Neutral	A Little	Somewhat	Very	
Hostile	1	2	3	4	5	6	7	Supportive
Cold	1	2	3	4	5	6	7	Warm
Insincere	1	2	3	4	5	6	7	Sincere
Rejecting	1	2	3	4	5	6	7	Accepting
Unenthusiastic	1	2	3	4	5	6	7	Enthusiastic

ID:_____

How many of the **helpful ideas** you received from this workshop were provided by:

	Hardly Any	A Few	Some	A Lot	Almost All
Other participants?	1	2	3	4	5
The trainers?	1	2	3	4	5
You?	1	2	3	4	5

How **confident** do you feel about doing the following things successfully?

	Not At All	A Little	Some	Pretty Much	A Great Deal
Introduce yourself in a way that emphasizes your skills	1	2	3	4	5
Imagine yourself as an adult in terms of work, relationships, community involvement and lifestyle	1	2	3	4	5
Develop a timeline to get to your adult self, including forks in the road and stumbling blocks	1	2	3	4	5
Take action in the present to make becoming like your desired adult self more likely	1	2	3	4	5
Break down everyday situations to see the problems to be solved	1	2	3	4	5
Ask for help in making plans for your future	1	2	3	4	5
Take needed classes to graduate and work toward your future self	1	2	3	4	5

ID:_____

Here are questions about **your expectations for the future**

	Not At All	A Little	Some	Pretty Much	A Great Deal
How much do you expect that difficulties and setbacks will arise in your efforts to do well in school and train for your future?	1	2	3	4	5
How much are you prepared to deal with difficulties and setbacks, that is, do you have plans or ideas about how to react and what to do next?	1	2	3	4	5
When a setback happens, *how much* will you be able to come up with alternatives and focus on moving forward?	1	2	3	4	5
How much do you feel that you may have to go through many setbacks and attempts before you get the job you like?	1	2	3	4	5

How many days of the School-to-Jobs workshop did you attend?_____

4.6 PARENT AND YOUTH SESSIONS

4.6.1 Sessions 1 and 2: Building an Alliance and Developing Communication Skills

4.6.1.1 OVERVIEW

Topics covered are introductions, review of previous sessions, points of concern, emerging themes, and active listening/taking the floor. Parents and youths pair up with a marble draw and introduce one another in terms of their strengths, skills, and experiences in school and the world of work (parents are thus not likely to be paired with their own child). Parents and youths separate to discuss concerns about the coming transitions from middle to high school and into adulthood. Parents and youths join to discuss themes that emerge in the issues raised by each. Trainers role-play active listening and taking the floor. Parents pair off with their own youth to try out being an active listener and taking the floor on points of concern from the previous discussion. Afterwards participants have a chance to process active listening and talk about ways that they can practice this skill in the time until the next session. At the end of each session, participants will be asked to rate how we are doing. They will also be asked to sign informed consent forms to allow us to stay in contact with them. If the STJ groups were 25 people, it may be necessary to run two sessions so that total attendance is not doubled. There are segments that are easier to run with two trainers.

4.6.1.2 ROOM SETUP

The start and end are in a circular setup with a board or newsprint so people can see each other as well as materials.

There should be a second room space so that when parents and youth separate they are not talking over one another.

There should be space for parents and students to pair off and practice with some privacy, though trainers need to circulate.

4.6.1.3 MATERIALS
- Having the floor/active listening sheets
- Pencils and paper
- Prepared-in-advance newsprint sheets with AIMS of SCHOOL to JOBS, definition of INTRODUCTION, definition of ACTIVE LISTENING, definition of HAVING the FLOOR.
- Newsprint and markers
- Nametags for parents and students
- Attendance and participation notebook
- Camera and film
- Food (foods that can be carried are especially good)

4.6.1.4 POINTS FOR REINFORCEMENT
1. Parents and youth are both concerned about the youth doing well.
2. Parents and youth have different perspectives about what they think are the most pressing problems facing youth in their transition to high school.
3. Parents are trying to do their best to help their children succeed.
4. Active listening is surprisingly difficult but can be done.

5. Parents and youth are willing to talk to each other about difficult problems if the other is willing to listen.

4.6.1.5 AGENDA

1. School-to-Jobs
2. Introductions
3. Concerns
4. Active listening and having the floor
5. Practice
6. Feedback and the future

4.6.1.5.1 School-to-Jobs Overview

For parents, who are joining us for the first time, welcome to School-to-Jobs. Today is the first youth/parent session: Communicating Concerns and Active Listening. I am ___ and this is ___ (trainers give your names.). And this is (Observer's name) who is observing the sessions to make sure we cover everything we are supposed to. The observer isn't actually a participant; she is just here to watch. School-to-Jobs is a program that is run jointly by ___ and _____ Middle School. It is a program about planning for the future and how school now is related to jobs students will have in the future. Can one of our students tell parents what we have been doing so far at School-to-Jobs? Youth are asked to volunteer an overview of what they have discussed to this point. After eliciting the youths' memories of what they did and why, trainers should provide a session-by-session review of the major points in order so parents get a feel for the sequence and "building on" that has occurred. Use the overview from Session 11. *"Good. Until now we looked at adult images, thought about role models, timelines, and how to get there and then spent some time thinking about strategies and ways to overcome obstacles and think about alternatives. Finally, everyone has had a chance to work on everyday problem solving and begin to think about the process of getting to high school, through high school, and to whatever training needed afterwards."* The trainer put up the prepared STJ goal sheet from Session 1.

> *School-to-Jobs AIM:*
> *Helping create a road map from school to the world of work.*
>
> *By:*
> *Connecting the present to the near (next year) and far (adult) future and working on strategies that can be used to attain near and far goals.*

4.6.1.5.2 Introductions

Since parents and students don't know each other yet, the first thing we are going to do is introductions. We worked on introductions in the first session of School-to-Jobs. (Allow for responses.) *Can any of the students tell what an introduction is?* Elicit responses. *When we began School-to-Jobs, we did introductions based on skills and abilities each person has to do well in school.* Hang preprinted newsprint from Youth Session 1.

An introduction is a way of presenting someone and getting a sense of someone as a person. Introductions are usually brief and share some personal information and information relevant to the context. Since our focus is School-to-Jobs, our introductions will focus on experiences with school or on the job, skills and capabilities, and effectiveness in the face of challenges. Instead of just introducing yourself, we'll have partners introduce each other. You will introduce the person with the same colored marble as you. Write down notes for yourself so you can do a good job introducing your partner to the group; you need his or her name and skill or ability for succeeding in school or in the world of work next year.

Okay, I am passing around two bags; parents take from one bag and students from another. That way you'll be introducing each other. Use two marble bags, one for parents and one for youth so that parents and youth have to work as partners. Those who choose like colors are paired and should move their chairs so that they are sitting in pairs. Give pairs a few minutes to learn about each other (name and skill or ability to help succeed at school, at work, or at finding work). Then have them go around in a circle and introduce each other. Ask a student to repeat the names, then a parent and so on. *Take a few minutes to get information; then we'll hear from all of the pairs.*

After pairs have introduced each other: *Who can say the names of everyone?* Try this once or twice. *Our first goal today will be to think about areas of concern for the coming year as students move through the eighth grade and hopefully into high school. What we'll do is first divide up into two groups—a parent group and a student group. Each group will list their concerns for themselves/their student. Then we'll come back into the large group and look at the commonalities and differences.*

4.6.1.5.3 Concerns

Assign one trainer per group; separate to different rooms if possible. In each room, the trainer tapes up newsprint labeled Areas of Concern. *So what are your areas of concern—issues you feel need to be worked on* (dealt with, taken care of, monitored, discussed) *in the coming year?* Samples are homework, grades, deciding what to do in high school, dating, curfew, freedom, and autonomy. . . any issues related to the coming year. The trainer should use multiple sheets and try to organize common topics together on the page as they come up. Reinforce participation, reinforce coming up with multiple topics, and reinforce any comments that connect concerns to previous concerns raised or to issues raised in previous School-to-Jobs sessions.

Okay, any other concerns? Let's head back to the other room and join the group.

Trainers tape up the concerns newsprint sheets. *First, let's read through what the concerns of the parents were.* Trainer, read the newsprint out loud. *What were the kinds of issues raised by parents?* Write on fresh newsprint the issues raised. Get involvement and groupings of issues. *Let's see what the students were concerned about.* Trainer, read the newsprint out loud. *What were the kinds of issues raised by students?* Write the issues raised on fresh newsprint. Get involvement and groupings of issues. Write on new newsprint in three sections. *What common concerns do parents and students raise? What concerns are raised only by parents? What concerns were raised only by students?* The group should end up seeing that both students and parents are concerned about school, but students also want autonomy and parents want to supervise. Students are also concerned about friends in a somewhat different way than parents are. *These sound like pretty important issues to talk about. Let's take a break and when we come back, we'll be working on communicating about these issues.*

BREAK (Provide Food)

4.6.1.5.4 Active Listening and Having the Floor

Before the break we talked about the concerns parents and students have for next year. These are all pretty important issues. When there is an important topic of concern, it is sometimes hard to communicate about it, especially since, as we just saw, even though there is some overlap, there are a lot of differences in the ways students and parents see the points of concern. The tricky thing with communicating about important issues is that the other person may want to tell you his or her own issues while you are trying to talk about something else. Sometimes you feel like you have already tried to talk about the issue before, so you don't really believe you can get the other person to listen.

Say that you needed to discuss a point of concern. How would you do it? Can someone give some examples of how communicating goes in your house? Give parents and students a chance to respond. *Okay, and how do you think communicating ought to go?*

The trainer elicits from parents and youth ideas as to how to best set up communication; ideas should be things such as pick a time when the other person has time to listen to you, speak in a way that the other person will listen—don't shout or call names, don't lecture, give the other person a chance to talk. Write all of this on newsprint. Reinforce how much they already know.

Read out loud the ideas. *Say we try these ideas—as a role-play. Then you can tell us how we did and maybe see other things to add.* Trainers role-play using only what was brought up, *only* the rules elicited. Role-play should make clear which rules were missing; usually these are the rules for the listener.

Okay, what was good about this? What did not work? The trainer should elicit the fact that rules for the listener were not included. *What should we add?* The trainer should write down—Get more ideas—especially the idea of turn taking and the need to have a chance to speak and also listen to the other on the issue you want to raise, but this means you have to give the other person a chance to raise his or her own issues and have a chance to speak and listen on that issue as well.

Okay, so let's go through all of our ideas for communicating: Trainer, read through the list out loud. *We have a short card with reminders for the speaker and the listener. What we focused on is how to be an active listener. Sometimes it is easy not to really listen to the other because you are busy getting your points ready for your turn to speak. But the idea here is that if you know you'll get a chance to speak you can really listen and make sure you understand what the speaker is saying. This will make for better communication and might help work on issues of concern. I'll pass these out.* Read out loud: *The rules for speaker are: Don't go on and on. Pause and let the listener check what out he or she has understood. Speak for yourself. The rules for the listener are: Listen for why things are important to the speaker. Check out your understanding. Ask for examples and explanations. Don't offer your own opinion or thoughts. Concentrate on what the speaker is saying.*

Can someone read out loud the rules for the speaker? Have someone read. *Can someone give examples of why these rules might help?* Discuss examples. *Okay, let's try rules for the listener; can someone read these out loud? How would this work* (get examples)?

4.6.1.5.5 Practice

What we will do now is practice using these rules. Everyone will divide up into pairs with their own parent. Pick a topic that you want to raise from the list of concerns we wrote together or another concern you have for next year. First, the parent picks and is the speaker for a few minutes and the student is the listener. Then the student gets to speak to the parent on this same topic and the parent is the listener. Because the parent started this topic, the parent then should have a chance to respond while the student listens again. After about 10 or 15 minutes, switch. Now the student gets to pick a topic of concern and be the speaker while the parent listens; then the parent is the speaker and the student listens. Because the student started this topic, the student then should have a chance to respond while the parent listens again. Take about 10 or 15 minutes for the second round as well.

It is hard to be an active listener so we will be going around the room checking on how you are doing with having the floor and being an active listener. Separate yourself so that it won't be too noisy to hear your partner.

Trainers should wander through the room, *actively* checking on communication; stop pairs that are off track and get them to do the active listening skills. Ask the pairs questions to make sure they are using all of the rules for whichever role they are playing. These include the following: Have you asked for examples or clarification? Have you paused to make sure the listener understands? If the listener asked you questions, did you respond to clarify before continuing?

BREAK

What was that like? In what ways was that different from the way you usually talk? (Get feedback from students and parents.) *When can this be helpful?* (Examples: important topics, ones you have already fought about, things that are ongoing.) *How might this way of talking help in these situations?* (Example: Knowing the other person will give you a chance to talk and will try to listen.) *What is hard about doing this?* (Look for barriers. For example: it seems quicker just to tell the student what to do because there are other kids and little time—this seems like it would take longer.) *What could you do to overcome these barriers if you wanted to use this skill?* (Elicit ideas.) *Could everyone practice this skill in the coming week before the next session? What about you—when could you guys do this?* (Get some commitment from each parent–student pair as to a time or place, etc.)

4.6.1.5.6 Feedback and the Future

Next time we will be inviting some community members so that we can learn about a valuable communication tool for finding out about jobs: informational interviewing. We look forward to seeing everyone again. The last thing we need for you to do for today is to fill out our evaluation sheets so we will know your opinions.

Thank you very much for participating and we will see you next session.

Trainers rate each member's participation and collect evaluation forms.

"The Floor"	
Rules for the Speaker	*Rules for the Listener*
• Don't go on and on.	• Listen for why things are important to the Speaker.
• Pause and let the Listener check out what he or she understood.	• Check out your understanding.
• Speak for yourself.	• Ask for examples and explanations.
	• Don't offer your own opinions or thoughts.
	• Concentrate on what the Speaker is saying.

4.6.1.7 BUILDING AN ALLIANCE, DEVELOPING COMMUNICATION SKILLS: SESSION EVALUATION

Thank you for participating in the School-to-Jobs program. We would like your feedback. Please rate this session by marking the number that fits your opinion and give you ideas for improvement.

To what extent was this session											
Boring	1	2	3	4	5	6	7	8	9	10	Interesting
Difficult	1	2	3	4	5	6	7	8	9	10	Easy
Not useful	1	2	3	4	5	6	7	8	9	10	Useful
To what extent did this session											
Provide no new way of thinking	1	2	3	4	5	6	7	8	9	10	Provide a new way of thinking
Provide no new information	1	2	3	4	5	6	7	8	9	10	Provide new information

We want to improve this session. What would make it better?

_____

_____

_____

4.6.2 Sessions 3 and 4: Informational Interviewing

4.6.2.1 OVERVIEW

Parents and youth think through how they got or plan to get a job. Discuss issues related to getting a job versus having a career plan. This leads to discussion of how to learn about jobs, careers, and occupations. The skill of informational interviewing is introduced, taught, and practiced. First, parents and youth practice on each other, and then community members join the group and are used to practice the skill and give feedback about how to do it in real life.

4.6.2.2 ADDITIONAL PARTICIPANTS

In order to run this session you will need to have an equal number of working community members as you have participant youths. Community members should be balanced by gender and reflect the racial-ethnic composition of youth participants. Community members should have occupations that match an expectable range of jobs for youth. Highly unusual jobs or occupations with extremely low likelihood of attainment are less useful for this session (even though they may be exciting) than are ones that youth can actually use as models. Community members are located via personal networks, invited to participate, and provided with a copy of the informational interview in advance. They should be told that youths will interview them about their job and that they will not be asked to give any prepared remarks. The goal is for youth to learn to talk with adults with jobs.

4.6.2.3 ROOM SETUP

This session requires multiple rooms and movement between rooms. First, parents and youth will meet together, and then they will need to be able to divide into pairs with a space of their own. When community members join the session, there needs to be space for each community member to be individually interviewed. These rooms should be contiguous so that youth can move easily from room to room. Finally, community members will meet in a room separately from parents and youth prior to joining them for the final discussion.

4.6.2.4 MATERIALS

- Worksheet on informational interviewing
- Pencils and paper
- Newsprint and markers
- Nametags for parents and students
- Attendance and participation notebook
- Camera and film
- Foods that can be carried are especially good; the session is long and food is a mood elevator.

4.6.2.5 POINTS FOR REINFORCEMENT

1. Every parent has some skills in finding and keeping a way to make a living.
2. Parents and youth want the youth to have a job or career that is interesting and provides for a reasonable standard of living.
3. Parents and youth have some knowledge about how to make career plans.
4. Asking questions helps make a realistic plan.

5. Parents and youth can ask questions about jobs, what they are like, and what are the skills needed to get them.

6. People in the community, whom you don't know, are most likely happy to answer these questions.

4.6.2.6 AGENDA

1. Last session
2. Getting a job or planning to get one
3. Informational interviewing—what is it?
4. Informational interviewing—practice
5. Informational interviewing with community members
6. Feedback and the future

4.6.2.6.1 Last Session

Greet everyone by name as they enter. *It is good to see everyone back again. Before we start today's session, let's review what we discussed and did last time.* Circulate an attendance list as you begin the first discussion. Ask for a volunteer from the group. Responses should include student session review, introductions, common concerns of parents and students, and active listening. Mention any of these points, if forgotten by volunteer. Thank volunteer for input. *That's right, we touched on a few different things last time. We found out that parents and students have similar and different concerns and that active listening is a good way of communicating those concerns. I hope some of you tried to use the communication skills we learned last time.* Get some feedback on how having the floor went at home and encourage people to keep using it as it gets easier with practice.

4.6.2.6.2 Getting a Job or Planning to Get One

Today we will be thinking more specifically about jobs. (To Parents): *Who is working or has worked in the past?* (Basically everyone). *One of the issues we have begun to think about is how youth can become the adult selves that they have described. One of the big areas of adulthood is a job. Let's try to list the ways adults get jobs. For example, how did you get the job you have now?* Trainers write on newsprint what parents are saying. (To Students): *What can you do to find out what kind of job you want to have?*

Trainers write youths' and parents' comments on separate newsprint sections. Youth and parents will be responding in a general open discussion; this may be dominated by parents first as they are telling facts—what they did. Youth are asked to say what they could do. Parents may add to this as well. One trainer tracks the youths' comments, and the other trainer tracks the parents' comments by writing them on newsprint. *Everyone has a lot of ideas about how to find out information about jobs he or she may want. What is the difference between having a job and having a career?* Elicit responses from both parents and students. Some parents may say that they currently have jobs, but they want their student to plan for a career. Ask parents to explain what they mean by this. All that is needed is to emphasize the more general points as parents make them. Jobs are distinguished from careers or occupations in that parents have jobs or ways to make sure that there is food on the table and a roof over their heads. Careers and occupations are planned for and trained for. Ask parents how they made plans for careers or decided on training. Add this to the list. Many parents will share that either they did not plan and assumed it would just happen or that they had children and therefore could not continue training. Some may say they have received training, but it turned out that the training did not get them the job they wanted, and so on. Trainers should keep writing and feeding back points as they emerge. The general problem issue that emerges here is that it is hard to know what jobs are available and it is difficult to figure out what training is needed for this job. Jobs that seem interesting from the outside may turn out to have unexpected negative aspects. Parents also may mention that there are things about jobs that turn out to be important which they did not think about before they had them—this includes such issues as whether there are opportunities for promotion and whether the skill to be learned can be used elsewhere. Parents may express frustration that they still really do not know enough about jobs in the marketplace. Youth will say that they really know even less so it seems impossible to really know what jobs they want or how to train for them. Someone may say that, in the real world, you need to know someone who has the kind of job you want so you can talk with him or her about it. This point will be your lead into introducing the concept of informational interviewing.

4.6.2.6.3 Informational Interviewing—What Is It?

As it turns out, one of the best ways to learn whether a job or career is really interesting for you—what it would be like every day to have this job, what training and prior experience are needed to get the job, and something about the conditions on the job—is to talk to other people who have the job you are interested in.

Talking with someone who has a job about that job is called informational interviewing. Often people think about calling to ask for a job—an employment interview—but informational interviewing is used to learn about a job or about the kinds of jobs available at a certain place.

The leader should write a heading on newsprint entitled "Informational Interviewing" and define it—a way of learning about possible jobs and careers from people who are currently working in that area or a similar area. *From what has already been said, what questions would be good to ask people who have jobs that you might be interested in? Is this something that any of you have ever done?*

4.6.2.6.4 Informational Interviewing—Practice

Now it is your turn to try informational interviewing. The trainer should start a new newsprint sheet entitled "Questions for Informational Interviewing." *Can we take a moment and come up with a few questions that you would ask someone who had the job/career you are interested in.* Participants will give questions such as "How much do you earn? And what are the benefits?" And so on. Trainers should list what is said on the newsprint. Reflect back on parents' comments as a source of questions. Reinforce questions that seem reasonable and think aloud about other ways to word questions that might seem too personal, for example, "How much do you make?" and help the group find a different way to ask them, for example, "How much do people in a position like yours earn?"

Read aloud the questions that have been generated.

Good, we have a list of good informational interviewing questions. We have prepared an informational interviewing question sheet with questions similar to the ones you thought of. What we will do is go through this list of questions, see whether there are some on our list that should be added, and then practice doing an informational interview.

Students will get a chance to practice by interviewing a parent (not your own) about the job she or he currently has or what she or he does to earn a living. First, have students read aloud the questions and reword them, if necessary, into questions that make sense to them or have words that they would use. Next, divide the group into parent-youth pairs, using the same marble task as in the Introductions activity. Parents and youth draw from separate bags containing equal numbers of different colored marbles, and those drawing the same color are paired up, except if they are related. Youth should interview a parent on a job the parent has or has had in the past. Then the parent should interview the youth on being a middle school student—this is to give the youth a sense of what being the target of an informational interview feels like.

So everyone can work on informational interviewing, parent and youth pairs move into separate parts of the room so that pairs do not distract each other. Pairs work together at practicing the interview.

BREAK (10 minutes)

4.6.2.6.4.1 PREPARING FOR INFORMATIONAL INTERVIEWING WITH COMMUNITY MEMBERS
Ask pairs to come back to the meeting room to discuss their experience. *Before proceeding with the next section, let's talk about how the interviewing process went with your partner.* Let the group discuss the process.

Community members who have agreed to have the group do informational interviews with them will soon join us. Each student will get to do an informational interview with each of the community members. What you should do is mark the questions you think you want to ask since, of course, you cannot ask any one person all of these questions. Students will be the informational interviewers. The parent who was your informational interviewing partner will go with you. Her or his job will be to watch you and write down anything she or he notices that could be helpful. They might write down follow-up questions that they would have asked to get more information or to understand better what the community member is saying. Parents should also write down what is good about the way the student is doing the interview and what could be improved. After all of the interviews are done, we will ask parents and students to talk about how it went and then we will ask community members how they think it went in separate rooms. Then everyone will have a chance to ask the community members questions. You will have 15 minutes with each person.

BREAK (5 minutes, depending on whether community members have arrived)

4.6.2.6.5 Informational Interviewing with Community Members
Community members should be scheduled to arrive at this point. They are introduced and then dispersed to separate contiguous rooms. Each youth and parent will have 15 minutes to do an informational interview. Trainers should knock on the door and say, "Excuse me, Mr./Mrs. X, your next appointment is here," in the event that pairs are not finishing and moving after 15 minutes. Trainers should move between rooms, listening from the hallway just to make sure that things are going well, but not going into rooms unless a major problem has occurred (e.g., the parent-partner has taken over the interview).

BREAK (5 minutes)

4.6.2.6.6 Feedback and Looking to the Future

When a full cycle of interviews has been completed, and all youth have interviewed all of the community members, the trainers will divide community members into one room and parents and youth to a second room. A facilitator leads each group.

In the parent-youth group: *Now that you have completed your informational interviews, how was the process for students, first?* Write down responses as youth talk. *Parents, what are some of the comments or points you wrote down during the interview?* Write these points on newsprint. This is also a time for hearing any comments about the community members or the interview situation. *Is there anything anyone else wants to add?*

In the community members group: *First, How was this experience and what could be improved about this experience? What made being a part of this process easy for the community members? What made it hard (if anything)?* Let the conversation flow but make sure that all questions are asked and discussed. Are there other community people whom they would like to see involved? This should be documented on newsprint. *What was useful in this session? Were there any questions that should be added or omitted?* This should also be documented on newsprint.

Next, bring both groups together for a joint session. *Now we will have a group discussion about how everyone felt about the informational interviewing process.* The newsprint sheets generated separately should be brought together, if relevant. Read aloud what parents thought youths could do to improve, get feedback from community members on the parents' suggestions, and ask what community members think was useful about what youth did or could be improved. List these comments on newsprint. To the community members: *What ideas or tips do they have about how to make contacts to set up informational interviews?*

To the youth: *How did you feel during the interviews?* Youth generally find the process interesting and not difficult. *Okay, so what about doing informational interviewing outside of School-to-Jobs. How would that work?* Trainers are to elicit whether youth can imagine doing this and how it would work. Youths should be prompted to suggest how to do this and what would stand in their way of doing it. Ask community members: *Are the youths' plans likely to work? What would happen if a youth called the community member's place of work and said, "My name is _____, I am 13 years old. I think I would like to work at a job like this one when I am grown up. Could I talk with someone about what you do?"* Community members should be prompted to describe both what would happen if someone called and what would be the best way to ask to do an informational interview. Community members should be prompted to talk about things like scheduling and making phone calls, what to wear, how long to expect to be there, and so on.

This session should be closed by having youth talk about the kinds of places that they might be interested in going to do an informational interview. Elicit ideas about how they could start. *Before we go, we have a session evaluation form that we would like you to fill out. We really appreciate your feedback.* Hand out evaluations to parents, students, and community members. Thank everyone: community members, parents, and youths.

Trainers rate each member's participation and pick up evaluation forms.

INFORMATIONAL INTERVIEWING WORKSHEET

1. I am interested in hearing about (name their type of work). Can you tell me a little about it here at (the place you are interviewing at)?

2. (If more than one job title is mentioned) I'd like to hear more about the job of

   _____

3. What is it like to do this job? Is there some daily routine?

4. What kind of person fits in best? What personal characteristics are the best fits for this job?

5. What type of training and previous experiences does it require?

6. Is there any on-going training? Can you describe it?

7. How would you describe the supervision received by a person in this position?

8. What equipment or machines, including computers and software are used in this job?

9. Are there special requirements or skills needed to have this job?

10. What is the range of salary generally paid to a person in this field?

11. Could you describe the work conditions or job setting (is it in an office, is it noisy and so on)?

12. What do you predict will be happening in this field in 5 or 10 years?

13. What opportunities are there for promotion?

14. What pose the most problems for people who have interviewed for or tried to train for this job?

15. How did you come to this job, what types of jobs or training did you have before?

16. What are some of the satisfactions of this job?

17. What are some of the headaches of this job?

18. Are there other people or organizations you recommend I contact for more information about this job?

19. Is there anything else you think I should know about this job?

Thank the person for his or her time and help and leave.

4.6.2.8 THE SCHOOLS-TO-JOBS PROGRAM
INFORMATIONAL INTERVIEWING

Informational Interviewing is way of learning about jobs that you may be interested in having in the future. By talking with someone who has a job or works in an area that you may be interested in, you can learn both more about the job and the training and skills needed on the job. Informational interviewing can help you come up with a plan for how to prepare for jobs you might be interested in later in the future.

Informational interviews can be done by phone or in person. If you are setting up an in-person meeting, be sure you know how to get there and exactly when you are supposed to meet. Be sure you ask with whom you will be meeting. Ask how to spell the name so you are not confused when you arrive. When the interview is finished, thank the person for his or her time and help, and leave. When you get home, it is a good idea to follow up with a short thank-you letter.

1. Before you go, be sure to double-check:

    a) Appointment DATE: _____ TIME: _____

    b) Name of person you will interview _____

    (CHECK SPELLING WITH SECRETARY IF UNSURE)

    c) Name of company or organization: _____

    d) Address: _____

    e) Record information on how to get to the interview. If you did not get directions, call back and ask. You can ask these questions of a secretary if there is one. Indicate whether you are coming by car or public transportation for better directions.

1. Greet the person, express enthusiasm at being there, and begin the interview.

2. Say "I am interested in hearing about being a (name of job or area). Can you tell me a little about what it is like?"

3. What is it like to do your job? What is the daily routine?

4. What personal characteristics help make a good (name of job or area of interest)?

5. What previous experiences help to do well?

6. Do you get training while you are on the job?

7. How are you supervised?

8. What special requirements are there, what skills are important?

9. What is it like to work here—is it quiet or noisy, do you work alone or with others?

10. What do you predict will be happening in this area of work in 5 or 10 years?

11. What are some of the satisfactions of having this job?

12. What are some of the headaches of having this job?

13. Is there anything else you think I should know about this job?

4.6.2.10 INFORMATIONAL INTERVIEW SESSION EVALUATION

Thank you for participating in the School-to-Jobs program. We would like your feedback. Please rate this session by marking the number that fits your opinion and give you ideas for improvement.

To what extent was this session											
Boring	1	2	3	4	5	6	7	8	9	10	Interesting
Difficult	1	2	3	4	5	6	7	8	9	10	Easy
Not useful	1	2	3	4	5	6	7	8	9	10	Useful
To what extent did this session											
Provide no new way of thinking	1	2	3	4	5	6	7	8	9	10	Provide a new way of thinking
Provide no new information	1	2	3	4	5	6	7	8	9	10	Provide new information

We want to improve this session. What would make it better?

_____

_____

_____

4.7 FIDELITY ASSESSMENT MEASURES

4.7.1 Summary

MEASURE	WHO RATES	WHEN RATED	WHAT IS RATED
Receipt of Treatment			
• Attendance	Trainer	Each session	Each student
• Active participation	Trainer	Each session	Each student
• Quality of participation	Observer	Rotating (5 students each session)	Each student
• Product content-analysis	Research staff	End of intervention	Student products
Delivery of Treatment			
• Fidelity checklists	Observer	Each session	Implementation
• Trainer engagement (labeled session quality)	Observer	Each session	Trainer skills
• Trainer established tone (Labeled session quality)	Observer	Each session	Trainer-group affect
• Student atmosphere	Participants	End of intervention	Emotional tone
• Skill presentation	Participants	End of intervention	Presentation of skills
• Holistic feel	Research staff	End of intervention focus group	Experience as whole

4.7.2 School-to-Jobs Observation Forms

SCHOOL-TO-JOBS OBSERVATION FORM

Youth Session 1

Site: _____   Trainer: _____

Group _____   Observer _____   Date ____/____/____

Task	Y	N	Detailed Trainer Activity	Y	N	Group Behavior	Y	N
Agenda hung								
Start on time			START TIME: _____					
Opening								
Welcome			Greet and welcome participants			Talk with trainer		
			Greet latecomers			Talk with each other		
Introductions			Trainer introduces self (Name, Organization)			Listen		
			States there is observer/videographer/camera in the room to observe trainer (improve program not grade students)			Acknowledge observer/ videographer if present		
Introduction								
Introduce the concept of introductions as goal oriented			Ask what an introduction is			Share ideas		
			Reinforce: is a way of saying who you are and what you can contribute					
			Different goals for introductions					
Introduce School-to-Jobs as success oriented			Show preprinted newsprint definition (Introduction)					
			Ask about skills and abilities for succeeding in school			Share ideas		

Task	Y	N	Detailed Trainer Activity	Y	N	Group Behavior	Y	N
Introductions task								
Group creation process			Explain activity			Listen		
			Pass out marbles			Take marble Find partner		
Creating sense of competence			Ask for questions					
			Circulate, check for understanding			Talk in pairs		
			Make big circle			Form circle		
			Ask youth to introduce partners/ask for repetition of names			Introduce partner, repeat names and skills		
			State specific plan for who is speaking					
			Take attendance					
			Trainer participates					
Expectations & concerns								
Elicit sense of self-control			Introduce new task, explain concept					
			Ask for examples			Participate		
			Use newsprint to write group expectations					
			Use newsprint to write group concerns					
			Reinforce and repeat 4 basic themes (seeing both my far and near future/developing strategies to work toward my future/seeing the path between now and my future/getting help (parents, community members, and teachers can be resources)			Listen		

Task	Y	N	Detailed Trainer Activity	Y	N	Group Behavior	Y	N
Rules								
Provide a sense of safety			Elicit group rules (everyone participates, no name calling)			Participate		
Everyone participates			Write on newsprint					
Goals								
			State goal			Listen		
			Show prepared newsprint					
Naming group								
			Explain activity					
			Give examples, elicit ideas			Participate		
			Call for a vote			Vote		
Schedule								
			Explain session schedule			Listen		
			Provide contact information			Write		
			Write on board					
			Review names					
[Line task]								
			Explain task, line up from youngest to oldest without talking (Encourage/when completed, ask month of birth)			Participate		
			Reinforce cooperation					
			Congratulate on success					

Task	Y	N	Detailed Trainer Activity	Y	N	Group Behavior	Y	N
Human knot task								
Group creation process			Explain task, stand in circle, cross arms in front and grab hands of two people across the circle, then without letting go of hands, get them uncrossed so that we are again in a circle			Participate		
			Trainer is part of the circle			Move, reform circle		
			Congratulate					
			Reinforce cooperation					
			Review—Ask participant to name all names (take attendance as this happens)			Respond		
Next session and good-byes								
			Summary statement: We discussed strengths to succeed					
			Connecting statement: Next session we will work on adult images			Listen		
			Pass out session evaluation forms (elicit help doing so)			Complete evaluation forms		
			Pass out snacks (elicit help doing so)			Eat		
			Ask for help rearranging the room			Rearrange room		
			Say good-byes/collect evaluation forms			Good-byes		
			Rate participant participation levels					
End on time			END TIME:					

Youth Session 2

Site: _____

Trainer: _____

Group _____

Observer _____

Date ____/____/____

Task	Y	N	Detailed Trainer Activity	Y	N	Group Behavior	Y	N
Agenda hung								
Start on time			START TIME: _____					
Opening								
Welcome			Greet participants and latecomers by name			Greet trainer and each other		
			Say pick up nametag. Take attendance					
			Say today is Session 2, Adult Images					
Bridging			Ask for what happened last session (Learned names about each other, expectations, concerns, games as a team, adding and building on each other's skills)			Participate, say what did and why		
Images								
Introduce the concept of adult images			Explain task—choosing pictures that represent images of yourself as an adult. Each to pick 3 to 5 pictures, what do they mean for you and when these will be true of you, afterwards share			Listen		
Create personal images			Make instructions clear/Ask for questions			Ask questions		
			Have participants begin			Move around room, picking pictures		
			Pass out snacks if people are finishing at different times			Eat		
			Mingle—check for understanding			Write ideas		

Task	Y	N	Detailed Trainer Activity	Y	N	Group Behavior	Y	N
Share			Have everyone rejoin circle			Eat		
			Explain task—show 1 picture and explain to group, while group listens and pays attention			Participate		
			Write participant responses on newsprint, clustering by themes			Listen		
Domains of adulthood								
Highlight various domains			Explain task—participant to call out what they thought was similar about everyone's adult images			Participate		
Reinforce personal competence in noticing connections, ability to contribute to the group			Highlight themes that emerge (e.g., jobs, family, friends, community involvement, lifestyle; trainer need only mention domains that did emerge)			Similarities, connections		
Next session and good-byes								
			Summary statement: Adult images can be about jobs, family, friends, community involvement, and lifestyle (only those group brought up or implied) (adult images + repeat themes)			Listen		
			Connecting statement: Next session we'll identify models and forces that help us work on those adult images that are goals			Listen		
			Pass out session evaluation forms (elicit help doing so)			Help, complete evaluation forms		
			Good-byes/collect evaluation forms			Say good-byes		
			Rate participant participation levels					
End on time			END TIME:					

SCHOOL-TO-JOBS OBSERVATION FORM

Youth Session 3

Date ____ / ____ / ____

Site: _____

Trainer: _____

Group _____

Observer _____

Task	Y	N	Detailed Trainer Activity	Y	N	Group Behavior	Y	N
Agenda hung								
Start on time			START TIME: _____					
Opening								
Welcome			Greet participants and latecomers by name			Greet trainer and each other		
			Say pick up nametag. Take attendance					
			Say today is Session 3, Positive Role Models and Negative Forces					
Bridging			Ask for what happened last session (picked pictures of adult images, when would happen and what had in common) (reinforce participation)			Participate		
			Ask for domains of adulthood that discussed and then add (lifestyle, career, relationship, community involvement)					
Role models and negative forces								
Adults images come from somewhere			Ask for what are positive models and negative forces.			Participate		
			Reinforce participation.					
			Use newsprint to write what they say					
			Define terms (positive role model—image of attained goal/supports work toward it, negative model—image of failure, undermines effort)			Discuss		
			Show preprinted newsprint definition					

Task	Y	N	Detailed Trainer Activity	Y	N	Group Behavior	Y	N
Those close to us, often parents, can support or tear down			Explain task/handout worksheets. Start with job domain—write/draw adult image and a positive and negative force for that adult image			Write goals/role models/force		
			Pass out snacks (elicit help doing so)			Eat		
			Mingle, help individually as needed					
			Have students organize into circle					
			Discuss models and negative forces. Have students give examples, write on newsprint as they do (cluster similar)			Participate		
			Read through positive model list			Listen, participate		
			Read through negative force list			Listen, participate		
			Say close people in our lives can be supporting					
			Say everyone has negative forces					
Next session and good-byes								
			Summary statement: Adult images can be about jobs, family, friends, community involvement, and lifestyle			Participate		
			Summary statement: We worked on role models and negative forces; everyone has both			Complete evaluation forms		
			Connecting statement: In the next session, we will work on timelines into the future			Say good-bye		
			Pass out session evaluation forms (elicit help doing so)			Help, say good-byes		
			Good-byes/collect evaluation forms					
			Rate participation					
End on time			END TIME:					

SCHOOL-TO-JOBS OBSERVATION FORM

Youth Session 4

Site: _____

Trainer: _____

Date ___/___/___

Group _____

Observer _____

Task	Y	N	Detailed Trainer Activity	Y	N	Group Behavior	Y	N
Agenda hung								
Start on time			START TIME: _____					
Opening								
Welcome			Greet participants and latecomers by name			Greet		
			Say pick up nametag. Take attendance			Listen		
			Say today is Session 4, Timelines			Participate		
Bridging			Ask about last session (domains of adulthood, positive and negative forces for career possible selves)			Give themes—jobs, family, community participation, friends, lifestyle		
			Trainer bridges last session and this session (Today we will begin to map out how to get from now to the future)					
Timelines activity								
Create sense of linear time			Ask what are timelines, ask for ideas			Participate		
			Write ideas on newsprint					
			Repeat examples (linear, history, now in future and future not for sure)					
			Reveal preprinted newsprint timeline (general)					

Task	Y	N	Detailed Trainer Activity	Y	N	Group Behavior	Y	N
Create sense of competence to handle choices, obstacles; reinforce naturalness of obstacles			Explain fork in the road			Listen		
			Explain obstacles-barriers-roadblocks					
Create timelines			Reveal preprinted timeline into the future					
			Explain the tasks—rough draft then on timeline, everything from now as far as can go, in order (at least 1 fork and 1 obstacle)					
			Pass out materials—tell to spread out			Help, spread out		
			Pass out snacks (elicit help doing so)			Eat		
			Repeat instructions as needed (out loud, individually)			Work		
			Circulate and provide help			Work		
Discuss timelines			Regroup Students (I know you are not done but. . .)			Regroup		
			Ask students to orient or turn chairs			Orient		
			Ask students to show timelines			Show timelines		
			Ask students to point to their fork in the road			Show forks		
			Ask students to point to their obstacle			Show obstacles		
			Get one or two students to state their fork			Participate		
			Get one or two different students to state their obstacle					
			Time permitting, suggest an additional step in the timeline for another student					

Task	Y	N	Detailed Trainer Activity	Y	N	Group Behavior	Y	N
Next session and good-byes								
			Summary statement: We discussed timelines, forks in the road, obstacles, and timelines into the future					
			Connecting statement: Next session is Session 5, Action Goals					
			Ask for help rearranging the room			Move desks, chairs		
			Pass out session evaluation forms (elicit help doing so)			Complete evaluation forms		
			Good-byes/collect evaluation forms			Say good-byes		
			Rate participation					
End on time			END TIME:					

SCHOOL-TO-JOBS OBSERVATION FORM

Youth Session 5

Site: _____ _____

Trainer: _____

Date ____ / ____ / ____

Group _____

Observer _____

Task	Y	N	Detailed Trainer Activity	Y	N	Group Behavior	Y	N
Agenda hung								
Start on time			START TIME: _____					
Opening								
Welcome			Greet participants/latecomers by name			Greet		
			Say pick up nametag. Take attendance			Listen		
			Say today is Session 5, Action Goals			Participate		
Bridging			Elicit description of last session activities.			Timelines, forks, obstacles		
			Reinforce key concepts: timelines, obstacles/forks in road					
			Ask about domains of adulthood			Jobs, family, lifestyle, community		
			Trainer bridges last session and this session (Say: action goals, timelines, adult images, positive and negative models)					
Action Goals								
Define term			What is a possible self? Elicit and reinforce idea that possible selves are attainable. Use newsprint to record responses			Listen		
			Before we talked about adult images, some were possible selves and others were dreams			Ask questions		
			What is the difference between a possible self and a dream?					

Task	Y	N	Detailed Trainer Activity	Y	N	Group Behavior	Y	N
			Reveal preprinted newsprint definitions (action goals)					
			Define terms (goal, action goal; an action goal has an adult possible self, closer possible self, strategy, and when and where actions occur; this takes the form of a sentence)					
Use worksheet to practice action goals			Explain task—write specific action goal for two domains of adulthood (because, I will, by, when-where)			Listen		
			Get help passing out handouts, snack			Help, eat		
			Ask group to spread out			Spread out, write		
			Circulate and provide help					
			Move back to circle			Move, help		
			Have students read their action goals (starting with someone who hasn't yet participated, going counterclockwise), use newsprint to cluster common themes by "I will" statements			Participate		
			For anyone who doesn't have today action, trainer helps, problem solves, and suggests working on different piece					
Next session and good-byes			Summary statement: Today we worked on action goals			Participate		
			Connecting statement: Next session we will work on possible selves and strategies					
			Pass out session evaluation forms (elicit help doing so)			Complete evaluation forms		
			Good-byes, collect evaluation/worksheets			Say good-byes		
			Rate participation					
End on time			END TIME:					

SCHOOL-TO-JOBS OBSERVATION FORM

Youth Session 6

Date ____ / ____ / ____

Group _____

Site: _____   Observer _____

Trainer: _____

Task	Y	N	Detailed Trainer Activity	Y	N	Group Behavior	Y	N
Agenda hung								
Start on time			START TIME: _____					
Opening								
Welcome			Greet participants and latecomers by name			Greet		
			Say: Pick up nametag. Take attendance					
			Say: This is Session 6, Possible Selves and Strategies					
Review of last session			Ask activities last session			Action goal, because, I will, by, when, where		
			Reinforce the concept of action goals (because, I will, by, when-where) link more distal goals to closer ones with activities to be done in certain times and contexts			Listen		
Bridging			Trainer statement of connection from last session to this session (last session we linked adult images to the next few years with action that could be done right now, this week)			Listen		
			This session we will focus on the really close future, next year.					
			Introduce new concepts (expected, to-be avoided possible selves, and strategies)					
			Reveal preprinted newsprint definitions (possible selves)					

Task	Y	N	Detailed Trainer Activity	Y	N	Group Behavior	Y	N
Connecting next year to strategies								
			Show preprinted strategies					
			Show blank poster board (left, middle, right)					
			Provide instructions for next year possible selves (focus on left only)					
Making poster boards			Explain use of Next Year Possivle Selves stickers (read and choose 5 expected, 5 to be avoided for you; can write your own, but after reading, do not pull off backing until picked best 5; choose expected for the left top and to be avoided for bottom)					
			Show with finger on board. Pass out sticker bag (repeat instructions read before peeling, only 5, top expected, bottom to be avoided)			Listen		
			Say move to your own space. Pass out boards (repeat instructions out loud)			Move, work		
			Ask for stickers back while explaining choosing strategies connecting to next year selves					
			Repeat instructions out loud and individually					
			Pass out strategy stickers (collect possible selves stickers)					
			Pass out snacks (elicit help doing so)			Eat		
			State instructions (ask if they are doing anything to work on a possible self and, if so, use a sticker to say what and place on board)			Raise hand for materials		
			Explains use of red markers, pass out red markers					

Task	Y	N	Detailed Trainer Activity	Y	N	Group Behavior	Y	N
			Explains use of red markers again out loud and individually					
			Walk through group continuously, helping, giving positive reinforcement, clarifying instructions					
			Explains use of blue markers					
			Ask for red back in exchange for blue					
			Circulate, look at boards, remark out loud; some possible selves have strategies we are using now, and they are marked with a red line; some possible selves have strategies we could be using but are not now, and they are marked with a blue line; some possible selves have no strategies, and the strategy space is blank.					
Next session and good-byes								
			Summary statement: Today worked on possible selves and strategies boards)			Listen		
			Connecting statement: Next session we will finish our poster boards by listing adult possible selves and seeing if there are pathways from next year to adulthood through current action			Complete evaluation forms		
			Pass out session evaluation forms (elicit help)					
			Good-byes			Move desks/chairs		
			Rate participation levels			Say good-byes		
End on time			END TIME:					

SCHOOL-TO-JOBS OBSERVATION FORM

Youth Session 7

Site: _____

Trainer: _____

Group _____

Observer _____

Date ____ / ____ / ____

Task	Y	N	Detailed Trainer Activity	Y	N	Group Behavior	Y	N
Agenda hung								
Start on time			START TIME: _____					
Opening								
Welcome			Greet participants and latecomers by name			Greet		
			Say: Pick up nametag. Take attendance					
			Say: Today is Session 7, Pathways to the Future			Listen		
Last session			Elicit description of activities last session			Poster board, stickers, possible self, strategies		
			Put up preprinted newsprint (possible selves and strategies)					
			Reinforce concepts (Possible selves are possible, not for sure, not just hopes. You can work on them with strategies. Strategies are things one does or can do now to make the possible real).					
Bridging			Trainer statement of connection from last session to this session (next year possible selves and strategies, connected with red lines if doing now, blue lines if could do).					
			Show poster board and point to right (adult possible selves)					
			Now we are going to do this part (point to right)					
			Show baggies. Say: I will give you a bag of expected and to be avoided adult selves. Read the stickers. Pick the best 5 expected and the best 5 to-be-avoided. Do not pull off backing.					

Task	Y	N	Detailed Trainer Activity	Y	N	Group Behavior	Y	N
Connecting next year and the future								
			Repeat instructions while passing back boards, ask to move			Move to space out		
			Repeat instructions while passing out adult stickers			Ask questions		
			Repeat instructions while circulating to look at boards, positively reinforce effort			Listen		
			Pass out snacks (elicit help doing so)			Eat		
			Explain markers and distribute. Say: Put the stickers back in the bag and I will trade you for a red marker. For each adult or to-be-avoided possible self, if a strategy that you are doing now can help you get to or avoid it, connect that strategy to the possible self with a red line.			Work on own		
			Circulate, repeat instructions, look at boards and check for understanding			Work on own		
			As students finish, offer to trade red markers with blue. Say: Look at the strategies you could use but are not using now. If any of these could help with adult possible selves; draw a blue line from the strategy to the possible self it could help.			Raise hands, swap markers		
			Circulate, repeat instructions, check boards			Work on board		
Sharing pathways								
			Ask students to move chairs, reorient to see each other's work			Move		
			Ask students to show their work			Show, listen		
			Define pathway					

Task	Y	N	Detailed Trainer Activity	Y	N	Group Behavior	Y	N
			Ask those with a red pathway to read a current pathway: strategy, next year, adult			Show, listen, talk		
			Ask those with a blue pathway to read a potential pathway: strategy could use, next year, adult			Show, listen, talk		
			Reinforce individual participation in activity					
			Make connection between next year and future (via strategies)			Listen		
			Define connection as pathways (strategy connects a next year self to adult self)					
			Ask students to share one pathway with the group (working around circle)			Share pathways		
Next session and good-byes								
			Summary statement: Today we worked on pathways			Listen		
			Connecting statement: Next session we will work difficult puzzles in life					
			Pass out session evaluation forms (elicit help doing so)			Complete evaluation forms		
			Pick up evaluation forms					
			Ask for help rearranging room					
			Good-byes			Say good-byes		
			Rate participant participation levels					
End on time			END TIME:					

SCHOOL-TO-JOBS OBSERVATION FORM

Youth Session 8

Site: _____

Trainer: _____

Date ____/____/____

Group _____

Observer _____

Task	Y	N	Detailed Trainer Activity	Y	N	Group Behavior	Y	N
Agenda hung								
Start on time			START TIME: _____					
Opening								
Welcome			Greet participants and latecomers by name			Greet		
			Say: Pick up nametag. Take attendance					
			Say: Today is Session 8, Puzzles					
Last session			Ask about last session activities			Possible selves, pathways, strategies, red, blue		
Bridging			Trainer statement of connection from last session to this session and overview of the questions addressed this session (sometimes it feels hard, impossible, so just have possible selves)					
			Elicit inoculation/vaccination discussion					
			Use newsprint to write student ideas					
			Today will work on inoculating from difficulty by solving puzzles that feel impossible					
			Reveal preprinted newsprint (Inoculation)					

Task	Y	N	Detailed Trainer Activity	Y	N	Group Behavior	Y	N
Solving Puzzle, 1								
			Provides puzzle activity instructions					
			Passes out Puzzle 1			Listen		
			Reads out loud					
			Asks students to work in groups to figure out how to solve (move to groups)			Move to groups		
			Have students regroup (orient to front) to give their plan of action and talk through how far they got in trying to solve the problem			Participate		
			Use newsprint to write out student plans, possible solution paths (or have students do it)					
			Reinforce cooperative participation, effort, ideas					
			Reinforce many ways to solve					
			Walk through Puzzle 1 solution					
			Reinforce that seems impossible before trying					
Solving Puzzle 2								
			Pass out snacks (elicit help doing so)			Eat		
			Get help passing out Puzzle 2			Help with passing out Puzzle 2		
			Read out loud Puzzle 2			Eat, listen		
			Asks students to work in groups to solve					
			Have students regroup (orient to trainer) to give their plan of action and talk through how far they got in trying to solve the problem			Participate		

Task	Y	N	Detailed Trainer Activity	Y	N	Group Behavior	Y	N
			Reinforce ways to solve the problem			Listen		
			Use newsprint					
			Write out student plans, possible solution paths (or has students do it)			Participate		
			Write out grid, as a possible solution path, solves out loud with students			Work as a group		
			Reinforces cooperative participation, effort, ideas					
			Reinforces responses that move toward problem solution					
			Show problem solution, reinforce how impossible it seems before trying					
Next session and good-byes								
			Summary statement: Everyday puzzles seem impossible; sometimes we need trial and error			Listen		
			Connecting statement: Next session we will practice dealing with everyday problems			Complete evaluation forms		
			Pass out session evaluation forms (elicit help doing so), pick up			Rearrange room		
			Good-byes			Say good-byes		
			Rate participation					
End on time			END TIME:					

SCHOOL-TO-JOBS OBSERVATION FORM

Youth Session 9

Site: _____

Trainer: _____

Date ____ / ____ / ____

Group _____

Observer _____

Task	Y	N	Detailed Trainer Activity	Y	N	Group Behavior	Y	N
Agenda hung								
Start on time			START TIME: _____					
Opening								
Welcome			Greet participants and latecomers by name			Greet		
			Say: Pick up nametag. Take attendance					
			Say: Today is Session 9, Solving Everyday Problems					
			Elicit description of activities in last session			Inoculation from difficulty, puzzles		
Last session			Trainer bridges last session and this session			Listen		
			Reinforce last session's concept (inoculation from thinking if it is difficult it is impossible). Say: often what is really difficult is not impossible; you just need to start to consider or plan.					
Bridging			Today I am going to give you an everyday problem. You will ask what you need to ask before solving it.					
			Then I will ask you for everyday problems you have. We will use what we learned to map out questions to ask before solving it.					

Task	Y	N	Detailed Trainer Activity	Y	N	Group Behavior	Y	N
Everyday Problem 1: Math								
			Have students move into groups			Move		
			Ask for student help to pass out math problem			Help		
			Read out loud math problem			Move into groups		
			Give students newsprint			Listen		
			Ask students to consider the questions they need to ask themselves to solve this			Work		
			Circulate, reinforce effort, ask questions					
			Have students hang up their newsprint or elicit their ideas and write it down			Participate		
			Have students move to one big circle			Move		
			Reinforce many solutions could do this as action goals: Because (adult image) I will (next year possible self) by (strategy) when and where during the day____), could do as timeline, with obstacles and forks, could do as asking for adult help (positive models, negative forces).			Participate		
Everyday Problems 2								
			Pass out snacks (elicit help doing so)			Eat		
			Ask: Think about a school problem like the math problem you faced (or are facing) in school			Listen		
			Have students write down problem, crumple it up and throw it on the floor in the middle of the room (should still be in circle)			Writes, throws paper on floor		

Task	Y	N	Detailed Trainer Activity	Y	N	Group Behavior	Y	N
			Trainer pushes all the problems toward himself or herself, takes four, and reads them out loud					
			Trainer provides reinforcement. Says: There are o many problems; everyone has at least one.					
			Now they are crumpled up.					
			Trainer reads out 4 problems, group selects one			Participate		
			Asks: What are questions to ask			Participate		
			Trainer stands with newsprint to write questions, writes in clusters by theme					
			Uses clusters to link back to the action goal, timeline, and possible self activities and for coming up with forks in the road obstacles, models to ask for help, negative forces to avoid					
Next session and good-byes								
			Summary statement: Today we looked at everyday problems			Listen		
			Connecting statement: More inoculation by looking at what you need to finish high school and get more training, such as college			Complete evaluation forms		
			Pass out session evaluation form (elicit help), pick up			Move desks, chairs		
			Good-byes			Say good-byes		
			Rate participation/label newsprint					
End on time			END TIME:					

SCHOOL-TO-JOBS OBSERVATION FORM

Youth Session 10

Date ____ / ____ / ____

Site: _____

Trainer: _____

Group: _____

Observer: _____

Task	Y	N	Detailed Trainer Activity	Y	N	Group Behavior	Y	N
Agenda hung								
Start on time			START TIME: _____					
Opening								
Welcome			Greet participants and latecomers by name			Greet		
			Say: Pick up nametag. Take attendance					
			Say: This is Session 10, Graduating			Participate		
Last session			Elicit description of activities			Solved math problem and everyday problems, used STJ activities to do it.		
Bridging			Last session we worked on everyday problems we with questions and STJ activities like timelines with forks in the road and obstacles, action goals, positive and negative forces. Today we are going to keep working on inoculation from difficulty.			Participate		
High School								
			Ask students to divide into groups or turn chairs			Move to groups		
			Explain activity (what does it take to graduate high school)			Listen		
			Circulate and check on groups' progress			Participate		

Task	Y	N	Detailed Trainer Activity	Y	N	Group Behavior	Y	N
			Move to one circle			Move, participate		
			Elicit students responses, write on newsprint (What classes, anything else? How many classes? Anything else? Attendance? Anything else? Behavior/citizenship)					
			Reinforce how much students know					
			Ask for help to pass out high school graduation requirements for own location					
			Read out loud					
			Ask for help connecting this to what students already said					
			Repeats process with a second high school					
			Highlights how not all high schools are the same but graduation requirements are the same					
			Facilitate connection of course names and content					
College			[Pass out snacks (elicit help doing so)]			[Eat]		
			Turn to your group work again			Turn and participate		
			Clarifies task: So we figured out graduating high school. We are going to do the same thing, for college, figuring out how to get from high school to college			Help		
			What do you need for college? Classes? Grades? What else?					
			Turns students back to center as they flag			Work in groups		
			Elicits and write responses on newsprint			Move		
			Passes out college entrance requirements			Participate		
			Helps link student statements to college					
			Repeats with another college, reading out loud the requirements and linking to student ideas					

Task	Y	N	Detailed Trainer Activity	Y	N	Group Behavior	Y	N
Next session and good-byes								
			Summary statement: Today we worked on finishing high school and getting to college			Listen		
			Connecting statement:: We will have a wrap-up session [and talk about inviting parents and community members]					
			Next session we will review all sessions and have a party					
			Pass out session evaluation form (elicit help), pick up			Complete evaluation form		
			Ask for help rearranging the room			Move desks, chairs		
			Good-byes			Say good-byes		
			Rate participation/label newsprint					
End on time			END TIME:					

SCHOOL-TO-JOBS OBSERVATION FORM

Youth Session 11

Site: _____ Group _____

Trainer: _____ [Observer _____]

Date ____ / ____ / ____

Task	Y	N	Detailed Trainer Activity	Y	N	Group Behavior	Y	N
Agenda hung								
Start on time			START TIME: _____					
Opening								
Welcome			Greet participants and latecomers by name			Greet		
			Say: Pick up nametag. Take attendance					
			Say: This is Session 11, Wrapping Up and Moving Forward. This is our last in-school STJ session; this is our wrapping up and looking forward session. I will ask you what we did each session and why, what was best, what was worst, and how to improve. This is also our STJ party					
Last session			Ask what happened last session			Get through high school, graduate to college		
Bridging			Trainer statement of connection from last session to this session and overview of this session (last session we worked on planning for—high school and college by knowing the requirements)			Listen		
Party								
			[Provide food and other party materials]			[Eat]		
			Ask to move desks/chairs to circle			Move desks to circle		

Task	Y	N	Detailed Trainer Activity	Y	N	Group Behavior	Y	N
What did we do at STJ?								
Review			Ask for what did in each of the previous sessions			Participate		
			Ask for help getting the right order			Participate		
			Write on newsprint					
			Elicit a reason for each session, how they connect					
Give voice to students			Ask for: favorite sessions, least liked sessions, what to change about program					
			Write responses on newsprint					
			Explain a connection between all sessions					
Next session and good-byes								
			Explain next phase of program			Help, eat		
			[Elicit from students' opinions about how adding parents will change/influence group]					
			Encourage students to participate in second phase					
			Pass out session evaluation forms			Complete evaluation form; say good-byes		
			Ask for help rearranging the room					
			Good-byes					
			Rate participation					
End on time			END TIME:					

SCHOOL-TO-JOBS OBSERVATION FORM

Parent and Youth Sessions

Session 1 & 2

Date ____/____/____

Site: _____   Group _____

Trainer: _____   Observer _____

Task	Y	N	Detailed Trainer Activity	Y	N	Group Behavior	Y	N
Agenda hung								
Start on time			**START TIME:** _____					
School-to-Jobs program			Elicit a review of activities			Participate		
			Reinforce student participation					
			Provide a STJ summary description and aim			Listen		
Introductions			Ask for students to tell what an introduction is			Participate, define		
			Define introduction			Listen		
			Model introductions by introducing one another (or oneself if a single trainer)					
			Pair students and parents for introductions; provide instructions for introducing partner			Interview partner		
			Ask for introductions			Perform introductions		
Concerns			Split parents and youth into two separate groups			Moves		
			Elicits concerns from parent group, writes on newsprint			Participates		
			Elicits concerns from youth group, writes on newsprint			Participates		
			Reconvene groups together			Moves		
			Tape up concerns from each group, read aloud			Listens		
			Directs examination of similarities, common themes, reinforces participation			Participates		
Break			Provides break for group			Mingles		

Task	Y	N	Detailed Trainer Activity	Y	N	Group Behavior	Y	N
Active listening and having the floor			Provide food			Eats		
			Elicit from parents and students best ways to communicate concerns to one another			Participate		
			Write responses on newsprint					
			Note that group possesses a lot of knowledge about communicating					
			Trainers role-play skit using only way to communicate brought up by group					
			Elicit responses from group about the role play (How was it? What should we add?)			Participate		
			Pass out handout rules for listener and speaker, read aloud					
Practice			Separate parent-child pairs to practice using communication rules to discuss a concern each has			Move		
			Circulate, help pairs to stick to rules when communicating			Talk with the handout		
Feedback and the future			Reconvene group			Move		
			Ask group about using rules when communicating			Participate		
			Encourage parents and students to use this method of communicating at home and with others			Respond		
			Provide information about next meeting. (Next time, we will work on how to find information about the kind of jobs you want in the future and we will have community members in those jobs providing additional information)					
			Encourage attendance at next session					
Evaluation			Provide session evaluation forms			Fill out, return		
Good-byes			Thank everyone for participation, good-byes			Good-byes		
End on time			TIME END: _____					

SCHOOL-TO-JOBS OBSERVATION FORM

Parent and Youth Sessions

Session 3 & 4

Site: _____ Group _____

Trainer: _____ Observer _____

Date ____ / ____ / ____

Task	Y	N	Detailed Trainer Activity	Y	N	Group Behavior	Y	N
Agenda Hung								
Start on time			**START TIME:** _____					
Opening			Greet student participants and parents by name			Greet trainers and each other		
			Circulate attendance list			Fill in		
Last meeting/ bridging			Elicit a review of last meeting's activities			Participate		
			Elicit rationale the activities (what learned)			Participate		
			Reinforce participation					
			Trainer states/reiterates (Last meeting we had a review of STJ, discussed common concerns of parents and students, and practiced communicating)			Listen		
			Feedback on how communication went at home. Encourage to keep using it					
			Today we figure out how to get information about the jobs and careers we want and learn a helpful skill to get information					
Getting a job or planning to get one			Elicit responses from parents about how do people find jobs; write responses on newsprint			Participate, listen		

Task	Y	N	Detailed Trainer Activity	Y	N	Group Behavior	Y	N
			Reinforce that most parents have this knowledge already			Listen		
			Elicit student responses about how people find out about the kind of jobs they want; write responses on newsprint			Participate, listen		
			Ask difference between job and career; write responses on newsprint			Participate, listen		
What is informational interviewing?			Introduce informational interviewing			Listen		
			Elicit questions that would be asked, write on newsprint			Participate		
			Pass out handout informational interviewing questions			Take forms		
Informational interviewing practice			Pair each parent with a youth partner (not their own) to practice interviewing techniques			Move		
			Circulate, insure each practices interviewing			Work in pairs		
			Reconvene all pairs and discuss interviewing process			Discuss		
Break			Provide a break			Mingle		
			Provide food			Eat		
			Reconvene the group			Rejoin		
Informational interviewing with community members			Introduce community members			Listen, greet community members		

Task	Y	N	Detailed Trainer Activity	Y	N	Group Behavior	Y	N
			Describe activity					
			Provide separate interview rooms for each community member					
			Have parent-youth pairs move from room to room doing informational interviews			Ask questions from list, write down or pay attention to responses, move		
Break			10-minute stretch and restroom break			Use break		
Feedback			Reconvene parents-youth in one room and community members in another			Return		
			Elicit responses about the interviewing (What went well? What can be added?)			Participate		
			Join all participants for final discussion			Reconvene		
			Encourage students to ask community members about doing this in the real world			Ask, listen		
Looking to the future			Encourage students to use informational interviewing technique in the future, provide handout for future use			Listen		
Evaluation			Pass out session evaluation forms			Complete evaluation forms		
Good-byes			Thank everyone for their participation, good-byes			Good-byes		
End on time			END TIME: _____					

4.7.3 Observer End-of-Session Ratings

4.7.3.1 SCHOOL-TO-JOBS END OF SESSION 1 OBSERVATION FORM

Date____/____/____   Observer_____   Site_____

Group _____   Trainers _____

1. **During today's session**, how many of the ideas about **introductions** were provided by participants compared to those provided by the trainers: *Circle one*

Trainers provided nearly all	Trainers provided most	Trainers provided somewhat more	Trainers & participants provided an equal amount	Participants provided somewhat more	Participants provided most	Participants provided nearly all
1	2	3	4	5	6	7

2. **During today's session**, the trainers: (5 = maximum appropriate given group activity)

Circle one number per item	Not at All	A Little	Some	Pretty Much	A Great Deal
a. Made supportive comments focused on participants' strengths?	1	2	3	4	5
b. Referred to participants by name?	1	2	3	4	5
c. Criticized participants' ideas?	1	2	3	4	5
d. Listened closely to participants' comments?	1	2	3	4	5
e. Responded using specific examples?	1	2	3	4	5
f. Provided equal opportunities for people to share their ideas?	1	2	3	4	5
g. Gave the group an opportunity to answer questions people asked?	1	2	3	4	5
h. Kept the group focused on topic?	1	2	3	4	5
i. Connected participants' ideas to program goals?	1	2	3	4	5
j. Self-disclosed to an appropriate degree if examples were needed?	1	2	3	4	5
k. Dwelt on individual participants' issues?	1	2	3	4	5

3. **During today's session** the trainers:

Circle one number per item	Disagree Strongly	Disagree Moderately	Disagree Slightly	Agree Slightly	Agree Moderately	Agree Strongly
a. Worked well together?	1	2	3	4	5	6
b. Were coordinated?	1	2	3	4	5	6
c. Referred to each other by name as appropriate?	1	2	3	4	5	6
d. Assisted each other with handouts and flipcharts?	1	2	3	4	5	6
e. Shared roles as appropriate?	1	2	3	4	5	6
f. Showed each other polite courtesy? (verbal or nonverbal)	1	2	3	4	5	6

4. **During today's session** the trainers were:

Circle one number per pair	Very	Some-what	A Little	Neither or Neutral	A Little	Some-what	Very	
a. Apathetic	1	2	3	4	5	6	7	Enthusiastic
b. Cold	1	2	3	4	5	6	7	Warm
c. Rejecting	1	2	3	4	5	6	7	Accepting
d. Tense	1	2	3	4	5	6	7	Relaxed
e. Hostile	1	2	3	4	5	6	7	Friendly
f. Insincere	1	2	3	4	5	6	7	Sincere
g. Unknowledgeable	1	2	3	4	5	6	7	Knowledgeable
h. Disorganized	1	2	3	4	5	6	7	Organized
i. Confusing	1	2	3	4	5	6	7	Clear

5. **During today's session** participants:

Circle one number per item	Not at All	A Little	Some	Pretty Much	A Great Deal
a. Used each other's names?	1	2	3	4	5
c. Listened to each other?	1	2	3	4	5
d. Engaged in workshop activities?	1	2	3	4	5
e. Shared ideas with each other?	1	2	3	4	5
f. Asked questions?	1	2	3	4	5

6. **During today's session**, group members were:

Circle one number per pair	Very	Some-what	A Little	Neither or Neutral	A Little	Some-what	Very	
a. Apathetic	1	2	3	4	5	6	7	Enthusiastic
b. Warm	1	2	3	4	5	6	7	Cold
c. Rejecting	1	2	3	4	5	6	7	Accepting
d. Tense	1	2	3	4	5	6	7	Relaxed
e. Hostile	1	2	3	4	5	6	7	Friendly
f. Insincere	1	2	3	4	5	6	7	Sincere
g. Indifferent	1	2	3	4	5	6	7	Supportive

NOTES

4.7.3.2 SCHOOL-TO-JOBS END OF SESSION 2 OBSERVATION FORM

Date_____/_____/_____   Observer_____   Site_____

Group _____   Trainers _____

1. During today's session, how many of the ideas about **adult visions** were provided by participants compared to those provided by the trainers:

Trainers provided nearly all	Trainers provided most	Trainers provided somewhat more	Trainers and participants provided equal amounts	Participants provided somewhat more	Participants provided most	Participants provided nearly all
1	2	3	4	5	6	7

2. **During today's session**, the trainers: (5 = maximum appropriate given group activity)

Circle one number per item	Not at All	A Little	Some	Pretty Much	A Great Deal
a. Made supportive comments focused on participants' strengths?	1	2	3	4	5
b. Referred to participants by name?	1	2	3	4	5
c. Criticized participants' ideas?	1	2	3	4	5
d. Listened closely to participants' comments?	1	2	3	4	5
e. Responded using specific examples?	1	2	3	4	5
f. Provided equal opportunities for people to share their ideas?	1	2	3	4	5
g. Gave the group an opportunity to answer questions that people asked?	1	2	3	4	5
h. Kept the group focused on topic?	1	2	3	4	5
i. Connected participants' ideas to program goals?	1	2	3	4	5
j. Self-disclosed to an appropriate degree if examples were needed?	1	2	3	4	5
k. Dwelt on individual participants' issues?	1	2	3	4	5

3. **During today's session** the trainers:

Circle one number per item	Disagree Strongly	Disagree Moderately	Disagree Slightly	Agree Slightly	Agree Moderately	Agree Strongly
a. Worked well together	1	2	3	4	5	6
b. Were coordinated	1	2	3	4	5	6
c. Referred to each other by name	1	2	3	4	5	6
d. Assisted each other	1	2	3	4	5	6
e. Shared roles as appropriate	1	2	3	4	5	6
f. Showed each other polite courtesy (verbal or nonverbal)	1	2	3	4	5	6

4. **During today's session,** the trainers were:

Circle one number per pair	Very	Some-what	A Little	Neither or Neutral	A Little	Some-what	Very	
a. Apathetic	1	2	3	4	5	6	7	Enthusiastic
b. Cold	1	2	3	4	5	6	7	Warm
c. Rejecting	1	2	3	4	5	6	7	Accepting
d. Tense	1	2	3	4	5	6	7	Relaxed
e. Hostile	1	2	3	4	5	6	7	Friendly
f. Insincere	1	2	3	4	5	6	7	Sincere
g. Unknowledgeable	1	2	3	4	5	6	7	Knowledgeable
h. Disorganized	1	2	3	4	5	6	7	Organized
i. Confusing	1	2	3	4	5	6	7	Clear

5. **During today's session,** participants:

Circle one number per item	Not at All	A Little	Some	Pretty Much	A Great Deal
a. Used each other's names?	1	2	3	4	5
b. Listened to each other?	1	2	3	4	5
c. Engaged in workshop activities?	1	2	3	4	5
d. Shared ideas with each other?	1	2	3	4	5
e. Asked questions?	1	2	3	4	5

6. **During today's session**, group members were:

Circle one number per pair	Very	Some-what	A Little	Neither or Neutral	A Little	Some-what	Very	
a. Apathetic	1	2	3	4	5	6	7	Enthusiastic
b. Cold	1	2	3	4	5	6	7	Warm
c. Rejecting	1	2	3	4	5	6	7	Accepting
d. Tense	1	2	3	4	5	6	7	Relaxed
e. Hostile	1	2	3	4	5	6	7	Friendly
f. Insincere	1	2	3	4	5	6	7	Sincere
g. Indifferent	1	2	3	4	5	6	7	Supportive

NOTES

4.7.3.3 School-to-Jobs End of Session 3 Observation Form

Date ＿＿ /＿＿ /＿＿   Observer ＿＿＿＿＿＿＿   Site ＿＿＿＿＿＿＿

Group ＿＿＿＿＿＿   Trainers ＿＿＿＿＿＿＿

1. **During today's session**, how many of the ideas about **role models and negative forces** were provided by participants compared to those provided by the trainers:

Trainers provided nearly all	Trainers provided most	Trainers provided somewhat more	Trainers and participants provided equal amounts	Participants provided somewhat more	Participants provided most	Participants provided nearly all
1	2	3	4	5	6	7

2. **During today's session**, the trainers: (5 = maximum appropriate given group activity)

Circle one number per item	Not at All	A Little	Some	Pretty Much	A Great Deal
a. Made supportive comments focused on participants' strengths?	1	2	3	4	5
b. Referred to participants by name?	1	2	3	4	5
c. criticized participants' ideas?	1	2	3	4	5
d. Listened closely to participants' comments?	1	2	3	4	5
e. Responded using specific examples?	1	2	3	4	5
f. Provided equal opportunities for people to share their ideas?	1	2	3	4	5
g. Gave the group an opportunity to answer questions that people asked?	1	2	3	4	5
h. Kept the group focused on topic?	1	2	3	4	5
i. Connected participants' ideas to program goals?	1	2	3	4	5
j. Self-disclosed to an appropriate degree if examples were needed?	1	2	3	4	5
k. Dwelt on individual participants' issues?	1	2	3	4	5

3. **During today's session** the trainers:

Circle one number per item	Disagree Strongly	Disagree Moderately	Disagree Slightly	Agree Slightly	Agree Moderately	Agree Strongly
a. Worked well together?	1	2	3	4	5	6
b. Were coordinated?	1	2	3	4	5	6
c. Referred to each other by name as appropriate?	1	2	3	4	5	6
d. Assisted each other with handouts and flipcharts?	1	2	3	4	5	6
e. Shared roles as appropriate?	1	2	3	4	5	6
f. Showed each other polite courtesy? (verbal or nonverbal)	1	2	3	4	5	6

4. **During today's session** the trainers were:

Circle one number per pair	Very	Some-what	A Little	Neither or Neutral	A Little	Some-what	Very	
a. Apathetic	1	2	3	4	5	6	7	Enthusiastic
b. Cold	1	2	3	4	5	6	7	Warm
c. Rejecting	1	2	3	4	5	6	7	Accepting
d. Tense	1	2	3	4	5	6	7	Relaxed
e. Hostile	1	2	3	4	5	6	7	Friendly
f. Insincere	1	2	3	4	5	6	7	Sincere
g. Unknowledgeable	1	2	3	4	5	6	7	Knowledgeable
h. Disorganized	1	2	3	4	5	6	7	Organized
i. Confusing	1	2	3	4	5	6	7	Clear

5. **During today's session** participants:

Circle one number per item	Not at All	A Little	Some	Pretty Much	A Great Deal
a. Used each other's names?	1	2	3	4	5
b. Listened to each other?	1	2	3	4	5
c. Engaged in workshop activities?	1	2	3	4	5
d. Shared ideas with each other?	1	2	3	4	5
e. Asked questions?	1	2	3	4	5

6. **During today's session**, group members were:

Circle one number per pair	Very	Some-what	A Little	Neither or Neutral	A Little	Some-what	Very	
a. Apathetic	1	2	3	4	5	6	7	Enthusiastic
b. Cold	1	2	3	4	5	6	7	Warm
c. Rejecting	1	2	3	4	5	6	7	Accepting
d. Tense	1	2	3	4	5	6	7	Relaxed
e. Hostile	1	2	3	4	5	6	7	Friendly
f. Insincere	1	2	3	4	5	6	7	Sincere
g. Indifferent	1	2	3	4	5	6	7	Supportive

NOTES

4.7.3.4 SCHOOL-TO-JOBS END OF SESSION 4 OBSERVATION FORM

Date____/____/____   Observer_____   Site_____

Group _____   Trainers _____

1. During today's session, how many of the ideas about **timelines** were provided by participants compared to those provided by the trainers:

Trainers provided nearly all	Trainers provided most	Trainers provided somewhat more	Trainers and participants provided equal amounts	Participants provided somewhat more	Participants provided most	Participants provided nearly all
1	2	3	4	5	6	7

2. **During today's session**, the trainers: (5= maximum appropriate given group activity)

Circle one number per item	Not at All	A Little	Some	Pretty Much	A Great Deal
a. Made supportive comments focused on participants' strengths?	1	2	3	4	5
b. Referred to participants by name?	1	2	3	4	5
c. Criticized participants' ideas?	1	2	3	4	5
d. Listened closely to participants' comments?	1	2	3	4	5
e. Responded using specific examples?	1	2	3	4	5
f. Provided equal opportunities for people to share their ideas?	1	2	3	4	5
g. Gave the group an opportunity to answer questions that people asked?	1	2	3	4	5
h. Kept the group focused on topic?	1	2	3	4	5
i. Connected participants' ideas to program goals?	1	2	3	4	5
j. Self-disclosed to an appropriate degree if examples were needed?	1	2	3	4	5
k. Dwelt on individual participants' issues?	1	2	3	4	5

3. **During today's session** the trainers:

Circle one number per item	Disagree Strongly	Disagree Moderately	Disagree Slightly	Agree Slightly	Agree Moderately	Agree Strongly
a. Worked well together?	1	2	3	4	5	6
b. Were coordinated?	1	2	3	4	5	6
c. Referred to each other by name as appropriate?	1	2	3	4	5	6
d. Assisted each other with handouts and flipcharts?	1	2	3	4	5	6
e. Shared roles as appropriate?	1	2	3	4	5	6
f. Showed each other polite courtesy? (verbal or nonverbal)	1	2	3	4	5	6

4. **During today's session** the trainers were:

Circle one number per pair	Very	Some-what	A Little	Neither or Neutral	A Little	Some-what	Very	
a. Apathetic	1	2	3	4	5	6	7	Enthusiastic
b. Cold	1	2	3	4	5	6	7	Warm
c. Rejecting	1	2	3	4	5	6	7	Accepting
d. Tense	1	2	3	4	5	6	7	Relaxed
e. Hostile	1	2	3	4	5	6	7	Friendly
f. Insincere	1	2	3	4	5	6	7	Sincere
g. Unknowledgeable	1	2	3	4	5	6	7	Knowledgeable
h. Disorganized	1	2	3	4	5	6	7	Organized
i. Confusing	1	2	3	4	5	6	7	Clear

5. **During today's session** participants:

Circle one number per item	Not at All	A Little	Pretty Some	A Great Much	Deal
a. Used each other's names?	1	2	3	4	5
b. Listened to each other?	1	2	3	4	5
c. Engaged in workshop activities?	1	2	3	4	5
d. Shared ideas with each other?	1	2	3	4	5
e. Asked questions?	1	2	3	4	5

6. **During today's session**, group members were:

Circle one number per pair	Very	Some-what	A Little	Neither Or Neutral	A Little	Some-what	Very	
a. Apathetic	1	2	3	4	5	6	7	Enthusiastic
b. Cold	1	2	3	4	5	6	7	Warm
c. Rejecting	1	2	3	4	5	6	7	Accepting
d. Tense	1	2	3	4	5	6	7	Relaxed
e. Hostile	1	2	3	4	5	6	7	Friendly
f. Insincere	1	2	3	4	5	6	7	Sincere
g. Indifferent	1	2	3	4	5	6	7	Supportive

NOTES

4.7.3.5 SCHOOL-TO-JOBS END OF SESSION 5 OBSERVATION FORM

Date____/____/____   Observer_____   Site_____

Group_____   Trainers_____

1. During today's session, how many of the ideas about **action goals** were provided by participants compared to those provided by the trainers:

Trainers provided nearly all	Trainers provided most	Trainers provided somewhat more	Trainers and participants provided equal amounts	Participants provided somewhat more	Participants provided most	Participants provided nearly all
1	2	3	4	5	6	7

2. **During today's session**, the trainers: (5 = maximum appropriate given group activity)

Circle one number per item	Not at All	A Little	Some	Pretty Much	A Great Deal
a. Made supportive comments focused on participants' strengths?	1	2	3	4	5
b. Referred to participants by name?	1	2	3	4	5
c. Criticized participants' ideas?	1	2	3	4	5
d. Listened closely to participants' comments?	1	2	3	4	5
e. Responded using specific examples?	1	2	3	4	5
f. Provided equal opportunities for people to share their ideas?	1	2	3	4	5
g. Gave the group an opportunity to answer questions that people asked?	1	2	3	4	5
h. Kept the group focused on topic?	1	2	3	4	5
i. Connected participants' ideas to program goals?	1	2	3	4	5
j. Self-disclosed to an appropriate degree if examples were needed?	1	2	3	4	5
k. Dwelt on individual participants' issues?	1	2	3	4	5

3. **During today's session** the trainers:

Circle one number per item	Disagree Strongly	Disagree Moderately	Disagree Slightly	Agree Slightly	Agree Moderately	Agree Strongly
a. Worked well together?	1	2	3	4	5	6
b. Were coordinated?	1	2	3	4	5	6
c. Referred to each other by name as appropriate?	1	2	3	4	5	6
d. Assisted each other with handouts and flipcharts?	1	2	3	4	5	6
e. Shared roles as appropriate?	1	2	3	4	5	6
f. Showed each other polite courtesy? (verbal or nonverbal)	1	2	3	4	5	6

4. **During today's session** the trainers were:

Circle one number per pair	Very	Some-what	A Little	Neither or Neutral	A Little	Some-what	Very	
a. Apathetic	1	2	3	4	5	6	7	Enthusiastic
b. Cold	1	2	3	4	5	6	7	Warm
c. Rejecting	1	2	3	4	5	6	7	Accepting
d. Tense	1	2	3	4	5	6	7	Relaxed
e. Hostile	1	2	3	4	5	6	7	Friendly
f. Insincere	1	2	3	4	5	6	7	Sincere
g. Unknowledgeable	1	2	3	4	5	6	7	Knowledgeable
h. Disorganized	1	2	3	4	5	6	7	Organized
i. Confusing	1	2	3	4	5	6	7	Clear

5. **During today's session** participants:

Circle one number per item	Not at All	A Little	Some	Pretty Much	A Great Deal
a. Used each other's names?	1	2	3	4	5
b. Listened to each other?	1	2	3	4	5
c. Engaged in workshop activities?	1	2	3	4	5
d. Shared ideas with each other?	1	2	3	4	5
e. Asked questions?	1	2	3	4	5

6. **During today's session**, group members were:

Circle one number per pair	Very	Some-what	A Little	Neither or Neutral	A Little	Some-what	Very	
a. Apathetic	1	2	3	4	5	6	7	Enthusiastic
b. Cold	1	2	3	4	5	6	7	Warm
c. Rejecting	1	2	3	4	5	6	7	Accepting
d. Tense	1	2	3	4	5	6	7	Relaxed
e. Hostile	1	2	3	4	5	6	7	Friendly
f. Insincere	1	2	3	4	5	6	7	Sincere
g. Indifferent	1	2	3	4	5	6	7	Supportive

NOTES

4.7.3.6 SCHOOL-TO-JOBS END OF SESSION 6 OBSERVATION FORM

Date____/____/____ Observer_____ Site_____

Group _____ Trainers _____

1. During today's session, how many of the ideas about **next year possible selves and strategies** were provided by participants compared to those provided by the trainers:

Trainers provided nearly all	Trainers provided most	Trainers provided somewhat more	Trainers and participants provided equal amounts	Participants provided somewhat more	Participants provided most	Participants provided nearly all
1	2	3	4	5	6	7

2. **During today's session**, the trainers: (5 = maximum appropriate given group activity)

Circle one number per item	Not at All	A Little	Some	Pretty Much	A Great Deal
a. Made supportive comments focused on participants' strengths?	1	2	3	4	5
b. Referred to participants by name?	1	2	3	4	5
c. Criticized participants' ideas?	1	2	3	4	5
d. Listened closely to participants' comments?	1	2	3	4	5
e. Responded using specific examples?	1	2	3	4	5
f. Provided equal opportunities for people to share their ideas?	1	2	3	4	5
g. Gave the group an opportunity to answer questions that people asked?	1	2	3	4	5
h. Kept the group focused on topic?	1	2	3	4	5
i. Connected participants' ideas to program goals?	1	2	3	4	5
j. Self-disclosed to an appropriate degree if examples were needed?	1	2	3	4	5
k. Dwelt on individual participants' issues?	1	2	3	4	5

PATHWAYS TO SUCCESS THROUGH IDENTITY-BASED MOTIVATION

3. **During today's session** the trainers:

Circle one number per item	Disagree Strongly	Disagree Moderately	Disagree Slightly	Agree Slightly	Agree Moderately	Agree Strongly
a. Worked well together?	1	2	3	4	5	6
b. Were coordinated?	1	2	3	4	5	6
c. Referred to each other by name as appropriate?	1	2	3	4	5	6
d. Assisted each other with handouts and flipcharts?	1	2	3	4	5	6
e. Shared roles as appropriate?	1	2	3	4	5	6
f. Showed each other polite courtesy? (verbal or nonverbal)	1	2	3	4	5	6

4. **During today's session** the trainers were:

Circle one number per pair	Very	Some-what	A Little	Neither or Neutral	A Little	Some-what	Very	
a. Apathetic	1	2	3	4	5	6	7	Enthusiastic
b. Cold	1	2	3	4	5	6	7	Warm
c. Rejecting	1	2	3	4	5	6	7	Accepting
d. Tense	1	2	3	4	5	6	7	Relaxed
e. Hostile	1	2	3	4	5	6	7	Friendly
f. Insincere	1	2	3	4	5	6	7	Sincere
g. Unknowledgeable	1	2	3	4	5	6	7	Knowledgeable
h. Disorganized	1	2	3	4	5	6	7	Organized
i. Confusing	1	2	3	4	5	6	7	Clear

5. **During today's session** participants:

Circle one number per item	Not at All	A Little	Some	Pretty Much	A Great Deal
a. Used each other's names?	1	2	3	4	5
b. Listened to each other?	1	2	3	4	5
c. Engaged in workshop activities?	1	2	3	4	5
d. Shared ideas with each other?	1	2	3	4	5
e. Asked questions?	1	2	3	4	5

6. **During today's session**, group members were:

Circle one number per pair	Very	Some-what	A Little	Neither or Neutral	A Little	Some-what	Very	
a. Apathetic	1	2	3	4	5	6	7	Enthusiastic
b. Cold	1	2	3	4	5	6	7	Warm
c. Rejecting	1	2	3	4	5	6	7	Accepting
d. Tense	1	2	3	4	5	6	7	Relaxed
e. Hostile	1	2	3	4	5	6	7	Friendly
f. Insincere	1	2	3	4	5	6	7	Sincere
g. Indifferent	1	2	3	4	5	6	7	Supportive

NOTES

4.7.3.7 SCHOOL-TO-JOBS END OF SESSION 7 OBSERVATION FORM

Date_____/_____/_____   Observer_____   Site_____

Group _____   Trainers _____

1. During today's session, how many of the ideas about **adult possible selves and pathways to the future** were provided by participants compared to those provided by the trainers:

Trainers provided nearly all	Trainers provided most	Trainers provided somewhat more	Trainers and participants provided equal amounts	Participants provided somewhat more	Participants provided most	Participants provided nearly all
1	2	3	4	5	6	7

2. **During today's session**, the trainers: (5 = maximum appropriate given group activity)

Circle one number per item	Not at All	A Little	Some	Pretty Much	A Great Deal
a. Made supportive comments focused on participants' strengths?	1	2	3	4	5
b. Referred to participants by name?	1	2	3	4	5
c. Criticized participants' ideas?	1	2	3	4	5
d. Listened closely to participants' comments?	1	2	3	4	5
e. Responded using specific examples?	1	2	3	4	5
f. Provided equal opportunities for people to share their ideas?	1	2	3	4	5
g. Gave the group an opportunity to answer questions that people asked?	1	2	3	4	5
h. Kept the group focused on topic?	1	2	3	4	5
i. Connected participants' ideas to program goals?	1	2	3	4	5
j. Self-disclosed to an appropriate degree if examples were needed?	1	2	3	4	5
k. Dwelt on individual participants' issues?	1	2	3	4	5

3. **During today's session** the trainers:

Circle one number per item	Disagree Strongly	Disagree Moderately	Disagree Slightly	Agree Slightly	Agree Moderately	Agree Strongly
a. Worked well together?	1	2	3	4	5	6
b. Were coordinated?	1	2	3	4	5	6
c. Referred to each other by name as appropriate?	1	2	3	4	5	6
d. Assisted each other with handouts and flipcharts?	1	2	3	4	5	6
e. Shared roles as appropriate?	1	2	3	4	5	6
f. Showed each other polite courtesy? (verbal or nonverbal)	1	2	3	4	5	6

4. **During today's session** the trainers were:

Circle one number per pair	Very	Some-what	A Little	Neither or Neutral	A Little	Some-what	Very	
a. Apathetic	1	2	3	4	5	6	7	Enthusiastic
b. Cold	1	2	3	4	5	6	7	Warm
c. Rejecting	1	2	3	4	5	6	7	Accepting
d. Tense	1	2	3	4	5	6	7	Relaxed
e. Hostile	1	2	3	4	5	6	7	Friendly
f. Insincere	1	2	3	4	5	6	7	Sincere
g. Unknowledgeable	1	2	3	4	5	6	7	Knowledgeable
h. Disorganized	1	2	3	4	5	6	7	Organized
i. Confusing	1	2	3	4	5	6	7	Clear

5. **During today's session** participants:

Circle one number per item	Not at All	A Little	Some	Pretty Much	A Great Deal
a. Used each other's names?	1	2	3	4	5
b. Listened to each other?	1	2	3	4	5
c. Engaged in workshop activities?	1	2	3	4	5
d. Shared ideas with each other?	1	2	3	4	5
e. Asked questions?	1	2	3	4	5

6. **During today's session**, group members were:

Circle one number per pair	Very	Some-what	A Little	Neither or Neutral	A Little	Some-what	Very	
a. Apathetic	1	2	3	4	5	6	7	Enthusiastic
b. Cold	1	2	3	4	5	6	7	Warm
c. Rejecting	1	2	3	4	5	6	7	Accepting
d. Tense	1	2	3	4	5	6	7	Relaxed
e. Hostile	1	2	3	4	5	6	7	Friendly
f. Insincere	1	2	3	4	5	6	7	Sincere
g. Indifferent	1	2	3	4	5	6	7	Supportive

NOTES

Date____/____/____   Observer_____   Site_____
Group _____   Trainers _____

1. During today's session, how many of the ideas about **solving puzzles** were provided by participants compared to those provided by the trainers:

Trainers provided nearly all	Trainers provided most	Trainers provided somewhat more	Trainers and participants provided equal amounts	Participants provided somewhat more	Participants provided most	Participants provided nearly all
1	2	3	4	5	6	7

2. **During today's session**, the trainers: (5 = maximum appropriate given group activity)

Circle one number per item	Not at All	A Little	Some	Pretty Much	A Great Deal
a. Made supportive comments focused on participants' strengths?	1	2	3	4	5
b. Referred to participants by name?	1	2	3	4	5
c. Criticized participants' ideas?	1	2	3	4	5
d. Listened closely to participants' comments?	1	2	3	4	5
e. Responded using specific examples?	1	2	3	4	5
f. Provided equal opportunities for people to share their ideas?	1	2	3	4	5
g. Gave the group an opportunity to answer questions that people asked?	1	2	3	4	5
h. Kept the group focused on topic?	1	2	3	4	5
i. Connected participants' ideas to program goals?	1	2	3	4	5
j. Self-disclosed to an appropriate degree if examples were needed?	1	2	3	4	5
k. Dwelt on individual participants' issues?	1	2	3	4	5

3. **During today's session** the trainers:

Circle one number per item	Disagree Strongly	Disagree Moderately	Disagree Slightly	Agree Slightly	Agree Moderately	Agree Strongly
a. Worked well together?	1	2	3	4	5	6
b. Were coordinated?	1	2	3	4	5	6
c. Referred to each other by name as appropriate?	1	2	3	4	5	6
d. Assisted each other with handouts and flipcharts?	1	2	3	4	5	6
e. Shared roles as appropriate?	1	2	3	4	5	6
f. Showed each other polite courtesy? (verbal or nonverbal)	1	2	3	4	5	6

4. **During today's session** the trainers were:

Circle one number per pair	Very	Some-what	A Little	Neither or Neutral	A Little	Some-what	Very	
a. Apathetic	1	2	3	4	5	6	7	Enthusiastic
b. Cold	1	2	3	4	5	6	7	Warm
c. Rejecting	1	2	3	4	5	6	7	Accepting
d. Tense	1	2	3	4	5	6	7	Relaxed
e. Hostile	1	2	3	4	5	6	7	Friendly
f. Insincere	1	2	3	4	5	6	7	Sincere
g. Unknowledgeable	1	2	3	4	5	6	7	Knowledgeable
h. Disorganized	1	2	3	4	5	6	7	Organized
i. Confusing	1	2	3	4	5	6	7	Clear

5. **During today's session** participants:

Circle one number per item	Not at All	A Little	Some	Pretty Much	A Great Deal
a. Used each other's names?	1	2	3	4	5
b. Listened to each other?	1	2	3	4	5
c. Engaged in workshop activities?	1	2	3	4	5
d. Shared ideas with each other?	1	2	3	4	5
e. Asked questions?	1	2	3	4	5

6. **During today's session**, group members were:

Circle one number per pair	Very	Some-what	A Little	Neither or Neutral	A Little	Some-what	Very	
a. Apathetic	1	2	3	4	5	6	7	Enthusiastic
b. Cold	1	2	3	4	5	6	7	Warm
c. Rejecting	1	2	3	4	5	6	7	Accepting
d. Tense	1	2	3	4	5	6	7	Relaxed
e. Hostile	1	2	3	4	5	6	7	Friendly
f. Insincere	1	2	3	4	5	6	7	Sincere
g. Indifferent	1	2	3	4	5	6	7	Supportive

NOTES

4.7.3.9 SCHOOL-TO-JOBS END OF SESSION 9 OBSERVATION FORM

Date ____/____/____   Observer _____   Site _____

Group _____   Trainers _____

1. During today's session, how many of the ideas about **working on everyday problems in school** were provided by participants compared to those provided by the trainers:

Trainers provided nearly all	Trainers provided most	Trainers provided somewhat more	Trainers and participants provided equal amounts	Participants provided somewhat more	Participants provided most	Participants provided nearly all
1	2	3	4	5	6	7

2. **During today's session**, the trainers: (5 = maximum appropriate given group activity)

Circle one number per item	Not at All	A Little	Some	Pretty Much	A Great Deal
a. Made supportive comments focused on participants' strengths?	1	2	3	4	5
b. Referred to participants by name?	1	2	3	4	5
c. Criticized participants' ideas?	1	2	3	4	5
d. Listened closely to participants' comments?	1	2	3	4	5
e. Responded using specific examples?	1	2	3	4	5
f. Provided equal opportunities for people to share their ideas?	1	2	3	4	5
g. Gave the group an opportunity to answer questions that people asked?	1	2	3	4	5
h. Kept the group focused on topic?	1	2	3	4	5
i. Connected participants' ideas to program goals?	1	2	3	4	5
j. Self-disclosed to an appropriate degree if examples were needed?	1	2	3	4	5
k. Dwelt on individual participants' issues?	1	2	3	4	5

3. **During today's session** the trainers:

Circle one number per item	Disagree Strongly	Disagree Moderately	Disagree Slightly	Agree Slightly	Agree Moderately	Agree Strongly
a. Worked well together?	1	2	3	4	5	6
b. Were coordinated?	1	2	3	4	5	6
c. Referred to each other by name as appropriate?	1	2	3	4	5	6
d. Assisted each other with handouts and flipcharts?	1	2	3	4	5	6
e. Shared roles as appropriate?	1	2	3	4	5	6
f. Showed each other polite courtesy? (verbal or nonverbal)	1	2	3	4	5	6

4. **During today's session** the trainers were:

Circle one number per pair	Very	Some-what	A Little	Neither or Neutral	A Little	Some-what	Very	
a. Apathetic	1	2	3	4	5	6	7	Enthusiastic
b. Cold	1	2	3	4	5	6	7	Warm
c. Rejecting	1	2	3	4	5	6	7	Accepting
d. Tense	1	2	3	4	5	6	7	Relaxed
e. Hostile	1	2	3	4	5	6	7	Friendly
f. Insincere	1	2	3	4	5	6	7	Sincere
g. Unknowledgeable	1	2	3	4	5	6	7	Knowledgeable
h. Disorganized	1	2	3	4	5	6	7	Organized
i. Confusing	1	2	3	4	5	6	7	Clear

5. **During today's session** participants:

Circle one number per item	Not at All	A Little	Some	Pretty Much	A Great Deal
a. Used each other's names?	1	2	3	4	5
b. Listened to each other?	1	2	3	4	5
c. Engaged in workshop activities?	1	2	3	4	5
d. Shared ideas with each other?	1	2	3	4	5
e. Asked questions?	1	2	3	4	5

6. **During today's session**, group members were:

Circle one number per pair	Very	Some-what	A Little	Neither or Neutral	A Little	Some-what	Very	
a. Apathetic	1	2	3	4	5	6	7	Enthusiastic
b. Cold	1	2	3	4	5	6	7	Warm
c. Rejecting	1	2	3	4	5	6	7	Accepting
d. Tense	1	2	3	4	5	6	7	Relaxed
e. Hostile	1	2	3	4	5	6	7	Friendly
f. Insincere	1	2	3	4	5	6	7	Sincere
g. Indifferent	1	2	3	4	5	6	7	Supportive

NOTES

Date____/____/____   Observer_____   Site_____

Group _____   Trainers _____

1. During today's session, how many of the ideas about working on **steps to graduating** were provided by participants compared to those provided by the trainers:

Trainers provided nearly all	Trainers provided most	Trainers provided somewhat more	Trainers and participants provided equal amounts	Participants provided somewhat more	Participants provided most	Participants provided nearly all
1	2	3	4	5	6	7

2. **During today's session**, the trainers: (5 = maximum appropriate given group activity)

Circle one number per item	Not at All	A Little	Some	Pretty Much	A Great Deal
a. Made supportive comments focused on participants' strengths?	1	2	3	4	5
b. Referred to participants by name?	1	2	3	4	5
c. Criticized participants' ideas?	1	2	3	4	5
d. Listened closely to participants' comments?	1	2	3	4	5
e. Responded using specific examples?	1	2	3	4	5
f. Provided equal opportunities for people to share their ideas?	1	2	3	4	5
g. Gave the group an opportunity to answer questions that people asked?	1	2	3	4	5
h. Kept the group focused on topic?	1	2	3	4	5
i. Connected participants' ideas to program goals?	1	2	3	4	5
j. Self-disclosed to an appropriate degree if examples were needed?	1	2	3	4	5
k. Dwelt on individual participants' issues?	1	2	3	4	5

3. **During today's session** the trainers:

Circle one number per item	Disagree Strongly	Disagree Moderately	Disagree Slightly	Agree Slightly	Agree Moderately	Agree Strongly
a. Worked well together?	1	2	3	4	5	6
b. Were coordinated?	1	2	3	4	5	6
c. Referred to each other by name as appropriate?	1	2	3	4	5	6
d. Assisted each other with handouts and flipcharts?	1	2	3	4	5	6
e. Shared roles as appropriate?	1	2	3	4	5	6
f. Showed each other polite courtesy? (verbal or nonverbal)	1	2	3	4	5	6

4. **During today's session** the trainers were:

Circle one number per pair	Very	Some-what	A Little	Neither or Neutral	A Little	Some-what	Very	
a. Apathetic	1	2	3	4	5	6	7	Enthusiastic
b. Cold	1	2	3	4	5	6	7	Warm
c. Rejecting	1	2	3	4	5	6	7	Accepting
d. Tense	1	2	3	4	5	6	7	Relaxed
e. Hostile	1	2	3	4	5	6	7	Friendly
f. Insincere	1	2	3	4	5	6	7	Sincere
g. Unknowledgeable	1	2	3	4	5	6	7	Knowledgeable
h. Disorganized	1	2	3	4	5	6	7	Organized
i. Confusing	1	2	3	4	5	6	7	Clear

5. **During today's session** participants:

Circle one number per item	Not at All	A Little	Some	Pretty Much	A Great Deal
a. Used each other's names?	1	2	3	4	5
b. Listened to each other?	1	2	3	4	5
c. Engaged in workshop activities?	1	2	3	4	5
d. Shared ideas with each other?	1	2	3	4	5
e. Asked questions?	1	2	3	4	5

6. **During today's session**, group members were:

Circle one number per pair	Very	Some-what	A Little	Neither or Neutral	A Little	Some-what	Very	
a. Apathetic	1	2	3	4	5	6	7	Enthusiastic
b. Cold	1	2	3	4	5	6	7	Warm
c. Rejecting	1	2	3	4	5	6	7	Accepting
d. Tense	1	2	3	4	5	6	7	Relaxed
e. Hostile	1	2	3	4	5	6	7	Friendly
f. Insincere	1	2	3	4	5	6	7	Sincere
g. Indifferent	1	2	3	4	5	6	7	Supportive

NOTES

Date_____/_____/_____   Observer_____   Site_____

Group _____   Trainers _____

1. During today's session, how many of the ideas about **what happened in School-to-Jobs** were provided by participants compared to those provided by the trainers:

Trainers provided nearly all	Trainers provided most	Trainers provided somewhat more	Trainers and participants provided equal amounts	Participants provided somewhat more	Participants provided most	Participants provided nearly all
1	2	3	4	5	6	7

2. **During today's session**, the trainers: (5 = maximum appropriate given group activity)

Circle one number per item	Not at All	A Little	Some	Pretty Much	A Great Deal
a. Made supportive comments focused on participants' strengths?	1	2	3	4	5
b. Referred to participants by name?	1	2	3	4	5
c. Criticized participants' ideas?	1	2	3	4	5
d. Listened closely to participants' comments?	1	2	3	4	5
e. Responded using specific examples?	1	2	3	4	5
f. Provided equal opportunities for people to share their ideas?	1	2	3	4	5
g. Gave the group an opportunity to answer questions that people asked?	1	2	3	4	5
h. Kept the group focused on topic?	1	2	3	4	5
i. Connected participants' ideas to program goals?	1	2	3	4	5
j. Self-disclosed to an appropriate degree if examples were needed?	1	2	3	4	5
k. Dwelt on individual participants' issues?	1	2	3	4	5

3. **During today's session** the trainers:

Circle one number per item	Disagree Strongly	Disagree Moderately	Disagree Slightly	Agree Slightly	Agree Moderately	Agree Strongly
a. Worked well together?	1	2	3	4	5	6
b. Were coordinated?	1	2	3	4	5	6
c. Referred to each other by name as appropriate?	1	2	3	4	5	6
d. Assisted each other with handouts and flipcharts?	1	2	3	4	5	6
e. Shared roles as appropriate?	1	2	3	4	5	6
f. Showed each other polite courtesy? (verbal or nonverbal)	1	2	3	4	5	6

4. **During today's session** the trainers were:

Circle one number per pair	Very	Some-what	A Little	Neither or Neutral	A Little	Some-what	Very	
a. Apathetic	1	2	3	4	5	6	7	Enthusiastic
b. Cold	1	2	3	4	5	6	7	Warm
c. Rejecting	1	2	3	4	5	6	7	Accepting
d. Tense	1	2	3	4	5	6	7	Relaxed
e. Hostile	1	2	3	4	5	6	7	Friendly
f. Insincere	1	2	3	4	5	6	7	Sincere
g. Unknowledgeable	1	2	3	4	5	6	7	Knowledgeable
h. Disorganized	1	2	3	4	5	6	7	Organized
i. Confusing	1	2	3	4	5	6	7	Clear

5. **During today's session** participants:

Circle one number per item	Not at All	A Little	Some	Pretty Much	A Great Deal
a. Used each other's names?	1	2	3	4	5
b. Listened to each other?	1	2	3	4	5
c. Engaged in workshop activities?	1	2	3	4	5
d. Shared ideas with each other?	1	2	3	4	5
e. Asked questions?	1	2	3	4	5

6. **During today's session**, group members were:

Circle one number per pair	Very	Some-what	A Little	Neither or Neutral	A Little	Some-what	Very	
a. Apathetic	1	2	3	4	5	6	7	Enthusiastic
b. Cold	1	2	3	4	5	6	7	Warm
c. Rejecting	1	2	3	4	5	6	7	Accepting
d. Tense	1	2	3	4	5	6	7	Relaxed
e. Hostile	1	2	3	4	5	6	7	Friendly
f. Insincere	1	2	3	4	5	6	7	Sincere
g. Indifferent	1	2	3	4	5	6	7	Supportive

NOTES

4.7.3.12 SCHOOL-TO-JOBS END OF SESSION PARENT AND YOUTH SESSION 1 AND 2 OBSERVATION FORM

Date_____/_____/_____   Observer_____   Site_____

Group _____   Trainers _____

1. **During today's session**, how many of the ideas about **prior sessions, goals, or communication skills** were provided by participants compared to those provided by the trainers: *Circle one*

Trainers provided nearly all	Trainers provided most	Trainers provided somewhat more	Trainers and participants provided equal amounts	Participants provided somewhat more	Participants provided most	Participants provided nearly all
1	2	3	4	5	6	7

2. **During today's session**, the trainers: (5 = maximum appropriate given group activity)

Circle one number per item	Not at All	A Little	Some	Pretty Much	A Great Deal
a. Made supportive comments focused on participants' strengths?	1	2	3	4	5
b. Referred to participants by name?	1	2	3	4	5
c. Criticized participants' ideas?	1	2	3	4	5
d. Listened closely to participants' comments?	1	2	3	4	5
e. Responded using specific examples?	1	2	3	4	5
f. Provided equal opportunities for people to share their ideas?	1	2	3	4	5
g. Gave the group an opportunity to answer questions that people asked?	1	2	3	4	5
h. Kept the group focused on topic?	1	2	3	4	5
i. Connected participants' ideas to program goals?	1	2	3	4	5
j. Self-disclosed to an appropriate degree if examples were needed?	1	2	3	4	5
k. Dwelt on individual participants' issues?	1	2	3	4	5

3. **During today's session** the trainers:

Circle one number per item	Disagree Strongly	Disagree Moderately	Disagree Slightly	Agree Slightly	Agree Moderately	Agree Strongly
a. Worked well together?	1	2	3	4	5	6
b. Were coordinated?	1	2	3	4	5	6
c. Referred to each other by name as appropriate?	1	2	3	4	5	6
d. Assisted each other with handouts and flipcharts?	1	2	3	4	5	6
e. Shared roles as appropriate?	1	2	3	4	5	6
f. Showed each other polite courtesy? (verbal or nonverbal)	1	2	3	4	5	6

4. **During today's session** the trainers were:

Circle one number per pair	Very	Somewhat	A Little	Neither or Neutral	A Little	Somewhat	Very	
a. Apathetic	1	2	3	4	5	6	7	Enthusiastic
b. Cold	1	2	3	4	5	6	7	Warm
c. Rejecting	1	2	3	4	5	6	7	Accepting
d. Tense	1	2	3	4	5	6	7	Relaxed
e. Hostile	1	2	3	4	5	6	7	Friendly
f. Insincere	1	2	3	4	5	6	7	Sincere
g. Unknowledgeable	1	2	3	4	5	6	7	Knowledgeable
h. Disorganized	1	2	3	4	5	6	7	Organized
i. Confusing	1	2	3	4	5	6	7	Clear

5. **During today's session** participants:

Circle one number per item	Not at All	A Little	Some	Pretty Much	A Great Deal
a. Used each other's names?	1	2	3	4	5
b. Listened to each other?	1	2	3	4	5
c. Engaged in workshop activities?	1	2	3	4	5
d. Shared ideas with each other?	1	2	3	4	5
e. Asked questions?	1	2	3	4	5

6. **During today's session**, group members were:

Circle one number per pair	Very	Somewhat	A Little	Neither or Neutral	A Little	Somewhat	Very	
a. Apathetic	1	2	3	4	5	6	7	Enthusiastic
b. Cold	1	2	3	4	5	6	7	Warm
c. Rejecting	1	2	3	4	5	6	7	Accepting
d. Tense	1	2	3	4	5	6	7	Relaxed
e. Hostile	1	2	3	4	5	6	7	Friendly
f. Insincere	1	2	3	4	5	6	7	Sincere
g. Indifferent	1	2	3	4	5	6	7	Supportive

NOTES

Date____/____/____   Observer_____   Site_____
Group _____   Trainers _____

1. During today's session, how many of the ideas about **informational inter-viewing** were provided by participants (youth and parents) compared to those provided by the trainers:

Trainers provided nearly all	Trainers provided most	Trainers provided somewhat more	Trainers and participants provided equal amounts	Participants provided somewhat more	Participants provided most	Participants provided nearly all
1	2	3	4	5	6	7

2. **During today's session**, the trainers: (5 = maximum appropriate given group activity)

Circle one number per item	Not at All	A Little	Some	Pretty Much	A Great Deal
a. Made supportive comments focused on participants' strengths?	1	2	3	4	5
b. Referred to participants by name?	1	2	3	4	5
c. Criticized participants' ideas?	1	2	3	4	5
d. Listened closely to participants' comments?	1	2	3	4	5
e. Responded using specific examples?	1	2	3	4	5
f. Provided equal opportunities for people to share their ideas?	1	2	3	4	5
g. Gave the group an opportunity to answer questions that people asked?	1	2	3	4	5
h. Kept the group focused on topic?	1	2	3	4	5
i. Connected participants' ideas to program goals?	1	2	3	4	5
j. Self-disclosed to an appropriate degree if examples were needed?	1	2	3	4	5
k. Dwelt on individual participants' issues?	1	2	3	4	5

3. **During today's session** the trainers:

Circle one number per item	Disagree Strongly	Disagree Moderately	Disagree Slightly	Agree Slightly	Agree Moderately	Agree Strongly
a. Worked well together?	1	2	3	4	5	6
b. Were coordinated?	1	2	3	4	5	6
c. Referred to each other by name as appropriate?	1	2	3	4	5	6
d. Assisted each other with handouts and flipcharts?	1	2	3	4	5	6
e. Shared roles as appropriate?	1	2	3	4	5	6
f. Showed each other polite courtesy? (verbal or nonverbal)	1	2	3	4	5	6

4. **During today's session** the trainers were:

Circle one number per pair	Very	Some-what	A Little	Neither or Neutral	A Little	Some-what	Very	
a. Apathetic	1	2	3	4	5	6	7	Enthusiastic
b. Cold	1	2	3	4	5	6	7	Warm
c. Rejecting	1	2	3	4	5	6	7	Accepting
d. Tense	1	2	3	4	5	6	7	Relaxed
e. Hostile	1	2	3	4	5	6	7	Friendly
f. Insincere	1	2	3	4	5	6	7	Sincere
g. Unknowledgeable	1	2	3	4	5	6	7	Knowledgeable
h. Disorganized	1	2	3	4	5	6	7	Organized
i. Confusing	1	2	3	4	5	6	7	Clear

5. **During today's session** participants:

Circle one number per item	Not at All	A Little	Some	Pretty Much	A Great Deal
a. Used each other's names?	1	2	3	4	5
b. Listened to each other?	1	2	3	4	5
c. Engaged in workshop activities?	1	2	3	4	5
d. Shared ideas with each other?	1	2	3	4	5
e. Asked questions?	1	2	3	4	5

6. **During today's session**, group members were:

Circle one number per pair	Very	Some-what	A Little	Neither or Neutral	A Little	Some-what	Very	
a. Apathetic	1	2	3	4	5	6	7	Enthusiastic
b. Cold	1	2	3	4	5	6	7	Warm
c. Rejecting	1	2	3	4	5	6	7	Accepting
d. Tense	1	2	3	4	5	6	7	Relaxed
e. Hostile	1	2	3	4	5	6	7	Friendly
f. Insincere	1	2	3	4	5	6	7	Sincere
g. Indifferent	1	2	3	4	5	6	7	Supportive

NOTES

4.7.4 Observer-Rated Student Participation Form
School-to-Jobs Individual Student Observation Form

School _____	Student Name _____
Group # _____	Student ID_____
Session#_____ Observer Name_____	Date___/___/___

During today's session, how much did **this student**:

Circle one number per item.		Not at all	A little	Some	Pretty much	A great deal
1.	Listen to trainers	1	2	3	4	5
2.	Listen to other students	1	2	3	4	5
3.	Follow instructions	1	2	3	4	5
4.	Participate in workshop activities	1	2	3	4	5
5.	Ask questions related to task	1	2	3	4	5
6.	Respond when called on to contribute	1	2	3	4	5
7.	Volunteer ideas	1	2	3	4	5
8.	Understand the point of the activities	1	2	3	4	5
9.	Take the activities seriously	1	2	3	4	5
10.	Enjoy the activities	1	2	3	4	5
11.	Do things not related to School-to-Jobs	1	2	3	4	5
12.	Distract other students from workshop activities	1	2	3	4	5

Notes: _____

_____

4.7.5 Student End of Intervention Ratings

DESCRIBE SCHOOL-TO-JOBS

My Student ID   ID:_____

Today's date. . . . .   ____ ____/____ ____/_____

                                                MONTH   DAY   YEAR

1.   These questions are about the **ideas you received from School-to-Jobs**. Circle one number for each item to describe how you feel.

	Hardly Any	A Few	Some	A Lot	Almost All
a. How many of the helpful ideas you received in School-to-Jobs came from **you**	1	2	3	4	5
b. How many of the helpful ideas you received in School-to-Jobs came from **other participants**	1	2	3	4	5
c. How many of the helpful ideas you received in School-to-Jobs came from **the trainers**	1	2	3	4	5

2.   These are ways to describe School-to-Jobs Trainers. Circle one number for each item to **describe your trainers**.

In School-to-Jobs my trainers	Not at all	A Little	Somewhat	Pretty Much	A lot
a. Understood my problems	1	2	3	4	5
b. Listened to my comments	1	2	3	4	5
c. Criticized my ideas	1	2	3	4	5
d. Used specific examples	1	2	3	4	5
e. Gave us all equal chance to participate	1	2	3	4	5
f. Gave us the chance to answer questions other students raised	1	2	3	4	5

3.   These are pairs of words to describe School-to-Jobs Trainers. For example, the first pair goes from Very Enthusiastic to Very Unenthusiastic. Circle one number for each word-pair to **describe your trainers**.

In School-to-Jobs my trainers were	Very	Somewhat	Neither	Somewhat	Very	
Enthusiastic	1	2	3	4	5	Unenthusiastic
Knowledgeable	1	2	3	4	5	Unknowledgeable
Warm	1	2	3	4	5	Cold
Clear	1	2	3	4	5	Confusing

ID: _____

4. **How did you feel during School-to-Jobs**? Circle one number to describe how you felt.

In School-to-Jobs	Not at all	A Little	Somewhat	Pretty Much	A lot
a. I felt comfortable participating and asking questions	1	2	3	4	5
b. I could trust others to listen to what I had to say	1	2	3	4	5
c. Others shared their experiences and difficulties working toward their futures	1	2	3	4	5
d. Other participants have the same problems I do	1	2	3	4	5
e. What we talked about was relevant for me	1	2	3	4	5
f. I was worried another group member would criticize me	1	2	3	4	5

5. These are pairs of words to **describe your School-to-Jobs group**. For each word-pair circle a number to describe your group.

In School-to-Jobs my group was	Very	Somewhat	Neither	Somewhat	Very	
Enthusiastic	1	2	3	4	5	Unenthusiastic
Knowledgeable	1	2	3	4	5	Unknowledgeable
Warm	1	2	3	4	5	Cold
Supportive	1	2	3	4	5	Unsupportive

6. These are questions about **your ability to do the things practiced in School-to-Jobs**. Circle one number for each item to describe **how sure you are that you can do it**.

I can	Not at all	A Little	Somewhat	Pretty Much	A lot
a. Introduce myself in a way that emphasizes my skills	1	2	3	4	5
b. Imagine myself as an adult (working, having family and friendships, a nice lifestyle, participating in my community)	1	2	3	4	5
c. Draw a future timeline, including obstacles and forks in the road.	1	2	3	4	5
d. Take action now to work toward my adult images	1	2	3	4	5
e. Break down everyday situations down into problems to be solved	1	2	3	4	5
f. Ask for help making plans	1	2	3	4	5
g. Plan my class schedule to meet my future goals	1	2	3	4	5

ID: _____

7. These are questions about your future. Circle one number for each item to describe how you feel.

In the future	Not at all	A Little	Somewhat	Pretty Much	A lot
a. **I will experience difficulties and setbacks** in my efforts to do well in school	1	2	3	4	5
b. **I have strategies to handle these difficulties** so I know what to do next	1	2	3	4	5
c. **I can come up with alternatives** when a setback happens	1	2	3	4	5
d. Other participants have the same problems I do	1	2	3	4	5
e. What we talked about was relevant for me	1	2	3	4	5
f. I felt concerned I would be criticized by another group member	1	2	3	4	5

8. How many days of the School-to-Jobs workshop did you attend? _____

4.8 OUTCOME ASSESSMENT MEASURES

4.8.1 School Records

Records should be obtained from the schools that participants attend; the data of interest are school grades and attendance.

4.8.2 Pathways for Youth: Teacher Survey

Your name _____   Student name and ID

School   _____   Label here

Below are items that describe students' classroom behavior. Please consider the behavior of the student named above over the time he or she has been in your class. Circle the number that indicates how often the student exhibits the behavior in your class. Please answer every item.

This student . . .	NEVER	HARDLY	SOMETIMES	MOST OF THE TIME	ALWAYS
1. Pays attention in class	1	2	3	4	5
2. Loses, forgets, or misplaces materials	1	2	3	4	5
3. Completes homework and in-class assignments	1	2	3	4	5
4. Comes late to class	1	2	3	4	5
5. Is persistent when confronted with difficult problems	1	2	3	4	5
6. Criticizes the importance of the subject matter	1	2	3	4	5
7. Does more than just the assigned work	1	2	3	4	5
8. Annoys peers or interferes with peers' work	1	2	3	4	5
9. Seems to think that this course is valuable	1	2	3	4	5
10. Is critical of peers who do well in school	1	2	3	4	5
11. Actively participates in class discussions	1	2	3	4	5
12. Needs to be reprimanded or sent to the office	1	2	3	4	5
13. Is verbally or physically abusive to the teacher	1	2	3	4	5
14. Engages me in conversation about subject matter before or after school or outside of class	1	2	3	4	5

Now, think of other youth in your school. Please circle the response that reflects how often this student associates with people who do the following things, use never, hardly, sometimes, most of the time, or always.

How often does this student associate with people who...	NEVER	HARDLY	SOMETIMES	MOST OF THE TIME	ALWAYS
15. Are friendly, helpful and dependable	1	2	3	4	5
16. Misbehave in school	1	2	3	4	5
17. Smoke cigarettes or chew tobacco	1	2	3	4	5
18. Use drugs or alcohol	1	2	3	4	5
19. Steal or vandalize	1	2	3	4	5
20. Get into fights	1	2	3	4	5
21. Do well in school/are academically motivated	1	2	3	4	5
22. Are involved in extracurricular activities	1	2	3	4	5

A few final questions. Please circle your response.

23. How well do you know this student?	NOT AT ALL	FAIRLY	VERY	EXTREMELY	
24. How confident are you in your rating of this student?	NOT AT ALL	FAIRLY	VERY	EXTREMELY	
25. To the best of your knowledge, was this student suspended this year (see attached calendar to mark)	NO	Unlikely	Probably	YES	DK

4.8.3 Youth Questionnaire

1. This is a survey. There are no right or wrong answers. For each section, please follow the directions and answer the questions as truthfully as you can, based on your own opinion.

2. All answers will be kept strictly confidential. This means that your name will not be on this questionnaire once you remove the label (it peels off) and no one other than research staff can connect the number on this questionnaire with your name; the information given during this questionnaire will not be connected with your name in research reports; and no one other than the research staff will know how you answered the questions.

3. This survey is optional and will not affect your grade.

4. You may skip any question if you are uncomfortable answering it.

5. If you have any questions about this survey, you can ask the staff member administering it, or call 1-877-PATHS4U.

Student number: _____

Who will you be next year? Each of us has some image or picture of what we will be like and what we want to avoid being like in the future. Think about next year—imagine what you'll be like, and what you'll be doing next year.

- In the lines below, write what you expect you will be like and what you expect to be doing next year.
- In the space next to each expected goal, mark NO (X) if you are not currently working on that goal or doing something about that expectation

Next year, I expect to be	Am I doing something to be this way		If yes, What I am doing now to be this way next year
	NO	YES	
(P1) _____			_____
(P2) _____			_____
(P3) _____			_____
(P4) _____			_____

and mark YES (X) if you are currently doing something to get to that expectation or goal.

- For each expected goal that you marked YES, use the space to the right to write what you are doing this year to attain that goal.

In addition to expectations and expected goals, we all have images or pictures of what we don't want to be like; what we don't want to do or want to avoid being. First, think a minute about ways you would **not** like to be next year—*things you are concerned about or want to avoid being like.*

- Write those concerns or selves to-be-avoided in the lines below.

Next year, I want to avoid	Am I doing something to avoid this		If yes, What I am doing now to avoid being that way next year
	NO	YES	
(P5) _____			_____
(P6) _____			_____
(P7) _____			_____
(P8) _____			_____

- In the space next to each concern or to-be-avoided self, mark NO (X) if you are not currently working on avoiding that concern or to-be-avoided self and mark YES (X) if you are currently doing something so this will not happen next year.
- For each concern or to-be-avoided self that you marked YES, use the space at the end of each line to write what you are doing this year to reduce the chances that this will describe you next year.

The next questions are **about the job you see yourself having as an adult**. Think about yourself as an adult; what job do you think you'll have? (If more than one, you can answer for the job you feel you will be most likely to have.)

J1)   What will you be doing in 10 years? _____

_____

J2)   Do you think you will have a job? ☐ YES ☐ NO
J3)   Do you need to finish high school to get this kind of job?   ☐ YES ☐ NO
J4)   Do you need to finish college to get this kind of job?   ☐ YES ☐ NO
        If NO—what other kind of training would you need? (describe it) _____

_____

J5)   How much money do you think people with the job you described earn a year?
        $_____

J6)   Put a checkmark next to the response that best describes how much farther you expect to go in school:

   ◊ Attend high school
   ◊ Obtain a GED
   ◊ Graduate from high school
   ◊ Attend a technical or vocational school or program after high school
   ◊ Receive training in the armed forces
   ◊ Attend a 2-year junior or community college
   ◊ Attend a 4-year college
   ◊ Attend a graduate or professional school or college

R1)   How would you describe your race or ethnicity? Which one of the following describes you best? Mark only one.

   ◊ African American
   ◊ Hispanic
   ◊ White
   ◊ Asian
   ◊ Native American
   ◊ Arab
   ◊ Other (write in_____):

R2) What does it mean to you to be a member of your race or ethnic group? Use examples from your everyday life of things you do that make you feel like a member of this group.

_____

_____

_____

These are statements people sometimes make about being a member of their own racial or ethnic group. The statements are written for African Americans. (If you are not African American, answer for your own racial or ethnic group.) There are no right or wrong answers; your opinion counts. For each statement, say **how close it is to your opinion** using the following scale, where 1 = strongly disagree; 2 = disagree; 3 = neither agree nor disagree; 4 = agree; and 5 = strongly agree.

	STRONGLY DISAGREE	DISAGREE	NEITHER AGREE NOR DISAGREE	AGREE	STRONGLY AGREE
R3) It is important to me to think of myself as an African American.	1	2	3	4	5
R4) I feel a part of the African American community.	1	2	3	4	5
R5) I have a lot of pride in what African Americans have done and achieved.	1	2	3	4	5
R6) I feel close to African Americans.	1	2	3	4	5
R7) If I am successful, it will help other African Americans.	1	2	3	4	5
R8) It is important for my family and the African American community that I succeed in school.	1	2	3	4	5
R9) Some people will treat me differently because I am African American.	1	2	3	4	5
R10) The way I look and speak influences what others expect of me.	1	2	3	4	5
R11) Things in the African American community are not as good as they could be because of lack of opportunity.	1	2	3	4	5
R12) It helps me when other African Americans do well.	1	2	3	4	5
R13) People might have negative ideas about my abilities because I am an African American.	1	2	3	4	5
R14) If I work hard and get good grades, other African Americans will respect me.	1	2	3	4	5

The following statements are about **how you act in school**.

How often do you	Never	Rarely	Sometimes	Often	Always
F1) Pay attention in class?	1	2	3	4	5
F2) Lose, forget, or misplace materials?	1	2	3	4	5
F2) Lose, forget, or misplace materials?	1	2	3	4	5
F3) Complete homework and in-class assignments?	1	2	3	4	5
F5) Work especially hard when you have to solve difficult problems?	1	2	3	4	5
F6) Feel some subjects (math, history, English, science) are not important to you?	1	2	3	4	5
F7) Do more work than your teacher assigns?	1	2	3	4	5
F8) Bother your classmates when they are working?	1	2	3	4	5
F9) Think your classes are valuable to your future?	1	2	3	4	5
F10) Think badly of students who do well in school?	1	2	3	4	5
F11) Participate in class discussions?	1	2	3	4	5
F12) Get disciplined by the teacher or sent to the office?	1	2	3	4	5
F13) Act mouthy and have an attitude with the teacher?	1	2	3	4	5
F14) Talk with the teacher after school or outside of class about what you are studying and learning?	1	2	3	4	5

These questions are about what you are normally like; answer about what is normal or typical for you.

S1a) How many hours a week do you usually spend doing homework?
_____ Hours

S1b) In one week, how much time do you usually spend doing homework:

0 hours a week	Less than 1 hour a week	1 hour a week	1–2 hours a week	2–3 hours a week	3–5 hours a week	5–10 hours a week	over 10 hours a week
0	1	2	3	4	5	6	7

S2) How often do you finish the homework that has been assigned?

Never	Occasionally (about 25% of the time)	About half of the time (about 50% of the time)	Often (about 75% of the time)	Always or almost always
1	2	3	4	5

S3) How seriously do you take your homework?

Not at all seriously	Not very seriously	50–50	Seriously	Very seriously
1	2	3	4	5

S4) What grades do you usually get in school?

Mostly F's	Mostly D's and F's	Mostly D's	Mostly C's and D's	Mostly C's	Mostly B's and C's	Mostly B's	Mostly A's and B's	Mostly A's
0	1	2	3	4	5	6	7	8

S5) How often are you absent from school or miss a class during the day?

More than once a week	Once a week or so	Once every few weeks	Once a month or so	Less than once a month	Once or twice a year	Never
1	2	3	4	5	6	7

S6) How often does a teacher make you leave the classroom because of your behavior?

More than once a week	Once a week or so	Once every few weeks	Once a month or so	Less than once a month	Once or twice a year	Never
1	2	3	4	5	6	7

During the summer (June, July, August), did you work for pay? ☐ Yes ☐ No

If so, how many hours a week did you work? _____ Hours

D1) How difficult or easy was it for you to understand the questions on this survey?

Very difficult	A little difficult	Not difficult or easy	A little easy	Very easy
1	2	3	4	5

We're done. Thank you for participating in the survey.

REFERENCES

Acemoglu, D., & Pischke, J. S. (2001). Changes in the wage structure, family income, and children's education. *European Economic Review, 45*, 890–904.

Adler, N. E., & Rehkopf, D. H. (2008). U. S. disparities in health: Descriptions, causes, and mechanisms. *Annual Review of Public Health, 29*, 235–252.

Allensworth, E., & Easton, J. Q. (2005). *The on-track indicator as a predictor of high school graduation.* University of Chicago Consortium on Chicago School Research.

Allensworth, E., & Easton, J. Q. (2007). *What matters for staying on-track and graduating in Chicago public high schools: A close look at course grades, failures, and attendance in the freshman year.* University of Chicago Consortium on Chicago School Research.

Altschul, I., Oyserman, D., & Bybee, D. (2006). Racial-ethnic identity in mid-adolescence: content and change as predictors of academic achievement. *Child Development, 77*(5), 1155–1169.

Altschul, I., Oyserman, D., & Bybee, D. (2008). Racial-ethnic self-schemas and segmented assimilation: Identity and the academic achievement of Hispanic youth. *Social Psychology Quarterly, 71*, 302–320.

Anderman, E. M., Anderman, L. H., & Griesinger, T. (1999). The relation of present and possible academic selves during early adolescence to grade point average and achievement goals. *Elementary School Journal, 100*, 3–17.

Anderson, C. L, Dietz, M., Gordon, A., & Klawitter, M. (2004). Discount rates in Vietnam. *Economic Development and Cultural Change, 52*, 873–887.

Andrews, D. A., Zinger, I., Hoge, R. D., Bonta, J., Gendreau, P., & Cullen, F. T. (1990). Does correctional treatment work? A clinically relevant and psychologically informed meta-analysis. *Criminology, 28*(3), 369–404.

Anthis, K. S., Dunkel, C. S., & Anderson, B. (2004). Gender and identity status differences in late adolescents' possible selves. *Journal of Adolescence, 27*(2), 147–152.

Archives for Children Trends Database. (2013). High school dropout statistics—2013. Retrieved from http://www.diploma2degree.org/info/tag/children-trends-database/

Aronson, J., Fried, C. B., & Good, C. (2002). Reducing the effects of stereotype threat on African American college students by shaping theories of intelligence. *Journal of Experimental Social Psychology, 38*, 113–125.

Arum, R., Roksa, J., & Cho, E. (2011). Improving undergraduate learning: Findings and policy recommendations from the SSRC-CLA longitudinal project. Social Science Research Council. Retrieved April 11, 2013, from: http://www.eric.ed.gov/PDFS/ED514983.pdf

Astin, A. W. (1993). *What matters in college? Four critical years revisited.* San Francisco: Jossey-Bass.

Atance, C., M. (2008). Future thinking in young children. *Current Direction in Psychological Science, 17*, 295–298.

Atance, C. M., & Jackson, L. K. (2009). The development and coherence of future-oriented behaviors during the preschool years. *Journal of Experimental Child Psychology, 102*, 379–391.

Atance, C. M., & Meltzoff, A. N. (2005). My future self: Young children's ability to anticipate and explain future states. *Cognitive Development, 20*, 341–361.

Babcock, P., & Marks, M. (2010). *Leisure college, USA: The decline in student study time.* Washington, DC: American Enterprise Institute for Public Policy Research.

Bachman, J. G., O'Malley, P. M., & Johnston, L. D. (1980). Correlates of drug use, Part I: Selected measures of background, recent experiences, and life-style orientations. *Monitoring the Future, Occasional Paper, 8*, 13–14.

Balfanz, R., Herzog, L., & MacIver, D. J. (2007). Preventing student disengagement and keeping students on the graduation path in urban middle-grades schools: Early identification and effective interventions. *Educational Psychologist, 42*, 223–235.

Bandura, A., & Mischel, W. (1965). Modifications of self-imposed delay of reward through exposure to live and symbolic models. *Journal of Personality and Social Psychology, 2*(5), 698–705.

Bargh, J. (2014). The historical origins of priming as the preparation of behavioral responses: Unconscious carry-over and contextual influences of real-world importance. *Social Cognition, 32*(Supplement), 209–224.

Bargh, J. A., & Ferguson, M. J. (2000). Beyond behaviorism: On the automaticity of higher mental processes. *Psychological Bulletin, 126*(6), 925–945.

Barnes, G. M., & Welte, J. W. (1986). Patterns and predictors of alcohol use among 7–12th grade students in New York State. *Journal of Studies on Alcohol and Drugs, 47*(01), 53–62.

Battistich, V., Solomon, D., Watson, M., Solomon, J., & Schaps, E. (1989). Effects of an elementary school program to enhance prosocial behavior on children's cognitive social problem-solving skills and strategies. *Journal of Applied Developmental Psychology, 10,* 147–169.

Beets, M. W., Flay, B. R., Vuchinich, S., Acock, A. C., Li, K., & Allred, C. (2008). School climate and teachers' beliefs and attitudes associated with implementation of the positive action program: A diffusion of innovations model. *Prevention Science, 9,* 264–275.

Benzion, U., Rapoport, A., & Yagil, J. (1989). Discount rates inferred from decisions: an experimental study. *Management Science, 35,* 270–284.

Bi, C. & Oyserman, D. (2014). Left behind or moving forward? Possible identities and strategies of rural Chinese children. Revise and resubmit, *Developmental Psychology.*

Bishaw, A. (2005). *Areas with concentrated poverty: 1999,* Census 2000 Special Reports, No. CENSR-16.

Blackwell, L. S., Trzesniewski, K. H., & Dweck, C. S. (2007). Implicit theories of intelligence predict achievement across an adolescent transition: A longitudinal study and an intervention. *Child Development, 78*(1), 246–263.

Bless, H., & Schwarz, N. (2010). Mental construal and the emergence of assimilation and contrast effects: The inclusion/exclusion model. In M. P. Zanna (Ed.), *Advances in Experimental Social Psychology, 42,* 319–373.

Borrelli, B., Sepinwall, D., Ernst, D., Bellg, A. J., Czajkowski, S., Breger, R., & Orwig, D. (2005). A new tool to assess treatment fidelity and evaluation of treatment fidelity across 10 years of health behavior research. *Journal of Consulting and Clinical Psychology, 73*(5), 852.

Boxer, P., Goldstein, S. E., DeLorenzo, T., Savoy, S., & Mercado, I. (2011). Education aspiration-expectation discrepancies: Relation to socioeconomic and academic risk-related factors. *Journal of Adolescence, 34,* 609–617.

Brehm, J. W. (1966). *A theory of psychological reactance.* New York: Academic Press.

Brehm, J. W., & Self, E. A. (1989). The intensity of motivation. *Annual Review of Psychology, 40,* 109–131.

Brehm, S. S., & Brehm, J. W. (1981). *Psychological reactance: A theory of freedom and control.* San Diego, CA: Academic Press.

Burgoon, M., Alvaro, E., Grandpre, J., & Voulodakis, M. (2002). Revisiting the theory of psychological reactance. In J. P. Dillard & M. Pfau (Eds). *The Persuasion Handbook* (pp. 213–232). Thousand Oaks, CA: Sage.

Brown, L. D., & Detterman, L. B. (1987). Small interventions for large problems: Reshaping urban leadership networks. *The Journal of Applied Behavioral Science, 23*(2), 151–168.

Bryant, A. L., Schulenberg, J. E., O'Malley, P. M., Bachman, J. G., & Johnston, L. D. (2003). How academic achievement, attitudes, and behaviors relate to the course of substance use during adolescence: A 6-year, multiwave national longitudinal study. *Journal of Research on Adolescence, 13*(3), 361–397.

Bryant, A. L., & Zimmerman, M. A. (2002). Examining the effects of academic beliefs and behaviors on changes in substance use among urban adolescents. *Journal of Educational Psychology, 94*(3), 621–637.

Building a Grad Nation. (2012). Civic enterprises, Everyone Graduates Center at Johns Hopkins University America's Promise Alliance for Excellent Education. http://www.civicenterprises.net/MediaLibrary/Docs/Building-A-Grad-Nation-Report-2012_ExecSum_v1.pdf

Bureau of Labor Statistics. (2010). *College enrollment and work activity of 2009 high school graduates* (USDL-10-0533). Retrieved July 2010 from http://www.bls.gov/ news.release/hsgec.nr0.htm

Cairns, R. B., Cairns, B. D., & Neckerman, H. J. (1989). Early school dropout: Configurations and determinants. *Child Development, 60*(6), 1437–1452.

Cauce, A. M., Comer, J. P., & Schwartz, D. (1987). Long term effects of a systems-oriented school prevention program. *American Journal of Orthopsychiatry, 57,* 127–131.

Chapman, C., Laird, J., Ifill, N., & Kewal Ramani, A. (2011). *Trends in high school dropout and completion rates in the United States: 1972–2009 compendium report.* Washington, DC: National Center for Education Statistics, Institute of Education Sciences, U.S. Department of Education.

Chapman, G. B., & Elstein, A. S. (1995). Valuing the future temporal discounting of health and money. *Medical Decision Making, 15*(4), 373–386.

Charnov, E. (1974). Optimal foraging, the marginal value theorum. *Theoretical Population Biology, 9,* 129–136.

Chen, P., & Vazsonyi, A. T. (2013). Future orientation, school contexts, and problem behaviors: A multilevel study. *Journal of Youth and Adolescence, 42*(1), 67–81.

Child Trends. Retrieved from: http://www.edweek.org/ew/dc/2013/gradrate_trend.html

Chirkov, V. I., & Ryan, R. M. (2001). Parent and teacher autonomy-support in Russian and U.S. adolescents: Common effects on well-being and academic motivation. *Journal of Cross-Cultural Psychology, 32*(5), 618–635.

Chowa, G., Masa, R., Wretman, C., & Ansong, D. (2012). *The impact of household possessions on youth's academic achievement in the Ghana Youth Save experiment: A propensity score analysis* (CSD Working Paper No. 12–17). St. Louis: Washington University, Center for Social Development.

Clark, L. F., Miller, K. S., Nagy, S. S., Avery, J., Roth, D. L., Liddon, N., & Mukherjee, S. (2005). Adult identity mentoring: Reducing sexual risk for African-American seventh grade students. *Journal of Adolescent Health, 37,* 337.e1–3337.e10.

Clinkinbeard, S. S., & Murray, C. I. (2012). Perceived support, belonging, and possible selves strategies among incarcerated juvenile offenders 1. *Journal of Applied Social Psychology, 42*(5), 1218–1240.

Clinkinbeard, S. S., & Zohra, T. (2012). Expectations, fears, and strategies juvenile offender thoughts on a future outside of incarceration. *Youth & Society, 44*(2), 236–257.

Cohen, J. (1992). A power primer. *Psychological Bulletin, 112*(1), 155–159,

Coleman, J. C. (1978). Current contradictions in adolescent theory. *Journal of Youth and Adolescence, 7*(1), 1–11.

Coleman, J., Herzberg, J., & Morris, M. (1977). Identity in adolescence: Present and future self-concepts. *Journal of Youth and Adolescence, 6*(1), 63–75.

Cook, T. D., Habib, F., Phillips, M., Settersten, R. A., Shagle, S. C., & Degirmencioglu, S. M. (1999). Comer's school development program in Prince George's County, Maryland: A theory-based evaluation. *American Educational Research Journal, 36,* 543–597.

Cook, T. D., Murphy, R. F., & Hunt, H. D. (2000). Comer's school development program in Chicago: A theory-based evaluation. *American Educational Research Journal, 37,* 535–597.

Costello, E., Mustillo, S., & Erkanli, A. (2003). Prevalence and development of psychiatric disorders in childhood and adolescence. *Archives of General Psychiatry, 60,* 837–844.

Cross, S., & Markus, H. (1991). Possible selves across the life span. *Human Development, 34,* 230–255.

Dalley, S., & Buunk, A. (2011). The motivation to diet in young women: Fear is stronger than hope. *European Journal of Social Psychology, 41,* 672–680.

DeParle, J. & Tavernise, S. (February 17, 2012). For women under 30, most births occur outside marriage *New York Times.* Retrieved February 18, 2012, from http://www.nytimes.com/2012/02/18/us/for-women-under-30-most-births-occur-outside-marriage.html?pagewanted=all&_r=0.

Destin, M. & Oyserman, D. (2009). From assets to school outcomes: How finances shape children's perceived possibilities and planned effort. *Psychological Science, 20,* 414–418.

Destin, M. & Oyserman, D. (2010) Incentivizing education: Seeing schoolwork as an investment, not a chore. *Journal of Experimental Social Psychology, 46,* 846–849.

Dewey, J. D. (1999). Reviewing the relationship between school factors and substance use for elementary, middle, and high school students. *Journal of Primary Prevention, 19*(3), 177–225.

Dillard, J. P., & Shen, L. (2005). On the nature of reactance and its role in persuasive health communication. *Communication Monographs, 72*, 144–168.

Dishion, T. J., McCord, J., & Poulin, F. (1999). When interventions harm: Peer groups and problem behavior. *American Psychologist, 54*(9), 755–764.

Durlak, J. A., & Dupre, E. P. (2008). Implementation matters: A review of research on the influence of implementation on program outcomes and the factors affecting implementation. *American Journal of Community Psychology, 41*, 327–350.

Durlak, J. A., Weissberg, R. P., Dymnicki, A. B., Taylor, R. B., & Schellinger, K. B. (2011). The impact of enhancing students' social and emotional learning: A meta-analysis of school-based universal interventions. *Child Development, 82*, 405–432.

Duval, T. S., & Wicklund, R. A. (1972). A theory of objective self-awareness. New York: Academic Press.

Dweck, C. S. (1999). *Self-theories: Their role in motivation, personality, and development.* Philadelphia: Psychology Press.

Dweck, C. (2006). *Mindset: The new psychology of success.* New York: Random House Digital.

Ebert, J. P., & Wegner, D. M. (2010). Time warp: Authorship shapes the perceived timing of actions and events. *Consciousness and Cognition: An International Journal, 19*, 481–489.

Ellickson, P. L., Tucker, J. S., Klein, D. J., & McGuigan, K. A. (2001). Prospective risk factors for alcohol misuse in late adolescence. *Journal of Studies on Alcohol and Drugs, 62*(6), 773–782.

Elliott, S. N. (1994, December). *The responsive classroom approach: Its effectiveness and acceptability in the District of Columbia Public Schools.* University of Wisconsin: Madison

Elliott, S. N. (1997). *The responsive classroom approach: Its effectiveness and acceptability in promoting social and academic competence.* Madison: University of Wisconsin, Madison. Prepared for the Northeast Foundation for Children.

Elliott, W. III. (2009). Children's college aspirations and expectations: The potential role of children's development accounts (CDAs). *Children and Youth Services, 31*, 274–283.

Elmore, K. & Oyserman, D. (2011). If 'we' succeed, 'I' can too: Identity-based motivation and gender in the classroom. *Contemporary Educational Psychology, 37*, 176–185.

Enright, R. D. (1980). An integration of social cognitive development and cognitive processing: Educational applications. *American Educational Research Journal, 17*, 21–41.

Entwisle, D. R., Alexander, K. L., & Olson, L. S. (2005). First grade and educational attainment by age 22: A new story. *American Journal of Sociology, 110*(5), 1458–1502.

EPE Research Center. (2007). *Gender gap in graduation.* Retrieved July 15, 2009, from http://www.edweek.org/rc/articles/2007/07/05/sow0705.h26.html

Epstude, K., & Peetz, J. (2012). Mental time travel: a conceptual overview of social psychological perspectives on a fundamental human capacity. *European Journal of Social Psychology, 42*, 269–275. doi:10.1002/ejsp.1867

Erikson, E. H. (1963). *Childhood and society* (2nd ed.). New York: Norton.

Erikson, E. H. (1980). *Identity and the life cycle* (Vol. 1). New York: Norton.

Ersner-Hershfield, H., Garton, M. T., Ballard, K., Samanez-Larkin, G. R., & Knutson, B. (2009). Don't stop thinking about tomorrow: Individual differences in future self-continuity account for saving. *Judgment and Decision Making, 4*(4), 280.

Ersner-Hershfield, H., Goldstein, D. G., Sharpe, W. F., Fox, J., Yeykelis, L., Carstensen, L. L., & Bailenson, J. N. (2011). Increasing saving behavior through age-progressed renderings of the future self. *Journal of Marketing Research, 48*(SPL), S23–S37.

Farrelly, M. C., Healton, C. G., Davis, K. C., Messeri, P., Hersey, J. C., & Haviland, M. L. (2002). Getting to the truth: Evaluating national tobacco countermarketing campaigns. *American Journal of Public Health, 92*, 901–907.

Farrington, C. A., Roderick, M., Allensworth, E., Nagaoka, J., Keyes, T. S., Johnson, D. W., & Beechum, N. O. (2012). *Teaching adolescents to become learners: The role of noncognitive factors in shaping school performance—A critical literature review.* Chicago: University of Chicago Consortium on Chicago School Research.

Feather, N. T. (1982). *Expectations and actions: Expectancy-value models in psychology.* Mahwah, NJ: Erlbaum.

Felner, R. D., Ginter, M., & Primavera, J. (1982). Primary prevention during school transitions: Social support and environmental structure. *American Journal of Community Psychology, 10*, 277–290.

Fine, M. (1991). *Framing dropouts: Notes on the politics of an urban public high school*. Albany, NY: State University of New York Press.

Finn, J. D. (1989). Withdrawing from school. *Review of Educational Research, 59*(2), 117–142.

Flay, B., Acock, A., Vuchinich, S., & Beets, M. (2006). Progress report of the randomized trial of positive action in Hawaii: End of third year of intervention (Spring, 2005). Unpublished manuscript. Corvallis: Oregon State University.

Flay, B. R., & Allred, C. G. (2003). Long-term effects of the positive action program—A comprehensive, positive youth development program. *American Journal of Health Behavior, 27*, S6–S21.

Flay, B. R., Allred, C. G., & Ordway, N. (2001). Effects of the positive action program on achievement and discipline: Two matched-control comparisons. *Prevention Science, 2*, 71–89.

Foster, E. M., Jones, D. E., & Conduct Problems Prevention Research Group. (2005). The high costs of aggression: Public expenditures resulting from conduct disorder. *American Journal of Public Health, 95*(10), 1767.

Foster, E. M., & Jones, D. (2006). Can a costly intervention be cost-effective?: An analysis of violence prevention. *Archives of General Psychiatry, 63*(11), 1284–1291.

Frederick, S., Loewenstein, G., & O'donoghue, T. (2002). Time discounting and time preference: A critical review. *Journal of Economic Literature, 40*(2), 351–401.

Fuhrer, J. C. (2000). Habit formation in consumption and its implications for monetary-policy models. *American Economic Review, 90*(3), 367–390.

Glade, A. C., Bean, R. A., & Vira, R. (2005). A prime time for marital/relational intervention: A review of the transition to parenthood literature with treatment recommendations. *The American Journal of Family Therapy, 33*(4), 319–336.

Gollwitzer, P. M. (1999). Implementation intentions: Strong effects of simple plans. *American Psychologist, 54*(7), 493.

Gonzales, M., Burgess, D., & Mobilio, L. (2001). The allure of bad plans: Implications of plan quality for progress toward possible selves and postplanning energization. *Basic and Applied Social Psychology, 23*, 87–108.

Grandpre, J., Alvaro, E. M., Burgoon, M., Miller, C. H., & Hall, J. R. (2003). Adolescent reactance and anti-smoking campaigns: A theoretical approach. *Health Communication, 15*, 349–366.

Greifeneder, R., Bless, H., & Pham, M. T. (2011). When do people rely on affective and cognitive feelings in judgment? A review. *Personality and Social Psychology Review, 15*, 107–141.

Guiffrida D. (2009). Theories of human development that enhance an understanding of the college transition process. *Teacher's College Record, 111*, 2419–2443.

Gupta, V., Hanges, P. J., & Dorfman, P. (2002). Cultural clusters: Methodology and findings. *Journal of World Business, 37*(1), 11–15.

Gylfason, T. (2001). Natural resources, education, and economic development. *European Economic Review, 45*, 847–859.

Hamman, D., Coward, F., Johnson, L, Lambert, M., & Zhou, L. (2013). Teacher possible selves: How thinking about the future contributes to the formation of professional identity. *Self and Identity, 12*, 307–336.

Hammett, T. M., Gaiter, J. L., & Crawford, C. (1998). Reaching seriously at-risk populations: Health interventions in criminal justice settings. *Health Education & Behavior, 25*(1), 99–120.

Hawkins, J. D., Catalano, R. F., Kosterman, R., Abbott, R., & Hill, K. G. (1999). Preventing adolescent health risk behaviors by strengthening protection during childhood. *Archives of Pediatrics and Adolescent Medicine, 153*, 226–234.

Heider, F. (1958). *The psychology of interpersonal relations*. Hoboken, NJ: Wiley.

Herlihy, C. (2007). *State and district-level supports for successful transition into high school*. Washington, DC: National High School Center.

Higgins, E. T. (1998). The aboutness principle: A pervasive influence on inference. *Social Cognition, 16*, 173–198.

Hill, J. P., & Holmbeck, G. N. (1986). Attachment and autonomy during adolescence. *Annals of Child Development, 3*, 145–189.

Hirschi, T. (1986). On the compatibility of rational choice and social control theories of crime. In T. Hirschi (Ed.), *The reasoning criminal: Rational choice perspectives on offending* (pp. 105–118). New York: Springer.

Hirschi, T. (2004). Self-control and crime. In R. F. Baumeister & K. D. Vohs (Eds.), *Handbook of self-regulation: Research, theory, and applications* (pp. 537–552). New York: Guilford Press.

Hirschi, T., & Gottfredson, M. (1990). *A general theory of crime.* Palo Alto, CA: Stanford University Press.

Hoyle, R., & Sherrill, M. (2006). Future orientation in the self-system: Possible selves, self-regulation, and behavior. *Journal of Personality, 74,* 1673–1696.

Ialongo, N. S., Werthamer, L., Kellam, S. G., Brown, C. H., Wang, S., & Lin, Y. (1999). Proximal impact of two first-grade preventive interventions on the early risk behaviors for later substance abuse, depression, and antisocial behavior. *American Journal of Community Psychology, 27,* 599–641.

Ingersoll, R. M. (2001). Teacher turnover and teacher shortages: An organizational analysis. *American Educational Research Journal, 38*(3), 499–534.

Iselin, A. M. R., Mulvey, E. P., Loughran, T. A., Chung, H. L., & Schubert, C. A. (2012). A longitudinal examination of serious adolescent offenders' perceptions of chances for success and engagement in behaviors accomplishing goals. *Journal of Abnormal Child Psychology, 40*(2), 237–249.

James, W. (1950). *The principles of psychology.* New York: Dover. (Original work published 1890)

Joe, S., Joe, E., & Rowley, L. L., (2009). Consequences of health risks for academic achievement. *Review of Research in Education, 33,* 283–309.

Johnson, J., Strange, M., & Madden, K. (2010). *The rural dropout problem: An invisible achievement gap.* Bethel, VT: Rural School and Community Trust.

Jordan, J. L., Kostandini, G., & Mykerezi, E. (2012). Rural and urban high school dropout rates: Are they different? *Journal of Research in Rural Education, 27,* 1–21.

Keough, K. A., Zimbardo, P. G., & Boyd, J. N. (1999). Who's smoking, drinking, and using drugs? Time perspective as a predictor of substance use. *Basic and Applied Social Psychology, 21*(2), 149–164.

Kim, Y., Sherraden, M., & Clancy, M. (March 2012). *Parental educational expectations by race and Hispanic origin: Evidence from the SEED OK experiment.* Paper presented at Assets and Education Research Symposium. Lawrence: University of Kansas, Lawrence, Kansas.

King, L. A. (2001). The health benefits of writing about life goals. *Personality and Social Psychology Bulletin, 27,* 798–807.

King, L. A., & Hicks, J. A. (2007). Whatever happened to" What might have been"? Regrets, happiness, and maturity. *American Psychologist, 62*(7), 625–636.

King, L. A., & Raspin, C. (2004). Lost and found possible selves, subjective well-being, and ego development in divorced women. *Journal of Personality, 72*(3), 603–632.

Kirby, D. (2002). The impact of schools and school programs upon adolescent sexual behavior. *Journal of Sex Research, 39*(1), 27–33.

Kirk, C. M., Lewis, R. K., Nilsen, C., & Colvin, D. Q. (2013). Foster care and college: The educational aspirations and expectations of youth in the foster care system. *Youth & Society. 45*(3), 307–323.

Klein, M. W. (1992). Big effects of small interventions: The informational role of intervention in exchange rate policy. *European Economic Review, 36*(4), 915–924.

Knox, M., Funk, J., Elliott, R., & Bush, E. G. (2000). Gender differences in adolescents' possible selves. *Youth & Society, 31*(3), 287–309.

Koepke, S., & Denissen, J. J. (2012). Dynamics of identity development and separation–individuation in parent–child relationships during adolescence and emerging adulthood–A conceptual integration. *Developmental Review, 32,* 67–88.

Kuh, G. D., Kinzie, J., Buckley, J. A., Bridges, B. K., & Hayek, J. C. (July 2006). *What matters to student success: A review of the literature.* Commissioned paper. National Postsecondary Education Cooperative (NPEC).

Labroo, A. A., Lambotte, S., & Zhang, Y. (2009). The "name-ease" effect and its dual impact on importance judgments. *Psychological Science, 20,* 1516–1522.

Lally, P., & Gardner, B. (2013). Promoting habit formation. *Health Psychology Review, 7*(suppl 1), S137–S158.

Lamb, M. (2011). Future selves: Motivation and autonomy in long term EFL learning trajectories. In G. Murray, X. Gao, & T. E. Lamb (Eds.), *Identity, motivation and autonomy in language learning: Independent learning*, (pp. 177–194). Tonawanda, NY: Second Language Learning.

Lamm, H., Schmidt, R. W., & Trommsdorff, G. (1976). Sex and social class as determinants of future orientation (time perspective) in adolescents. *Journal of Personality and Social Psychology, 34*(3), 317–326.

Landau, M., Oyserman, D., Keefer, L., & Smith, G. C. (2014) The college journey and academic engagement: How metaphor use enhances identity-based motivation. *Journal of Personality and Social Psychology, 106*, 679–698.

Lantz, P., House, J., Lepkowski, J., Williams, D., Mero, R., & Chen, J. (1998). Socioeconomic factors, health behaviors, and mortality. *Journal of the American Medical Association, 279*, 1703–1708.

Lapsley, D., & Yeager, D. S. (in press). Moral character education. In W. M. Reynolds, G. E. Miller, & I. B. Weiner (Eds.). *Handbook of Psychology: Vol. 7. Educational Psychology, 2nd ed.*, NJ: John Wiley and Sons Inc.

Levin, H., Belfield, C., Muenning, P., & Rouse, C. (2007). *The costs and benefits of an excellent education for all of America's children.* New York: Teachers College, Columbia University.

Lewis, N. Jr. & Oyserman, D. (2014). When does the future begin? Temporal granularity and psychological relevance. Paper under editorial review.

Liberman, N., & Förster, J. (2008). Expectancy, value and psychological distance: A new look at goal gradients. *Social Cognition, 26*, 515–533.

Liberman, N. & Trope, Y. (2008*). The psychology of transcending the here and now. Science, 322*, 1201–1205.

Little, B. R. (1983). Personal projects a rationale and method for investigation. *Environment and Behavior, 15*(3), 273–309.

Little, B. R. (1989). Personal projects analysis: Trivial pursuits, magnificent obsessions, and the search for coherence. In D. M. Buss et al. (Eds.), *Personality Psychology* (pp. 15–31). New York: Springer-Verlag.

Loeb, S., Darling-Hammond, L., & Luczak, J. (2005). How teaching conditions predict teacher turnover in California schools. *Peabody Journal of Education, 80*(3), 44–70.

Madeira, C. (2009). *Estimating the beliefs of economic agents.* Phd dissertation, Evanston, IL: Northwestern University.

Maton, K. I., & Zimmerman, M. A. (1992). Psychological predictors of substance abuse among urban black male adolescents. *Drugs & Society, 6*(1–2), 79–114.

Marcia, J. E. (1980). Identity in adolescence. In J. Adelson (Ed.), *Handbook of Adolescent Psychology*, vol 9, 159–187, New York, New York: Wiley and Sons.

Markus, H., & Nurius, P. (1986). Possible selves. *American Psychologist, 41*(9), 954–969.

Mazor, A., & Enright, R. D. (1988). The development of the individuation process from a social-cognitive perspective. *Journal of Adolescence, 11*, 29–47.

McGuire, W. J., & Padawer-Singer, A. (1976). Trait salience in the spontaneous self-concept. *Journal of personality and social psychology, 33*(6), 743–754.

MacIntyre, P. D., Mackinnon, S. P., & Clément, R. (2009). The baby, the bathwater, and the future of language learning motivation research. In Z. Dornyei & E. Ushioda (Eds.), *Motivation, Language Identity and the L2 self*, pp. 43–65, Tonawanda, NY: Multilingual Matters.

McTigue, E. M., & Rimm-Kaufman, S. E. (2011). The responsive classroom approach and its implications for improving reading and writing. *Reading & Writing Quarterly, 27*, 5–24.

Meevissen, Y., Peters, M., & Alberts, H. (2011). Become more optimistic by imagining a best possible self: Effects of a two week intervention. *Journal of Behavior Therapy and Experimental Psychiatry, 42*, 371–378.

Mello, Z. R., Anton-Stang, H. M., Monaghan, P. L., Roberts, K. J., & Worrell, F. C. (2012). A longitudinal investigation of African American and Hispanic adolescents' educational and occupational expectations and corresponding attainment in adulthood. *Journal of Education for Students Placed at Risk (JESPAR), 17*(4), 266–285.

Mello, Z. R. (2009). Racial/ethnic group and socioeconomic status variation in educational and occupational expectations from adolescence to adulthood. *Journal of Applied Developmental Psychology, 30,* 494–504.

Mercer, J. (2010). *Child development: Myths and misunderstandings.* Thousand Oaks, CA: Sage.

Metcalfe, J., & Mischel, W. (1999). A hot/cool-system analysis of delay of gratification: Dynamics of willpower. *Psychological Review, 106*(1), 3–19.

Mezulis, A. H., Abramson, L. Y., Hyde, J. S., & Hankin, B. L. (2004). Is there a universal positivity bias in attributions? A meta-analytic review of individual, developmental, and cultural differences in the self-serving attributional bias. *Psychological Bulletin, 130*(5), 711–747. doi:10.1037/0033-2909.130.5.711

Miller, C. H., Burgoon, M., Grandpre, J. R., & Alvaro, E. M. (2006). Identifying principal risk factors for the initiation of adolescent smoking behaviors: The significance of psychological reactance. *Health Communication, 19*(3), 241–252.

Miller, G. A., Galanter, E., & Pribram, K. H. (1960). *Plans and the structure of behavior.* New York: Holt, Rinehart & Winston.

Miller, S. R. (1998). Shortcut: High school grades as a signal of human capital. *Educational Evaluation and Policy Analysis, 20*(4), 299–311.

Miller, W. R. (2000). Rediscovering fire: Small interventions, large effects. *Psychology of Addictive Behaviors, 14*(1), 6.

Milligan, K., Moretti, E., & Oreopoulos, P. (2004). Does education improve citizenship? Evidence from the United States and the United Kingdom. *Journal of Public Economics, 88*(9), 1667–1695.

Mortenson, T. (2010). Family income and higher education opportunity 1970 to 2009. *Postsecondary Education Opportunity,* number 211, 1–16. Retrieved August 18, 2014 from http://www.postsecondary.org/last12/221_1110pg1_16.pdf

Mrazek, P. B., & Haggerty, R. J. (Eds.). (1994). *Reducing risks for mental disorders: Frontiers for preventive intervention research: Summary.* Washington, DC. National Academies Press.

Murru, E. C., & Martin Ginis, K. A. (2010). Imagining the possibilities: The effects of a possible selves intervention on self-regulatory efficacy and exercise behavior. *Journal of Sport & Exercise Psychology, 32,* 537–554.

National Center for Education Statistics. (2010). *The Condition of Education 2010.* NCES 2010-028. Retrived May 18, 2012, from: http://eric.ed.gov/PDFS/ED509940.pdf

Nation, M., Crusto, C., Wandersman, A., Kumpfer, K. L., Seybolt, D., Morrissey-Kane, E., & Davino, K. (2003). What works in prevention: Principles of effective prevention programs. *American Psychologist, 58*(6–7), 449.

Neild, R. C., Balfanz, R., & Herzog, L. (2007). An early warning system. *Educational Leadership, 65,* 28–33.

Nesse, R. (2009). Explaining depression, neuroscience is not enough: Evolution is essential. In C. Pariante, R. Nesse, D. Nutt, & L. Wolpert (Eds.), *Understanding depression: A translational approach* (pp. 17–35). New York: Oxford University Press.

Norman, C., & Aron, A. (2003). Aspects of possible self that predict motivation to achieve or avoid it. *Journal of Experimental Social Psychology, 39,* 500–507.

Nurra, C. & Oyserman, D. (2014) From future self to current action: A matter of psychological relevance. Manuscript under editorial review.

Norman, C., & Aron, A. (2003). Aspects of possible self that predict motivation to achieve or avoid it. *Journal of Experimental Social Psychology, 39,* 500–507.

Nurmi, J. E., (1991). How do adolescents see their future? A review of the development of future orientation and planning. *Developmental Review, 11,* 1–59.

Oettingen, G., Pak, H., & Schnetter, K. (2001). Self-regulation of goal-setting: Turning free fantasies about the future into binding goals. *Journal of Personality and Social Psychology, 80,* 736–753.

Ogilvie, D. M. (1987). The undesired self: A neglected variable in personality research. *Journal of Personality and Social Psychology, 52,* 379–385.

Oreopoulos, P. (2007). Do dropouts drop out too soon? Wealth, health and happiness from compulsory schooling. *Journal of public Economics, 91*(11), 2213–2229.

Oreopoulos, P., & Salvanes, K. G. (2011). Priceless: The nonpecuniary benefits of schooling. *The Journal of Economic Perspectives, 25*(1), 159–184.

Orfield, G., Losen, D., Wald, J., & Swanson, C. (2004). *Losing our future: How minority youth are being left behind by the graduation rate crisis*. Cambridge, MA: The Civil Rights Project at Harvard University.

Ouellette, J. A., Hessling, R., Gibbons, F. X., Reis-Bergan, M. J., & Gerrard, M. (2005). Using images to increase exercise behavior: Prototypes vs. possible selves. *Personality and Social Psychology Bulletin, 31*, 610–620.

Oyserman, D. (1993). Who influences identity: Adolescent identity and delinquency in interpersonal context. *Child Psychiatry and Human Development, 23*, 203–214.

Oyserman, D. (2001). Self-concept and identity. In A. Tesser & N. Schwarz (Eds.), *Blackwell handbook of social psychology*, pp. 499–517. Malden, MA: Blackwell Press.

Oyserman, D. (2007) Social identity and self-regulation. In A. Kruglanski & T. Higgins (Eds.), *Handbook of social psychology* (2nd ed.) pp. 432–453). New York: Guilford Press.

Oyserman, D. (2008). Racial-ethnic self-schemas: Multidimensional identity-based motivation. *Journal of Research in Personality, 42*(5), 1186–1198.

Oyserman, D. (2009). Identity-based motivation: Implications for action-readiness, procedural readiness, and consumer behavior. *Journal of Consumer Psychology, 19*, 250–260.

Oyserman, D. (2013). Not just any path: Implications of identity-based motivation for disparities in school outcomes. *Economics of Education Review, 33*, 179–190.

Oyserman, D., Brickman, D., Bybee, D., & Celious, A. (2006). Fitting in matters: Markers of in-group belonging and academic outcomes. *Psychological Science, 17*(10), 854–861.

Oyserman, D., Brickman, D., & Rhodes, M. (2007). School success, possible selves, and parent school involvement. *Family Relations, 56*(5), 479–489.

Oyserman, D., Bybee, D., Terry, K., & Hart-Johnson, T. (2004). Possible selves as roadmaps. *Journal of Research in Personality, 38*, 130–149.

Oyserman, D., Bybee, D. & Terry, K. (2006). Possible selves and academic outcomes: How and when possible selves impel action. *Journal of Personality and Social Psychology, 91*, 188–204.

Oyserman, D., & Destin, M. (2010). Identity-based motivation: Implications for intervention. *The Counseling Psychologist, 38*(7), 1001–1043.

Oyserman, D., Destin, M., & Novin, S. (in press). The context-sensitive power of possible selves. *Self and Identity*. doi:10.1080/15298868.2014.965733

Oyserman, D., Elmore, K., & Smith, G. (2012). Self, self-concept, and identity. In M. Leary & J. Tangney (Eds.), *Handbook of self and identity* (2nd ed. pp. 69–104). New York: Guilford Press.

Oyserman, D. & Fryberg, S. A. (2006). The possible selves of diverse adolescents: Content and function across gender, race and national origin. In J. Kerpelman & C. Dunkel (Eds.), *Possible selves: Theory, research, and applications* (pp. 17–39). Huntington, NY: Nova.

Oyserman, D, Fryberg, S., & Yoder, N. (2007). Identity-based motivation and health. *Journal of Personality and Social Psychology, 93*, 1011–1027.

Oyserman, D., Gant, L. & Ager, J. (1995). A socially contextualized model of African American identity: Possible selves and school persistence. *Journal of Personality and Social Psychology, 69*, 1216–1232.

Oyserman, D., Harrison, K., & Bybee, D. (2001). Can racial identity be promotive of academic efficacy? *International Journal of Behavioral Development, 25*, 379–385.

Oyserman, D., & James, L. (2011). Possible identities. In S. Schwartz, K. Luyckx, & V. Vignoles (Eds.), *Handbook of identity theory and research* (pp. 117–145). New York: Springer-Verlag.

Oyserman, D., & James, L. (2009). Possible selves: From content to process. In K. Markman, W. M. P. Klein, & J. A. Suhr (Eds.), *The handbook of imagination and mental stimulation* (pp. 373–394). New York: Psychology Press.

Oyserman, D., Johnson, E., & James, L. (2011). Seeing the destination but not the path: Effects of socioeconomic disadvantage on school-focused possible self content and linked behavioral strategies. *Self and Identity, 10*(4), 474–492.

Oyserman, D., Kemmelmeier, M., Fryberg, S., Brosh, H., & Hart-Johnson, T. (2003). Racial-ethnic self-schemas. *Social Psychology Quarterly, 66*, 333–347.

Oyserman, D., & Markus, H. R. (1990a). Possible selves and delinquency. *Journal of Personality and Social Psychology, 59*(1), 112–125.

Oyserman, D., & Markus, H. (1990b). Possible selves in balance: Implications for delinquency. *Journal of Social Issues, 46*(2), 141–157.

Oyserman, D., Novin, S., Smith, G., Elmore, K., & Nurra, C. (2014). From school difficulty to school possibility: How interpretation of experienced difficulty matters. Manuscript under editorial review.

Oyserman, D., & Sakamoto, I. (1997). Being Asian American: Identity, cultural constructs and stereotype perception. *Journal of Applied Behavioral Science, 33*, 435–453.

Oyserman, D., Sakamoto, I., & Lauffer, A. (1998) Cultural accommodation: Hybridity and the framing of social obligation. *Journal of Personality and Social Psychology, 74*, 1606–1618.

Oyserman, D., & Saltz, E. (1993). Competence, delinquency, and attempts to attain possible selves. *Journal of Personality and Social Psychology, 65*(2), 360–374.

Oyserman, D., Smith, G. C., & Elmore, K. (2014). Identity-based motivation: Implications for health and health disparities. *Journal of Social Issues, 70*(2), 206–225.

Oyserman, D., Terry, K., & Bybee, D. (2002). A possible selves intervention to enhance school involvement. *Journal of Adolescence, 24*, 313–326.

Palys, T. S., & Little, B. R. (1983). Perceived life satisfaction and the organization of personal project systems. *Journal of Personality and Social Psychology, 44*(6), 1221–1230

Papi, M. (2010). The L2 motivational self system, L2 anxiety, and motivated behavior: A structural equation modeling approach. *System, 38*, 467–479.

Papi, M. & Abdollahzadeh, E. (2012). Teacher motivational practice, student motivation, and possible L2 selves: An examination in the Iranian EFL context. *Language Learning, 62*, 571–594.

Pascarella, E. T., & Terenzini, P. T. (2005). *how college affects students:* Vol. 2, *A third decade of research*. San Francisco: Jossey-Bass.

Paulson, M. J., Coombs, R. H., & Richardson, M. A. (1990). School performance, academic aspirations, and drug use among children and adolescents. *Journal of Drug Education, 20*(4), 289–303.

Peters, M, Flink, I., Boersma, K. & Linton, S. (2010). Manipulating optimism: Can imagining a best possible self be used to increase positive future expectancies? *The Journal of Positive Psychology: Dedicated to Furthering Research and Promoting Good Practice, 5*, 204–211.

Phinney, J. S. (1990). Ethnic identity in adolescents and adults: review of research. *Psychological Bulletin, 108*(3), 499–514.

Phinney, J. S. (1992). The multigroup ethnic identity measure a new scale for use with diverse groups. *Journal of Adolescent Research, 7*(2), 156–176.

Pizzolato, J. E. (2007). Impossible selves investigating students' persistence decisions when their career-possible selves border on impossible. *Journal of Career Development, 33*(3), 201–223.

Poulin, F., Dishion, T. J., & Burraston, B. (2001). 3-year iatrogenic effects associated with aggregating high-risk adolescents in cognitive-behavioral preventive interventions. *Applied Developmental Science, 5*(4), 214–224.

Pronin, E., Olivola, C. Y., & Kennedy, K. A. (2008). Doing unto future selves as you would do unto others: Psychological distance and decision making. *Personality and Social Psychology Bulletin, 34*(2), 224–236.

Radloff, L. (1977). The CES-D scale: A self-report depression scale for research in the general population. *Applied Psychological Measurement, 1*, 385–401.

Radloff, L., & Locke, B. (2000). Center for Epidemiologic Studies Depression Scale (CESD). In Taskforce for the Handbook of Psychiatric Measures (Eds.), *Handbook of psychiatric measures: American Psychiatric Association* (pp. 523–526). Washington, DC: American Psychiatric Association.

Raynor, J. O. (1969). Future orientation and motivation of immediate activity: An elaboration of the theory of achievement motivation. *Psychological Review, 76*, 606–610.

Reich, J. W., & Robertson, J. L. (1979). Reactance and norm appeal in anti-littering messages. *Journal of Applied Social Psychology, 9*, 91–101.

Rimm-Kaufman, S. E., Fan, X., Chiu, Y.-J., & You, W. (2007). The contribution of the responsive classroom approach on children's academic achievement: Results from a three year longitudinal study. *Journal of School Psychology, 45*, 401–421.

Roberts, R., Attkisson, C., & Rosenblatt, A. (1998). Prevalence of psychopathology among children and adolescents. *American Journal of Psychiatry, 155*, 715–725.

Roderick, M. (2003). What's happening to the boys? Early high school experiences and school outcomes among African American male adolescents in Chicago. *Urban Education 38*(5), 538–607.

Roese, N. & Olson, J. (2007). Better, stronger, faster: self-serving judgment, affect regulation, and the optimal vigilance hypothesis. *Perspectives on Psychological Science, 2*, 124–141.

Rosenbaum, J. E., Deil-Amen, R., & Person, A. E. (2006). *After admission: From college access to college success.* New York, New York: Russell Sage Foundation.

Rotheram, M. J. (1982). Social skills training with underachievers, disruptive, and exceptional children. *Psychology in the Schools, 19*, 532–539.

Russell, J., Alexis, D., & Clayton, N. (2010). Episodic future thinking in 3- to 5-year-old children: The ability to think of what will be needed from a different point of view. *Cognition, 114*, 56–71.

Ruvolo, A. P., & Markus, H. (1992). Possible selves and performance: The power of self-relevant imagery. *Social Cognition, 10*, 95–124.

Sacker, A., & Schoon, I. (2007). Educational resilience in later life: Resources and assets in adolescence and return to education after leaving school at age 16. *Social Science Research, 36*, 873–896.

Schwartz, M. B., Thomas, J. J., Bohan, K. M., & Vartanian, L. R. (2007). Intended and unintended effects of an eating disorder educational program: Impact of presenter identity. *International Journal of Eating Disorders, 40*, 187–192.

Schwarz, N. (1998). Accessible content and accessibility experiences: The interplay of declarative and experiential information in judgment. *Personality and Social Psychology Review, 2*, 87–99.

Schwarz, N. (2002). Situated cognition and the wisdom of feelings: Cognitive tuning. In L. Feldman Barrett & P. Salovey (Eds.), *The wisdom in feelings* (pp. 144–166). New York: Guilford.

Schwarz, N. (2004). Meta-cognitive experiences in consumer judgment and decision making. *Journal of Consumer Psychology, 14*, 332–348.

Schwarz, N. (2010). Meaning in context: Metacognitive experiences. In B. Mesquita, L. F. Barrett, & E. R. Smith (Eds.), *The mind in context* (pp. 105–125). New York: Guilford Press.

Schwarz, N. (2012). Feelings-as-information theory. In P. Van Lange, A. Kruglanski, & E. T. Higgins (Eds.), *Handbook of theories of social psychology* (pp. 289–308). New York: Sage.

Schwarz, N., Bless, N., Strack, F., Klumpp, G., Rittenauer-Schatka, H., & Simons, A. (1991). Ease of retrieval as information: Another look at the availability heuristic. *Journal of Personality and Social Psychology, 61*, 195–202.

Schwarz, N., & Clore, G. L. (2007). Feelings and phenomenal experiences. In A. W. Kruglanski & E. Higgins (Eds.), *Social psychology: Handbook of basic principles* (2nd ed., pp. 385–407). New York: Guilford Press.

Schwarz, N., & Oyserman, D. (2001). Asking questions about behavior: Cognition, communication, and questionnaire construction. *American Journal of Evaluation, 22*, 127–160.

Seidman, E., & French, S. E. (1997). Normative school transitions among urban adolescents: When, where, and how to intervene. In H. Walberg, O. Reyes, & R. Weissberg (Eds.), *Children and youth: Interdisciplinary perspectives. Issues in children's and families' lives* (Vol. 7, pp. 166–189). Thousand Oaks, CA: Sage.

Seidman, E., & French, S. E. (2004). Developmental trajectories and ecological transitions: A two-step procedure to aid in the choice of prevention and promotion interventions. *Development and Psychopathology, 16*(4), 1141–1159.

Segal, H. G., DeMeis, D. K., Wood, G. A., & H. L. (2001). Assessing future possible selves by gender and socioeconomic status using the anticipated life history measure. *Journal of Personality, 69*(1), 57–87.

Seginer, R., & Halabi-Kheir, H. (1998). Adolescent passage to adulthood: Future orientation in the context of culture, age, and gender. *International Journal of Intercultural Relations, 22*(3), 309–328.

Shapiro, J. (2005). Is there a daily discount rate? Evidence from the food stamp nutrition cycle. *Journal of Public Economics, 89*, 303–325.

Sheldon, K., & Lyubomirsky, S. (2006). How to increase and sustain positive emotion: The effects of expressing gratitude and visualizing best possible selves. *Journal of Positive Psychology, 1*, 73–82.

Silvestrini, N., & Gendolla, G. H. E. (2013). Automatic effort mobilization and the principle of resource conservation: One can only prime the possible and justified. *Journal of Personality and Social Psychology, 104*, 803–816.

Smith, E. & Collins, E. C. (2010). Situated social judgments. In L. Feldman Barrett, B. Mesquita, & E. R. Smith (Eds.), *The mind in context* (pp. 126–145). New York: Guilford.

Smith, G. C., James, L., Varnum, M., & Oyserman, D. (2014) Give up or get going? Productive uncertainty in uncertain times. *Self and Identity, 13*, 681–700.

Smith, G. C., & Oyserman, D. (2014). Just not worth my time? Experienced difficulty and time investment. Manuscript under editorial review.

Snipes, J., Fancsali, C., & Stoker, G. (2012). Student academic mindset interventions. Retrieved from online http://www.impaqint.com/sites/default/files/project-reports/impaq%20 student%20academic%20mindset%20interventions%20report%20august%202012.pdf

Steele, C. M. (1997). A threat in the air: How stereotypes shape intellectual identity and performance. *American Psychologist, 52*, 613–629.

Steinberg, L., Graham, S., O'Brien, L., Woolard, J., Cauffman, E., & Banich, M. (2009). Age differences in future orientation and delay discounting. *Child Development, 80*(1), 28–44.

Steinberg, L., & Silverberg, S. B. (1986). The vicissitudes of autonomy in early adolescence. *Child Development, 57*, 841–851.

Strauss, K., Griffin, M. A., & Parker, S. K. (2012). Future work selves: How salient hoped-for identities motivate proactive career behaviors. *Journal of Applied Psychology, 97*(3), 580–598.

Thaler, R. (1981). Some empirical evidence on dynamic inconsistency. *Economic Letters, 8*, 201–207.

Toldson, I. A., Woodson, K. M., Braithwaite, R., Holliday, R. C., & De La Rosa, M. (2010). Academic potential among African American adolescents in juvenile detention centers: Implications for reentry to school. *Journal of Offender Rehabilitation, 49*(8), 551–570.

Trope, Y., & Liberman, N. (2003). Temporal construal. *Psychological Review, 110*, 403–421.

Trusty, J. (2000). High educational expectations and low achievement: Stability of educational goals across adolescence. *Journal of Educational Research, 93*, 356–395.

Tulving, E. (1985). Memory and consciousness. *Canadian Psychology/Psychologie Canadienne, 26*(1), 1–12.

Tversky, A., & Kahneman, D. (1973). Availability: A heuristic for judging frequency and probability. *Cognitive Psychology, 5*, 207–232.

Uno, M., Mortimer, J. T., Kim, M., & Vuolo, M. (2010). "Holding on" or "coming to terms" with educational underachievement: A longitudinal study of ambition and attainment. In S. Shulman & J.-E. Nurmi (Eds.), The role of goals in navigating individual lives during emerging adulthood. *New Directions for Child and Adolescent Development, 130*, 41–56.

van Gelder, J. L., Hershfield, H. E., & Nordgren, L. F. (2013). Vividness of the future self predicts delinquency. *Psychological Science, 24*(6), 974–980.

Vansteenkiste, M., Simons, J., Soenens, B., & Lens, W. (2003). How to become a lifelong exerciser: The importance on presenting a clear future goal in an autonomy-supportive way. *Journal of Sport Exercise Psychology, 26*(2), 232–250.

Vignoles, V., Manzi, C., Regalia, C., Jemmolo, S., & Scabini, E. (2008). Identity motives underlying desired and feared possible future selves. *Journal of Personality, 76*, 1165–1200.

Wakslak, C. J., Nussbaum, S., Liberman, N., & Trope, Y. (2008). Representations of the self in the near and distant future. *Journal of Personality and Social Psychology, 95*(4), 757.

Walton, G. M., & Cohen, G. L. (2011). A brief social-belonging intervention improves academic and health outcomes of minority students. *Science, 331*, 1447–1451.

Wandersman, A. (2003). Community science: Bridging the gap between science and practice with community-centered models. *American Journal of Community Psychology, 31*(3–4), 227–242.

Weber, M. (1967). *Subjective meaning in the social situation*. In G. B. Levitas (Ed.), *Culture and consciousness: Perspectives in the social sciences* (pp. 156–169). New York: Braziller.

Webley, P., & Nyhus, E. K. (2006). Parents' influence on children's future orientation and saving. *Journal of Economic Psychology, 27*(1), 140–164.

Weissberg, R. P., & Greenberg, M. T. (1998). School and community competence-enhancement and prevention programs. In W. Damon, I. Sigel, & A. K. Renninger (Eds.), *Child psychology in practice* (pp. 877–954). Hoboken, NJ: John Wiley & Sons.

Whitehead, D. (2005). In pursuit of pleasure: health education as a means of facilitating the "health journey" of young people. *Health Education, 105*(3), 213–227.

Wigfield, A. (1994). Expectancy-value theory of achievement motivation: A developmental perspective. *Educational Psychology Review, 6*(1), 49–78.

Wigfield, A., & Eccles, J. (2000), Expectancy-value theory of achievement motivation, *Contemporary Educational Psychology, 25*, 68–81.

Wildhagen, T. (2009). Why does cultural capital matter for high school academic performance? An empirical assessment of teacher-selection and self-selection mechanisms as explanations of the cultural capital effect. *The Sociological Quarterly, 50*, 173–200.

Wheeler, Mark A.; Stuss, Donald T.; Tulving, E. (1997). Toward a theory of episodic memory: The frontal lobes and autonoetic consciousness. *Psychological Bulletin, 121*, 331–354.

Wood, W., & Neal, D. T. (2007). A new look at habits and the habit-goal interface. *Psychological Review, 114*(4), 843.

Woolley, M. M., Rose, R. A., Orthner, D. K., Akos, P. T., & Jones-Sanpei, H. (2013). Advancing academic attainment through career relevance in the middle grades: A longitudinal evaluation of CareerStart, *American Educational Research Journal*. Published online before print May 29, 2013. doi:10.3102/0002831213488818

Wicklund, R. A. (1974). *Freedom and reactance.* Potomac, MD: Erlbaum.

Xu, J., & Schwarz, N. (2009). Do we really need a reason to indulge? *Journal of Marketing Research, 46*(1), 25–36.

Yeager, D. S., & Walton, G. M. (2011). Social-psychological interventions in education: They're not magic. *Review of Educational Research, 81*, 267–301.

Yerkes, R. M., & Dodson, J. D. (1908). The relation of strength of stimulus to rapidity of habit-formation. *Journal of Comparative Neurology and Psychology, 18*(5), 459–482.

Zhu, S., Tse, S., Cheung, H-S, & Oyserman, D. (2014). Will I get there? Effects of parental support on children's possible selves. *British Journal of Educational Psychology*. Article first published online: 16 Jun 2014. doi:10.1111/bjep.12044

Zimbardo, P. G., & Boyd, J. N. (1999). Putting time in perspective: A valid, reliable individual-differences metric. *Journal of Personality and Social Psychology, 77*(6), 1271.

Zimmerman, M. A., & Maton, K. I. (1992). Life-style and substance use among male African American urban adolescents: A cluster analytic approach. *American Journal of Community Psychology, 20*(1), 121–138.

Zimmerman, M. A., & Schmeelk-Cone, K. H. (2003). A longitudinal analysis of adolescent substance use and school motivation among African American youth. *Journal of Research on Adolescence, 13*(2), 185–210.

INDEX